# CORPORATE PERFORMANCE

# CORPORATE PERFORMANCE

## The
## *Key to*
## *Public Trust*

by

## Francis W. Steckmest

with a
Resource and Review Committee
for
The Business Roundtable

*HD*
*2785*
*.S67*

*201056*

**McGraw-Hill Book Company**

New York    St Louis    San Francisco    Auckland
Bogotá    Singapore    Johannesburg    London
Madrid    Mexico    Montreal    New Dehli
Panama    São Paulo    Hamburg
Sydney    Tokyo    Paris
Toronto

**Library of Congress Cataloging in Publication Data**

Steckmest, Francis W.
  Corporate performance.

  Includes index.
  1. Corporations. 2. Industry—Social aspects.
3. Corporations—Political activity. I. Business
Roundtable. II. Title.
HD2731.S73        658        81-8347
                                      AACR2

1234567890    DODO    8987654321

The editors for this book were William R. Newton and Beatrice E.
Eckes, the designer was Mark E. Safran, and the production
supervisor was Teresa F. Leaden. It was set in Melior by Black Dot,
Inc.

ISBN 0-07-009306-7

Printed and bound by R. R. Donnelley & Sons Company.

# Contents

# Preface

The Business Roundtable is an association of chief executives of major American corporations. Its principal purposes are to provide a forum for the examination of economic issues facing the nation, to develop reasoned positions on those issues, and thereby to contribute to the formation of public policy.

From its inception the Roundtable has paid close attention to the opinions and attitudes of the American public. We have listened. We have tried to be open-minded. As business leaders we bring our own point of view, but we are convinced of the importance of a lively debate on national goals and the means of attaining them.

To this end, the Roundtable occasionally sponsors research on the role of large corporations in the life of the country. This study, *Corporate Performance: The Key to Public Trust*, will, it is hoped, improve understanding of the public issues of corporate performance and governance both in the corporate community and among other audiences.

The book focuses on corporate issues from the viewpoints of the general public, relevant interest groups, and corporate executives. It is based on a study made by members of a Resource and Review Committee, chaired by the book's principal author, Francis W. Steckmest, of the Shell Oil Company. The book critically examines various aspects of corporate behavior. Although possible responses are suggested, it was not the intent to set standards of corporate performance.

The book may be controversial within and beyond the business community. It involves countless matters of judgment, and the author and the committee members had complete freedom to reach their own conclusions. If arguments are provoked, that will be in keeping with the

Roundtable's ambition to stimulate substantive discussion and further understanding of the larger corporation. I have no doubt that the greater the understanding of corporations among the public, the less likely are unwarranted governmental controls over business. I also believe that greater responsiveness by corporate leadership to reasonable public expectations will have a similar result.

Obviously, if business organizations are to help maintain and improve our free society, they must be successful. What this book addresses is the view, with which I agree, that continuing success involves more than the provision of needed goods and services at a profit; it requires as well a broad sensitivity to the public interest. We are reminded that nothing in history, precedent, or any of our laws guarantees a continuing role for large corporations. That assurance can be achieved only by a job well done.

**Clifton C. Garvin, Jr.**
*Chairman, Exxon Corporation*
*Chairman, The Business Roundtable*

# The Resource and
# Review Committee

**Francis W. Steckmest,** consultant, public affairs, Shell Oil Company, is a graduate of the University of California at Berkeley in political science and economics. Subsequent to service as a United States naval intelligence officer, Steckmest served as personnel director of Shell's research organization and then as manager of the companywide functions of employee training and communication, college recruitment, manager education, and executive development and succession planning. During the past 12 years Steckmest has consulted on emerging public policy issues, particularly those involving the large corporation. He is a member of the Conference Board's Public Affairs Research Council, a director and a former vice chairman of the Public Affairs Council, and a founder and vice president of the Forum Club of Houston. For 10 years, he was a member of the Board of Visitors of the Duke University School of Engineering and currently is a fellow of the Center for Public Policy of the University of Houston.

**Godfrey E. Briefs** was executive assistant to the vice president and chief economist of the General Motors Corporation while a member of the committee. Prior to assuming this position in 1980, he was director, legal economics, for 8 years. Briefs has B.A. and M.A. degrees in economics from Georgetown University and both an M.P.A. from the Kennedy School of Public Administration and a Ph.D. in international economics from Harvard University. He has had extensive experience in interpreting and forecasting business conditions and in writing and speaking on the economic and legal implications of public policy, particularly as they affect industry. In July 1981, Briefs became chief economist of the minority staff of the Banking, Finance, and Urban Affairs Committee of the U.S. House of Representatives.

**Kirk O. Hanson** is a lecturer in business administration at the Stanford University Graduate School of Business. He is a graduate of Stanford University and the Stanford Graduate School of Business and conducted research in business administration at the Harvard Graduate School of Business Administration. He was the founder of the National Affiliation of Concerned Business Students, and has been an assistant regional director for the National Alliance of Business, director of corporate policy for Chicago United, and a consultant on social and political policy to more than twenty corporations. He has written several articles on corporate social and political involvement and on business ethics and devotes considerable time to executive education in these fields.

**Edmund P. Hennelly** is general manager of public affairs for Mobil Oil Corporation. He holds degrees in both law and engineering, has taught the latter at the university level, and has worked and published in both fields. His naval service during World War II was as a civil engineering officer. Prior to joining Mobil, he practiced law with Cravath, Swaine & Moore in New York and as assistant general counsel in the Central Intelligence Agency and at Time Inc. His principal focus at Mobil has been, and remains, government relations and public policy. Hennelly is active in organizations concerned with public policy, including service as cochairman of the Conference Board's Public Affairs Research Council and as a director of the Tax Council, the Public Affairs Council, the Business Council of New York State, and the National Council on the Aging. He is also a trustee of Hamburg Savings Bank, Brooklyn, New York; of Marymount College, Tarrytown, New York; and of the Austin Riggs Center, Stockbridge, Massachusetts.

**Daniel S. Hirshfield,** assistant director of corporate communications for Union Carbide Corporation, is the holder of a Ph.D. degree in American history from Harvard. He has held positions in the Office of the Secretary of Health, Education, and Welfare, the White House staff, and several major corporations. Hirshfield is the author of *The Lost Reform: A History of the Campaign for Compulsory Health Insurance* and has been on the faculties of Boston College and Brandeis University.

**Carl B. Kaufmann** is executive assistant in the Public Affairs Department of E. I. du Pont de Nemours & Co. His career has been as a journalist and as a public affairs and educational consultant and manager in industry. His group in Du Pont has the principal responsibility for speech writing for senior executives. He is author of a book, *Man Incorporate,* which explores the role of large corporations in the American economy and society.

**James F. Langton** is senior vice president, social policy, of the Bank of America. His responsibilities are concerned with the bank's programs in the areas of consumerism, minority-group aspirations, the environment, and other areas of corporate performance. A graduate of Boston College, he served as an officer in the U.S. Coast Guard, a reporter with the *Boston Daily Post,* and national public relations director for Junior Achievement, Inc., prior to joining the Bank of America. He is past president of the San Francisco Bay Area Chapter of the Public Relations Society of America and the Public Relations Workshop of New York.

**Steven Markowitz,** general manager, government relations, of the Continental Group, Inc., is a graduate of Harpur College in economics and holds an M.Phil. degree in economics from George Washington University. After a year as an economist for the International Ladies' Garment Workers' Union, Markowitz served 6 years as a legislative assistant and economic adviser to a member of the U.S. House of Representatives. At Continental, he has developed a department that serves as an interface between the company and all levels of government, both domestic and international.

**Peter Vanderwicken** is president of Peter Vanderwicken Inc., a consulting firm concerned particularly with corporate relations and public policy issues. He is a graduate of Princeton University in history and subsequently was a staff reporter on *The Wall Street Journal,* a national economic correspondent of *Time,* and an associate editor of *Fortune.* Vanderwicken has extensive experience in the fields of public policy analysis and strategic planning and has conducted studies and written feature articles on corporate financial and legal issues. He has served as a consultant to the Business Roundtable's Task Forces on Economic Organization and Corporate Constituencies. Prior to founding his consulting firm in 1978, Vanderwicken was director of public affairs at Booz, Allen & Hamilton.

**Ian Wilson** is a staff member of SRI International's Strategic Environment Center, which he joined in October 1980 after a 25-year career with General Electric Company. A graduate of Oxford University, he first worked with Imperial Chemical Industries Ltd. in London prior to moving to the United States, where he joined General Electric. There he held a variety of positions in public relations, press relations, and management education and development. Wilson helped establish GE's Business Environment Studies and subsequently moved into corporate headquarters, where he concentrated on strategic planning and public issues research and its application. He is a member of the North American Society for Corporate Planning and the World Future Society, author of *Corporate Environments of the Future: Planning for Major Change* (Presidents Association, 1976) and numerous articles and papers, and coauthor of *The Business Environment of the Seventies* (McGraw-Hill, 1970) and *The Future World of Work* (Presidents Association, 1980).

# Introduction

This book is a critical examination of the public policy issues that have been generated by public concern about many aspects of the performance of large corporations. The study which led to this book was originally made to provide chief executive officers who are members of the Business Roundtable with fresh insight and an overall perspective on these issues and their causes and to serve as a basis for them to determine what, if any, changes they should make in their companies' policies, strategy and tactics, organization, or performance. The basic purpose of the book is thus to encourage the many large companies that constitute the corporate community to earn public trust and confidence by their performance in critical areas of public concern.

In addition to company officers and directors, the book was written for other corporate managers and professional staff members, government officials, editors and journalists, professors and students, attorneys, public accountants, consultants, and others who deal with or want to learn about large corporations and their evolving role. To be of optimum use to this broader audience, the manuscript of the study was prepared as a book without change in basic content but with more numerous examples and other explanatory material. A major addition, for example, was Part Three, "The Corporate Governance Issues," a subject already quite familiar to chief executives. Developing the study into this book was done without any sacrifice in freedom or candor to offer criticism of corporate performance and executive behavior.

To present the corporate performance and governance issues in proper context, the book is organized in five parts with a set of recommendations.

- Part One places the large corporation in the public policy arena by examining the broad nature of corporate performance and the types of issues it has generated. Corporate performance is considered in the context of the fundamental public concern about corporate power, a concept that suffuses all the corporate issues, and corporate accountability, a function of both externally and internally imposed constraints on corporate management's decision-making authority.

- Part Two focuses on the twelve corporate performance issues. Each is defined, and its causes and importance are given. This introduction in each case is followed by discussion of the positions and activities of the various interests that are concerned with the issue, corporate initiatives and actions that deal with the causes of the issue, and the outlook for the issue in the foreseeable future.

- Part Three is devoted to the corporate governance issues of corporate chartering, shareholder rights, and boards of directors. The interaction and causal relationship between the corporate performance and governance issues is explained, the initiatives and actions taken by corporate managements and other private-sector groups to help resolve the governance issues are described, and effective corporate performance is advocated as a basis of resolving both sets of issues.

- Part Four is concerned with the corporate executive and the public policy environment. Three subjects are covered: (a) executive conduct that has adversely affected the large corporation; (b) the external environment—the social, economic, political, and technological context of the corporate issues; and (c) the status of the other major participants in the public policy process, such as government, the media, and public-interest groups with whose representatives corporate executives must relate, cooperate, or often compete in the process of formulating public policies or resolving public issues.

- Part Five sets forth the findings and conclusions as a challenge to corporate managements to address the corporate performance issues and make progress in dealing with them. At the outset, three related subjects are discussed: (a) the impact of the corporate performance issues on the evolving social and political role of the large corporation, (b) a new concept of voluntary corporate accountability as an alternative to greater government control, and (c) the need for the development of corporate executives who are as effective in managing the public policy dimension as executives must be in managing the other aspects of their work. In the conclusion, the corporate performance and governance issues are brought together in terms of their significance to the future of the large corporation and the private enterprise system.

• "Recommendations" deals with fixed areas of assessment for chief executive officers and board members regarding their company's ability to manage the functions that are central to corporate performance and governance and to deal with the external environment, particularly the public policy process.

The corporate issues that are the focus of this book are considered from the viewpoints of the general public, relevant interest groups, and corporate executives. Because public and interest-group viewpoints on many aspects of corporate performance and governance are formed largely without direct experience or managerial perspective, they are often discounted by executives and others as misguided perceptions. However, public perceptions, accurate or inaccurate, have the effect of reality, and to ignore them is quite the same as ignoring a public attitude based on direct experience.

Similarly, many executives tend to discount the validity or significance of criticism and proposed reforms that are espoused and dramatized by antibusiness activists. They recognize that much activist activity reflects a fundamental anti-big-business populism and has avowed purposes that range from greater government control to extreme changes in the United States social, economic, and political system.

While most corporate executives recognize that there have been numerous instances of publicly unacceptable corporate performance, they rarely agree with the activists' proposals. Many people do, however, accept much of the activists' criticism, and consequently many aspects of corporate performance have become subjects for public debate and government action. It follows, then, that unless corporate managements are to default to the critics' objective of far greater governmental control, they must understand the critics' viewpoints and proposals, as well as the genuine concerns of many people, and be prepared to respond either by disproving them or by changing performance voluntarily in response to them.

Many corporate leaders do recognize the need for improvements in corporate performance. Readers will note that most of the criticism of corporate performance in this book is documented by statements of prominent corporate executives and advocates of the business community. Criticism by peers and known friends was thought to be more credible to top executives to whom the study was addressed than that of corporate adversaries and, it was hoped, would also serve as worthy evidence to others.

Readers will also notice that the many general references to "public attitudes" and "public concerns" are not footnoted. To avoid the tedium of voluminous footnotes, we asked a preeminent authority on contemporary public attitudes about corporations, Prof. Seymour Martin Lipset of Stanford University and coeditor of *Public Opinion*, to review the manuscript, and he confirmed the authenticity of the references.

The public policy issues discussed in this book affect almost all large United States corporations. While the issues are also of concern to smaller companies, they are generally discussed in terms of the problems and initiatives taken by large corporations such as those in the *Fortune* 500. Whereas companies in that category are heterogeneous in many respects, they are, in common, highly visible objects of public observation and government attention. Although the same or similar corporate issues exist in other countries and United States companies are affected by them there, the issues are dealt with as matters of United States public policy.

*Corporate Performance: The Key to Public Trust* had its origins as an individual project that would never have been completed without the collaboration of the members of the Resource and Review Committee and the encouragement and support of many other people. In conducting studies on public policy issues, I became aware that no one had arrayed the principal corporate performance issues, described them coherently and systematically in the context of the public policy process, considered their interrelationships, and examined their impact on the evolving role of the large corporation. Yet, to produce such holistic knowledge in a timely fashion seemed too comprehensive a project to accomplish alone.

Fortunately, a coincidence of needs and interests was recognized by Robert M. Estes, a former senior vice president and general counsel of the General Electric Company. As a special counsel to the Business Roundtable Task Force on Economic Organization, Robert Estes knew that the missing subject in the panoply of studies sponsored by the task force was a critical analysis of the performance of the large corporation, and he recommended my unfulfilled project to satisfy that need.

The Business Roundtable was an ideal sponsor. Robert M. Hatfield, then chairman of the Continental Group, Inc., and chairman of the task force, gave solid encouragement from the start. Thomas S. Thompson, vice president, corporate affairs, and Robert Hatfield's administrator of the task force, was enthusiastic and supportive from start to finish and beyond. He was ably assisted by Steven Markowitz.

One of my first steps was to recruit several people with substantial corporate experience and in-depth knowledge of public issues and the public policy process as a Resource and Review Committee. This carefully selected group agreed to be a source of ideas and to review drafts of the subject material of our study. The committee met for intensive discussions on six occasions over a period of 2 years, and, in addition, individual members and I had innumerable conversations and a great deal of correspondence.

Several committee members made contributions far beyond the basic purpose of resource and review. Kirk Hanson was in on the planning from the formation of the committee and initiated drafts on "Legal and Ethical Behavior," "Social Performance," and "Executive Compensation and Perquisites." Carl Kaufmann prepared the chapter "Quality of Working Life" and introduced "Employee Citizenship Rights." Dan Hirshfield initiated the draft of "Health, Safety, and the Environment."

Peter Vanderwicken played an invaluable role. In addition to input based on his broad perspective of large corporations, his rich experience as a business editor contributed to the editorial features of the book.

John H. Tatlock, III, an associate in my office during much of the project, provided valuable assistance in drafting "Political Participation" and a great deal of ideation and research on many of the chapters. Mark Lowry performed the important task of checking references, reviewing copy, and proofreading the final manuscript.

The following people and organizations prepared background papers that were used as resource material in preparing the text: Courtney Brown, dean emeritus, Graduate School of Business, Columbia University; the Council of Better Business Bureaus by Richard Aszling, vice president (retired), General Foods Corporation; John L. Holcomb, formerly research director, Foundation for Public Affairs and now a professor of business and public policy at the University of Maryland; Professors Richard F. Walton and Leonard A. Schlesinger, Harvard Graduate School of Business Administration; Arnold P. Weber, professor of economics and president, University of Colorado; and the Financial Executives Research Foundation by William H. Beaver, Thomas D. Dee II Professor of Accounting, Stanford Graduate School of Business.

More than thirty business and academic authorities generously gave their time to review manuscripts. Their comments were encouraging in confirming the need for *Corporate Performance: The Key to Public Trust* not only in the business community and schools of management but for use by professional practitioners and students of government, law, journalism, economics, psychology, sociology, and science and engineering. The following reviewers made suggestions, many of which were incorporated in the book. We are grateful to all and acknowledge our sincere appreciation to them here: Herbert E. Alexander, director, Citizens' Research Foundation, University of Southern

California; L. Earle Birdzell, Jr., consultant; David W. Brady, professor of political science, Rice University; Courtney C. Brown, dean emeritus, Graduate School of Business, Columbia University; Rogene Buchholz, professor of management, University of Texas at Dallas; George D. Daly, dean, College of Social Sciences, University of Houston; Richard A. Edwards, senior vice president, Metropolitan Life Insurance Company; Robert L. Fegley, staff executive, chief executive officer, communications, General Electric Company; Wallace C. Fulton, vice president, the Equitable Life Assurance Society of the United States; David Gottlieb, professor of sociology, University of Houston; Richard S. Hait, manager, public relations, the Procter & Gamble Company; Kenneth Harwood, professor of communication, University of Houston; Walter G. Held, professor and founder of the Business and Public Policy Center, American University; J. C. Jacobsen, controller, Shell Oil Company; H. W. Judson, manager, consumer relations (retired), Shell Oil Company; Gerald Keim, associate professor of management and leader of the Business and Public Policy Group, Texas A&M University; Eugene R. Kline, vice president, public affairs, Bethlehem Steel Corporation; J. Clayburn LaForce, dean, Graduate School of Management, University of California at Los Angeles; Thomas F. McGarry, vice president, corporate communications, Pitney Bowes, Inc.; Ira M. Millstein, senior partner, Weil, Gotshal & Manges; William E. Moffett, vice president, Public Affairs, Gulf Oil Corporation; R. D. Mullineaux, general manager, health, safety, and environment, Shell Oil Company; Frederick L. Neumann, Price Waterhouse Professor of Auditing, University of Illinois; A. J. O'Brien, manager, internal controls, Shell Oil Company; James E. Post, professor of management and public policy, Boston University; Lee E. Preston, professor and director, Center for Business and Public Policy, University of Maryland; Andrew J. Schroeder, vice president, public affairs, General Foods Corporation; L. William Seidman, vice chairman, Phelps Dodge Corporation; S. Prakash Sethi, professor, School of Management and Administration, and director, Center for Research in Business and Social Policy, University of Texas at Dallas; John K. Tabor, partner, Reavis & McGrath; Wayne E. Thompson, senior vice president, Dayton Hudson Corporation (retired); and David Vogel, professor, Schools of Business Administration, University of California at Berkeley.

Beyond these acknowledgments and thanks, I have a deep sense of gratitude for the encouragement, freedom, and support given by the management of my company. Since 1970 three successive vice presidents of public affairs steadfastly supported my work on corporate public policy issues: Charles A. Foster, Jr., initiated me into public policy studies; his successor, Harry E. Walker, gave the go-ahead on the project that led to this book; and his successor, Philip J. Carroll, Jr., has patiently seen me through completion of it. They, like the Roundtable officers, gave me complete freedom in every step, from organizing the project to the completion of the book.

While both the authors of background papers and those who reviewed manuscripts provided important information or suggestions and the Resource and Review Committee members concur with the contents and conclusions, I am solely responsible for the text of the book.

**Francis W. Steckmest**
*Consultant, Public Affairs*
*Shell Oil Company*

## PART ONE

# The Large Corporation in the Public Policy Arena

A merican corporations, both large and small, have achieved an impressive record of performance in improving the human condition. Along with the contributions of government, education, the professions, and other institutions and operating within the freedoms and constraints of the private enterprise system, they have enabled our society to create unprecedented economic well-being and standards of living. In virtually every field from agriculture to xerography, large corporations in particular have used their ability to mobilize people, capital, and technology to increase human productivity, security, income, and welfare. They have generated or contributed to many of this century's most notable economic, technological, and social achievements. These benefits not only have been salutary to the American people but have, in numerous cases, been extended by the operation of private enterprise in many other nations.

Notwithstanding those historic achievements, large United States corporations and their leaders have suffered severe losses of public confidence. While trust in all institutions and their leaders has declined since the late 1960s, the losses of confidence in large corporations and corporate executives have been among the most serious. Corporate executives can take little comfort from the generalized and diffuse nature of diminished public confidence, since the decline of trust in the large corporation as an institution has been attended by extraordinary public criticism, the unparalleled imposition of government controls, and burgeoning public expectations and demands for improved corporate performance in many ways. These are the conditions that have set the corporate public policy agenda as described in Chapter 1.

The contemporary concern about the effects of corporate performance has been spurred by some leaders of public-interest groups who focus public attention on aberrant corporate performance by conducting well-publicized demonstrations, lobbying, and litigation. Those activities have been employed with vigor and effectiveness, and they have been instrumental in helping to make the large corporation a central topic of public and political debate in our society. Thus, contemporary examination of the economic performance of the large corporation has been joined by a more emotional debate about the nature amd extent of "corporate power" and "corporate accountability" as discussed in Chapter 2.

# CHAPTER 1

# The Corporate
# Public Policy Agenda

Clearly our society now demands something more of the large corporation than its traditional role provides. There is ample evidence that in a wide range of areas, from legal and ethical behavior to the impact of technology, many previously acceptable or unquestioned aspects of corporate performance have become unacceptable to large segments of the public and have become prominent issues of national public policy. While large corporations can rightfully share credit with government, education, the professions, and other institutions for economic and social progress, they also share blame for certain societal problems and the unsatisfactory performance of the economy.

Many of the new expectations and much of the criticism reflect a greatly broadened view of the large corporation that includes important social and political functions and responsibilities arising from its basic economic activity. A factor contributing to this phenomenon is that the external social and political environment has become a steadily more decisive element in corporate affairs. There is scarcely any major trend or problem—social, economic, political, or technological—that does not, to some degree, affect the large corporation or that is not, in turn, affected by it. In this environment, the large United States corporation has become a subject of great public interest, and various aspects of corporate performance have themselves become important issues on the public policy agenda.

## THE CORPORATE PERFORMANCE ISSUES

Because of the broadened view of the large corporation, the concept of "corporate performance" has also become much broader. Traditionally, corporate performance has referred primarily to financial results, the bottom line, the size of net profits, or the return on investment. But to many people corporate performance has assumed other meanings that they believe are equally valid. Those people are concerned with how corporate performance affects them as customers, shareholders, employees, neighbors, and citizens as well as with its effects on the social and physical environments. As a result, corporations have been increasingly judged by their overall performance—by the social, political, and technological impacts as well as by the economic and financial results.

The corporate performance issues discussed in this book reflect the broadened view of the corporation. They are marketplace performance, profit, financial reporting and control, public disclosure, legal and ethical behavior, quality of working life, employee citizenship rights, health, safety, and the environment, technological innovation, political participation, social performance, and executive compensation and perquisites. Not only do these issues reflect the broader view of the large corporation, they also have these further characteristics: they are common to large corporations, they require top-management decision making and accountability, and they have affected and will continue to affect the role of the large corporation and the nature of the private enterprise system.

## THE CORPORATE GOVERNANCE ISSUES

Most of the corporate performance issues reflect underlying questions about how corporate managements should be accountable for use of their decision-making authority or, from some critics' viewpoint, their use of corporate power. This public concern has been magnified by people who believe that neither individual laws and regulations nor actions by corporate managements can achieve their views of acceptable corporate performance. Those people contend that questions of corporate performance can be resolved only by imposing reforms of corporate governance and limitations on corporate size. They also contend that while large corporations have become quasi-public in their nature, they are governed essentially as private institutions and therefore should be made more accountable to a variety of interests.

These arguments have been instrumental in propagating the corporate governance issues involving corporate chartering, shareholder rights, and boards of directors.

## THE CORPORATE ISSUES IN THE REAGAN ERA

Shortly before his inauguration, President Reagan called attention to the fact that the United States is virtually alone among the industrialized nations in the adversarial nature of the relationship between its government and the business-industrial sector. In explaining that his administration would have a keen appreciation of the need to end that adversarial relationship, Reagan, however, cautioned that "it does not follow that our purpose will be to protect business or to help one business or industry stifle competition by another."[1]

President Reagan advocates policies that are intended to create a more favorable economic environment and less government control over individuals and institutions, including business. The large corporation, as an important means to help achieve the President's goals, can only benefit, for example, from the rolling back of various regulations and the adoption of tax policies that encourage capital formation. However, public criticism of the large corporation remains, and the question of government control is at the heart of the corporate performance and governance issues. The reason is not that the general public favors government control over private freedom or does not support our economic system but that people see government as the only means of control when the market system or corporate management, or both, fail to control corporate malpractices. Public confidence and trust are likely to improve only when most people are generally satisfied with all aspects of corporate performance.

Despite their cheering in the wake of the 1980 elections, corporate executives, more than ever, are on trial to deliver results. With less government involvement in corporate decisions, they have greater opportunity to help build a capital base, increase productivity and international competitiveness, provide jobs, improve real income, and handle some societal problems by greater reliance on market forces. Corporate managements will be severely criticized if the results are unimpressive or antisocial.

William M. Batten, chairman of the New York Stock Exchange, has

[1]Ronald Reagan, "Business and Government in the 1980s," a report prepared for the Public Affairs Council, Washington, January 1981; also published in The Wall Street Journal, Jan. 9, 1981, p. 18.

pointed out that an essentially probusiness environment "offers Corporate America an opportunity to do all of the constructive, responsible things business always said it would do if only the climate were more favorable." He cautioned, however, that if the public is dissatisfied with how business conducts itself in a favorable environment, then "both the Administration and business are likely to be very vulnerable in November 1984."[2] Meanwhile, public dissatisfaction with large corporations and distrust of corporate executives could well interfere with the ability of the Reagan administration to attain and retain many of the remedial policies it seeks, particularly those that would be beneficial to corporations.

The 1980 elections thus offered corporate managements no excuse to avoid facing up to the corporate performance and governance issues. Nor do other arguments offer plausible hope that these issues will "go away and stay away," even though corporate executives point out rightly that in many ways performance is better than the public's perception of it. It can be argued, equally convincingly, that corporations are blamed for some problems that are mostly created elsewhere. Moreover, there are no simple and conclusive methods for dealing with many of these issues. While all that may be true, the responsibility for corporate performance and governance rests on management's doorstep. Leading executives themselves have long made this point, urging their colleagues to address performance issues squarely. When chairman of General Motors, Thomas A. Murphy said that "the clock is running on free enterprise and it is later than we think. I want to make certain that we recognize that all the fault does not lie elsewhere—much of it lies in our business community, and perhaps in our own organizations."[3]

The challenge thus is critical for managements to understand and respond to public concerns about large corporations. Such responses require effective management of the broader dimensions of corporate performance and active participation in the public policy process by which laws and regulations are formulated or alternative solutions are reached. Essential to managing these broader dimensions and participating in the public policy process, as broadly defined, is an understanding of the public's perception of corporate power and the balancing factor of corporate accountability.

[2]William M. Batten, "Why I Do Not Want to Talk about Corporate Governance," Bracebridge H. Young Memorial Address of the National Conference of the American Society of Corporate Secretaries, Inc., June 25, 1981.

[3]Thomas A. Murphy, "The Corporation and Public Opinion: Economic Freedom or Government Control," address to the Associated Industries of New York, Lake Placid, N.Y., Sept. 24, 1976; reprinted in *Vital Speeches of the Day*, Nov. 1, 1976.

# CHAPTER 2

# Corporate Power
# and Accountability

Regardless of the economic and social contributions of corporations, their size, scope, and impacts on people engender public concern that corporate managements have discretionary powers which can be and sometimes are used in disregard of or, in some cases, in wayscontrary to various views of what constitutes the public interest. The contemporary concern about corporate power is that important management authorities are substantially unrestrained—that corporate executives have significant discretion to make critical decisions affecting the lives of many people.

The belief that corporate managements wield excessive power is a sensitive issue for a pluralistic democratic society. It is almost always cited as underlying the causes of public policy issues involving corporations. Examples of unsatisfactory corporate performance are used to focus public attention on the extent to which large corporations and their managements have the day-to-day power to affect people, other institutions, and the social, political, and physical environments. In the end, public debate about corporate performance issues centers on this question: How should the managements of large corporations be held accountable for their use of power?

The manner in which this question is resolved by corporate management, government, and relevant interest groups will determine the balance between private and government control. That balance, in turn, will greatly affect both the future of the large corporation and the character of American society.

7

## CORPORATE POWER

"Corporate power" generally eludes straightforward definition and measurement. While it is obvious that the officers of large corporations possess extensive authority needed to manage a business, corporate executives often regard corporate power as illusory and the term itself as adversarial rhetoric. The authority of corporate officers is subject to many and often conflicting constraints by such corporate constituents as governments, competitors, shareholders, customers, employees, unions, the media, public-interest groups, and the intellectual community, as well as being constrained by the complexity of the large companies which top executives are presumed to control. In contrast, leaders and members of various corporate constituencies usually believe that the power of large corporations and their managements is enormous. As a result, whatever the complaint or demand, their purposed remedy involves another constraint on management, usually some form of government control. John D. deButts, the former chairman of the American Telephone & Telegraph Co., commented on corporate power in this way:

> It makes very little difference that we who are presumed to be so powerful have very little occasion to feel that way. It makes very little difference that in real life the range of options open to management decision is—except at very high risk—much more restricted than the public imagines it to be. And it makes very little difference that for a very long time we have had such a degree of government regulation over virtually every aspect of business operations as to leave very little question as to where the real power over the economy actually resides.
> However, what counts in this regard is not so much power as it is the perception of power. So long as business management is perceived as exercising power unchecked by public surveillance or countervailing force, it risks further infringement on areas of private decision and— eventually—the deterioration of the incentives that make enterprise enterprising.[1]

Corporate executives derive power from their management of a variety of financial, physical, technological, and human resources. The impact of management decisions is magnified by corporate size, whether measured in terms of a single corporation or aggregated on an industrywide, national, or international scale. Corporate power is manifested by such management actions as opening and closing plants or introducing or withdrawing products, all of which affect customers,

[1]John D. deButts, foreword to Chester Burger, *The Chief Executive: Realities of Corporate leadership,* CBI Publishing Company, Inc., Boston 1978, p. x.

employees, communities, and shareholders in different and sometimes contrary ways. For example, a corporate action that may benefit customers and shareholders may adversely affect a community. The concepts of corporate power and large size create another anomaly: when the performance of a large corporation satisfies general public expectations, few people raise serious questions about "bigness" or the proper use of corporate power; when corporate performance, such as environmental pollution, adversely affects people, large corporations are criticized as "too powerful"; yet, when a large corporation falters or fails, its management is characterized as "too weak."

The power issue becomes particularly acute when public and political opinion reaches a flash point of discontent over corporate performance. As a consequence, government control of corporate size and power becomes a rallying point for advocates of both specific regulations concerning corporate performance and, even more drastically, government controls on corporate governance and corporate size.

Americans are apprehensive about the power inherent in other large institutions such as government and labor. Still, the large corporation is in many ways a special object of public concern. For example, many individuals, as consumers, neighbors, employees, or shareholders, expect high standards of performance from large corporations and often feel relatively powerless when in business dealings their expectations are not met.

Government officials frequently target large corporations for special attention in enforcing laws and regulations in part to set an example for smaller, "less powerful" companies. Media, public-interest groups, and government officials reinforce public apprehensions of power by citing alleged or actual corporate malpractices as evidence of management misuse of corporate power that requires corrective action. Politicians have long used "the big corporation" as a favorite campaign opponent and "curbing the big monied interests" as an effective campaign slogan. Critics of capitalism use examples of corporate misconduct to attack the United States political and economic system at home and overseas.

Some critics charge that the power exercised by corporate managements is illegitimate because chief executive officers or boards of directors, or both, have preempted control from the shareholder-owners of corporations. Other critics of corporate governance contend that the power of large corporations can be regarded as legitimate only when fundamental changes are enacted, such as public representation on boards of directors and almost unlimited disclosure of corporate decision making and its effects. A few critics argue that privately controlled corporations are incompatible with a democratic society.

Public perception of corporate power is magnified by concern about the motivation and behavior of executives. For example, in a study of large institutions, Professors Seymour Martin Lipset and William Schneider of the Hoover Institution on War, Revolution and Peace concluded that top corporate executives are perceived as being driven by different motives from those of leaders of other social institutions, such as medicine, religion, law, and education, whose purposes are seen as essentially selfless and intended to benefit the whole society. Corporations and their executives, by contrast, are seen as motivated by self-interest. "The public view," Lipset and Schneider concluded, "is that business people are motivated by economic self-interest and, thus, concentrated power in the hands of the self-interested is inherently dangerous and untrustworthy."[2] This is not a new perception, but as Clifton C. Garvin, Jr., chairman of the Exxon Corporation and the 1980–1981 chairman of the Business Roundtable, has observed, "The impression that all business is strictly self-serving is more pervasive now than it perhaps has ever been."[3]

Power at the disposal of corporate managements is highly visible and personally affects or is a potential threat to a great variety of people, other institutions, and their interests. As a result, the phenomenon of corporate power raises the question of how corporate managements are or should be held accountable for the exercise of the power inherent in managing large corporations.

## CORPORATE ACCOUNTABILITY

The perception of substantially unrestrained power held by corporate managements suffuses all the performance and governance issues discussed in this book and is among the most important and fundamental public concerns about the large corporation. While corporate executives deny that they possess the vast amount of power imputed to them, it is not sufficient to contend that they possess little power. But the existence of corporate power does not mean that the use of that power is unlimited or unrestrained.

Large corporations have high public and political visibility; their activities are monitored by consumers, employees, politicians, govern-

[2]Seymour Martin Lipset and William Schneider, *The Confidence Gap: How Americans View Their Institutions,* Macmillan Publishing Co., Inc., New York, 1981. Copyright © 1981, The Trustees of Columbia University in the City of New York. Reprinted by permission of The Free Press.

[3]Clifton C. Garvin, address given at the Harvard Business Club International Dinner, New York, Apr. 16, 1980.

ment regulators, the media, labor, shareholders, public-interest groups, and the general public. Of all company managements, those of large corporations are among the least able to avoid public scrutiny of abuses of power. Thus, the size of the large corporation inherently provides a check on potential management abuse of power.

In considering the relationships between corporate accountability, corporate performance, and corporate power, it is helpful to review restraints on corporate power. In addition to the body of general laws applicable to everyone, Ira Millstein and Salem M. Katsh of Weil, Gotshal & Manges classify the legal restraints in these categories:[4]

- *State chartering laws and Securities and Exchange Commission (SEC) requirements.* State corporation laws provide both procedural and substantive prohibitions on corporate managers, precluding them, for example, from significantly changing the rights of shareholders without their approval, from taking personal advantage of corporate opportunities, and from failing to exercise due diligence in managing the corporation's activities. The trend of judicial decisions and SEC initiatives has been both to broaden the scope of shareholder interests (e.g., corporate compliance with foreign-country boycotts) and substantially to increase the risk of liability and public exposure for corporate managers who improperly disregard these interests.

- *Competition imposed by the market system.* The market pressures companies to compete for consumer preferences in a wide variety of ways, from quality products and services to increased productivity and innovative production methods. Indeed, notwithstanding the explosion in government regulation over the past half century, the competitive market system is still the principal means of making the corporation accountable to society's economic needs and wants. Direct governmental controls have been placed upon corporate performance through trade regulation and securities laws for the purpose of protecting the competitive market system.

- *Constraining influences of tax law.* The tax law, by means of monetary incentives and penalties, promotes and discourages various corporate activities in the areas of capital formation, resource allocation, and employment. Many provisions of the tax law also constrain corporate behavior in ways clearly unintended by Congress and encourage activities that other provisions flatly discourage. Walter B. Wriston, chairman of Citibank/Citicorp, gave an example of that

[4]Ira M. Millstein and Salem M. Katsh, *The Limits of Corporate Power*, Macmillan Publishing Co., Inc., New York, 1981. Copyright © 1981, The Trustees of Columbia University in the City of New York. Reprinted by permission of The Free Press.

phenomenon when he referred to the government's writing tax laws that encourage corporate managements to make a takeover bid rather than build new facilities and then putting the Justice Department to work probing for antitrust problems.[5]

- *Direct government controls which regulate corporate performance.* Corporate managers are well aware of the vast array of restrictions, including regulations of union-management relations, equal employment, occupational safety and health, the environment, consumer protection, political activity, and energy. These regulations can substantially influence the decision-making process of the large corporation in many ways, some unintended.

There are three other constraints on corporate managements in their use of power in managing corporate affairs:

- *Public pressures.* Individuals, the media, and public-interest groups that feel they have a stake in how corporations behave are active in pursuing their interests. In many cases, they originate or highlight corporate issues that later come to the forefront of national attention. As a result, in the last decade many corporate managements have developed a sensitivity to the concerns generated by others.

- *Peer pressure.* Subtle but important pressures are generated by the managements of large corporations on each other. Corporate and executive performance is observed and discussed within the corporate community. For example, a violation of law may well diminish the violator's professional reputation and social standing; significant failure in protecting worker health and the environment may create greater attention than a new marketing strategy. Corporate performance and the quality of top executives are comprehensively covered in the business literature that executives read. They are also the subjects of speeches and informal discussions in chief-executive peer groups such as the Business Council, the Business Roundtable, the Business–Higher Education Forum, and meetings or retreats of the Conference Board and the Committee for Economic Development. Although little noticed by the public or even by the media or critics, the peer pressures that result are a substantial constraint against malpractice. More important, they are an incentive for socially and politically acceptable performance.

- *Voluntary corporate accountability.* An alternative to ever-increasing government-imposed accountability is the concept of voluntary ac-

[5]Walter B. Wriston, "The Consent of the Governed: Add Your Own Two Cents Worth," *Enterprise*, February 1981, p. 9.

countability. This concept is based on effective management participation in the public policy process and sensitive interaction with
constituent interests that manifest a sense of voluntary accountability
to the broader society. This emerging process, discussed in Chapter
22, may ease public pressures for additional compulsory corporate
accountability.

Except for voluntary corporate accountability, all the foregoing types
of accountability provide rigorous external limitations on the exercise
of power by corporate managements. Voluntary corporate accountability can provide whatever restraints on the potential misuse of power by
executives and managers that a corporate management wishes to adopt
and enforce. Yet, if corporate performance engenders broad public
concern that corporate power is being abused, all seven forms of
accountability—no matter how well understood by the public in
principle—will be discredited as inadequate on quantitative and qualitative grounds.

Responsible exercise of power and accountability for its use are the
twin themes that underlie this book. Most of the individual performance issues discussed in the following chapters reflect in the end those
fundamental concerns about large corporations in our society. Of
course, corporations and their managements are judged by their performance as experienced or perceived by the public and not by the
processes they use to plan, execute, or account for their performance.

# PART TWO

# The Corporate Performance Issues

T he twelve United States domestic policy issues discussed in Part Two have arisen from the concerns of critics and the public about large corporations and their executives. There are, of course, many other issues that involve large corporations, but these twelve are specifically concerned with corporate performance and governance, they are common to large corporations, and they are matters that require corporatewide policies and top-management decisions. Although these issues are applicable to most companies, they are discussed largely in terms of examples and actions of large corporations.

While the twelve issues are not new, each continues to evolve and change as it is affected by the external environment, by pressures brought by government, the media, and the other public policy participants, and by the quality of individual company performance and that of large corporations as a whole. What is offered here that may be new to many executives and others interested in corporations and public policy is a descriptive analysis of the issues in this format. In each chapter, the issue is introduced by a definition, a statement about its importance, and a discussion of its causes. This summary introduction is followed by a comprehensive brief about the nature, evolution, and status of the issue and the principal parties involved, examples of corporate initiatives and actions in dealing with the issue and its causes, and the outlook for the issue in the foreseeable future.

15

As an overview, the chapters are a comprehensive but not an exhaustive exploration of each issue and all its facets. As a result, some practitioners or other authorities may regard the treatment of their specialties as incomplete or even superficial. Also, it was not possible to evaluate the validity or lack of validity of each criticism of corporate performance. The criticisms and justifications are cited because they help explain public attitudes, the behavior of government officials, the media, and interest groups, and the workings of the public policy process that have already affected the large corporation and its management in substantial ways.

# CHAPTER 3

# Marketplace Performance

***The Issue*** • The basic charter of business is to produce useful, safe, and reliable goods and services for society. Yet many people feel that business is not performing well enough in meeting their expectations in the marketplace. What are those expectations, and how can corporation managements address them more effectively?

***Importance*** • There is substantial evidence of customer dissatisfaction with corporate marketplace performance. One obvious manifestation of consumers' discontent has been their support for more extensive government regulation of business's marketplace practices. When chairman of General Motors, Thomas A. Murphy concluded: "The increasing regulation by government is a reaction to the mood of a large segment of the public that is disappointed, dissatisfied, and disenchanted with the everyday performance of American business, especially big business."[1] Other indications and consequences of widespread consumer dissatisfaction are the increased sales of some imported products such as automobiles, the rising tide of

[1]Thomas A. Murphy, "The Corporation and Public Opinion: Economic Freedom or Government Control," address to the Associated Industries of New York, Lake Placid, N.Y., Sept. 24, 1976. Reprinted in *Vital Speeches of the Day*, Nov. 1, 1976.

17

product liability lawsuits, and the expanded concept of corporate liability recognized by the courts.

Beyond the specific problems that flow from consumer dissatisfaction with business, there are more general consequences. Public disappointment with corporate performance in providing goods and services involves other performance issues, such as corporate legal and ethical behavior, disclosure of relevant information, and impact on health, safety, and the environment. In combination, these issues reinforce each other and have contributed to the erosion of general public confidence in business, lessened support for the private enterprise system, and encouragement of antibusiness activists.

*Causes* • When consumers believe that they have been poorly served by business in such areas as product quality, price, safety and information, packaging and labeling, advertising, credit, or redress of grievances, their dissatisfaction erupts into anger and frustration, generating public support for greater government control of business.

A Business Roundtable report on the business agenda for the 1980s recognized this issue:

> The experience of business in the postwar era of "rising expectations" has given it a sharpened awareness of the importance of reading consumer concerns accurately and responding to them. The considerable increase in the size of business units—especially in retailing but also in manufacturing—has tended inevitably to create an impression of impersonality or unconcern on the part of companies that supply consumers with their daily needs. Business knows this is not a healthy situation and is dedicated to correcting it.[2]

## PUBLIC ATTITUDES TOWARD MARKETPLACE PERFORMANCE

The things that consumers expect of the companies whose products and services they purchase are not difficult to determine. Nor do they change over time, although their organized expression may seem to have become more strident and articulate in recent years. Basically, these are the marketplace expectations of the American consumer:

[2]*Yes, Business Has an Agenda*, Business Roundtable, report of Mar. 17, 1980, p. 7.

- Quality products and dependable services at reasonable prices
- Competent and concerned sales and service personnel
- Convenient and well-planned sales and customer service facilities
- Honest and informative advertising
- Reliable and readily available information to facilitate sound purchase decisions and proper use of products
- Prompt and efficient handling of complaints and grievances
- Absence of fraud and deception
- Safe and wholesome products and services

Besides these expectations, many consumers have come to expect other characteristics in large corporations, such as fair and considerate treatment of employees, suppliers, dealers, and others with whom they do business, protection of the environment, and a sense of public accountability.

A well-known consumer relations survey has shown the gap between public expectations and business performance as a whole.[3] In identifying the concerns that trouble consumers most, the survey found that eight of the top ten relate directly to the performance of business in the marketplace. In descending order of concern, these are (1) the high price of everything, (2) the poor quality of many products, (3) the failure of some companies to live up to the claims of their advertising, (4) the poor quality of aftersales service and repairs, (5) the feeling that some manufacturers do not care about their customers, (6) products breaking or failing soon after purchase, (7) misleading packaging or labeling, and (8) the feeling that it is futile to complain about consumer problems because businesses will not redress grievances.

Despite the breadth and intensity of consumer dissatisfaction indicated by that survey and many others, the picture is not entirely gloomy. Although Americans are displeased with the performance of business, they have by no means given up on business. A sizable majority continues to look to business as the source of economic strength and growth and as the wellspring of needed innovation.

The natural subjectivity of the individual consumer is also a factor to be taken into account. The purchase of a product or service is the average person's most frequent (perhaps only) contact with large corporations, and it follows that failure to meet consumer expectations

---

[3]*Consumerism at the Crossroads*, survey conducted by Louis Harris and Associates, Inc., and the Marketing Science Institute for Sentry Insurance, 1977.

may produce an exaggerated impact on public attitudes. Moreover, an individual's attitude may not be drawn from firsthand experience but from what he or she has heard about the experiences of others.

The public's increased awareness of marketplace performance has been encouraged by two significant developments. One is the widespread adoption by elementary and secondary schools of courses dealing with consumer concerns and rights. The other is the great increase in coverage of consumer issues by the media. Many newspapers and television stations now have consumer affairs editors and consumer "action line" features. These developments have increased public sensitivity to corporate marketplace performance.

Consumer dissatisfaction and the political action which it spawns cannot be viewed as a discrete public issue. While the corporate executive understandably addresses this dissatisfaction as a distinct problem, in the public mind it is part of a larger mosaic. Consumers do not draw sharp lines between marketplace failures and other sources of annoyance in shaping their attitudes toward business. They lump their experiences and perceptions without any particular effort at sorting them. An example of that phenomenon is the annoyance of some consumers with product packaging—a concern that extends beyond criticism of a marketing practice to public concerns about litter, environmental damage if the packaging is not biodegradable, and waste of resources if the packaging is viewed as excessive.

Thus what appears to be a marketplace issue merges with other performance issues, such as corporate legal and ethical behavior, profit, health, safety, and the environment, political participation, and social performance. The public's lack of distinction between marketplace disappointments and other criticisms of business magnifies general antibusiness attitudes. Politicians and business critics understand this all too human trait and take full advantage of it. They understand that it is easier for the average citizen to comprehend marketplace shortfalls and other perceived faults of business than complex, esoteric issues such as corporate governance. Hence, they capitalize on the political appeal inherent in consumerism.

More broadly, many consumers feel that large corporations are remote, impersonal, and unresponsive. They believe that corporations take advantage of inflation and rising raw-material costs to conceal excessive price increases and profiteering. These perceptions of business, although not directly related to disappointments with products and services, tend to reinforce the adverse attitudes arising from marketplace disappointments, and vice versa.

Finally, among the factors underlying the issue, it must be noted that consumers are apparently aware that not all companies are guilty of the shortcomings they attribute to business, but nevertheless they seem to hold business as a whole accountable for inadequate performance in the marketplace. And they look to business leadership, particularly executives of large corporations, to devise and enforce the self-discipline within their companies that will produce needed remedies and set positive examples within the corporate community.

## GOVERNMENT AND CONSUMER-GROUP ACTIONS

Although legislation to protect the consumer has gained prominence as a political vogue in the last two decades, it is by no means a recent development. The establishment of the Interstate Commerce Commission in 1887, for instance, was an early federal legislative action aimed at curbing abuses by the railroad industry.

The current era of legislative controls on marketing practices began in 1962 with the amendments to the Food, Drug, and Cosmetic Act that required generic labeling and pretesting of drugs for safety and efficacy. That was followed by a spate of new laws covering everything from packaging and labeling to cigarette advertising, flammable fabrics, and consumer credit and from freedom of information to protection of privacy. Many of these measures were of the so-called "truth-in" variety. More consumer legislation was enacted in the 1970s than in the entire prior history of the nation.

The largest element of the consumer movement is the Consumer Federation of America, a coalition of organizations whose more than 200 members include state and local consumer groups, rural electric co-ops, credit union leagues, national labor unions, and other interest groups. In addition to the Consumer Federation and several other national organizations, there are countless local and national organizations of every character. Some of them are committed to such disruptive actions against business as boycotts, class-action lawsuits, and defiant rallies. Others are constructive and moderate, interested in improved corporate performance and willing to work collaboratively with business toward common ends. Obviously, a major challenge to business in this whole area is to distinguish among the various groups, identify those which have hidden agendas and are committed to disruption, and proffer cooperation to those with which productive joint action is possible. A number of large corporations have begun to see the potential value in collaborative efforts with consumer-oriented groups. An interesting example is the Food Safety Council, which was established several years ago as a joint undertaking of the food industry and representatives of consumer organizations and public agencies to try to bring order into the chaotic area of safety standards for food ingredients.

## CORPORATE INITIATIVES AND ACTIONS

The first and most self-evident need is to make every feasible effort to meet consumers' expectations. Several corporate leaders have observed this. Said James L. Ferguson, chairman of General Foods Corporation: "We've got to give the customers their money's worth. All the well designed efforts to cope with the march of consumerism will come to nothing if the goods and services we turn out don't measure up, especially to the claims of our advertising."[4]

Beyond giving customers their money's worth, a growing number of companies, reports the Business Roundtable, are meeting bona fide consumer concerns in ways such as these: voluntary additions to label information, meticulous documentation of advertising claims, increased corporate disclosure, and programs of self-regulation. In addition, many large corporations have developed thoughtful and well-executed programs aimed at meeting specific expectations of consumers. These include toll-free telephone service for customer inquiries about problems or service, effective methods for prompt and responsive complaint handling, and worthwhile consumer information.

Additionally, a number of trade and business organizations have instituted industrywide programs supported by their constituent companies. One that is often cited for its effectiveness is the Major Appliance Consumer Action Panel (MACAP), which, as its name implies, was created by the major-appliance industry to see that consumers receive prompt and satisfactory handling of complaints. Other industries have emulated this successful example.

Seeing the need to organize properly to respond to burgeoning marketplace pressure, many corporations in recent years have added consumer affairs departments. In the last decade, managers of this new business function make up the Society of Consumer Affairs Professionals in Business (SOCAP), with more than 1000 members representing most of the large corporations in consumer goods industries. SOCAP has earned respect as a clearinghouse of useful ideas and a force for the

[4]James L. Ferguson, "Consumerism Revisited," address to the annual meeting of the American Association of Advertising Agencies, White Sulphur Springs, W. Va., May 17, 1974.

elevation of business standards and corporate effectiveness in identifying and meeting consumer needs.

As the overall business advocate of the consumer, the Council of Better Business Bureaus (CBBB) has many effective programs. Its National Business-Consumer Arbitration Program provides for effective settlement of disputes between businesses and their customers, with more than 20,000 businesses in ninety-four cities having precommitted themselves to accept the outcome of arbitration. CBBB is the parent of another national effort to attack a frequent source of consumer complaint: deceptive advertising. The National Advertising Division of CBBB, since its inception in 1970, has handled more than 1600 cases, of which about one-third have been based on consumer complaints and slightly more than that on the National Advertising Division's own monitoring function.

The experiences of corporate managements that are deeply involved in the retail marketplace suggest that the elements of a successful consumer relations strategy must include these actions:

- Identify and understand the consumer issues relating to their specific businesses. Consumer issues vary from industry to industry, but they meld in the public's development of attitudes toward business.
- Identify and understand the relationship between marketplace issues and nonmarketplace issues. Environmental protection, opposition to nuclear energy, civil rights, equal opportunity, and other causes that have little or no relation to marketing are nonetheless linked with marketplace issues by the critics of business and the consumers they influence.
- Establish responsibility within the company for consumer response and consumer satisfaction among the major corporate management functions and include them in setting objectives.
- Require the development of effective programs within the company and encourage effective efforts by the business associations which the company supports.
- Engage in positive dialogue with responsible leaders of the consumer movement and with legislators and other government officials.
- By the same token, refute promptly and effectively incorrect assertions or irresponsible actions by consumer activists, and oppose openly legislative proposals that are demonstrably counterproductive.

Some people believe that the defeat in 1978 of a bill proposing a new federal consumer protection agency marked a turning point in government regulation of business. While the efforts of business in opposition to the measure were effective, another reason for its demise was public objection to more bureaucracy.

## THE OUTLOOK

The outlook for the consumer movement, whether or not it has peaked, is that it remains a very potent political force at both national and local levels. Consumer protection continues to be a popular interest of numerous members of Congress and state and local legislators. While the rapid expansion of consumer protection offices was taking place at the federal level, a parallel development was occurring at the state and local level. Many states and most major cities now have influential consumer affairs departments as part of their administrations. Another phenomenon has been the growth in the number and power of unofficial consumer protection organizations. According to Richard Aszling, former vice president of General Foods,

> It would be a self-deception to think that the consumer movement today continues to be the lengthened shadow of Ralph Nader, who first came to attention when he challenged the safety of the automobile. A decade ago, perhaps, the movement was a disconnected assortment of charismatic—and usually self-appointed—"spokesmen" like Nader. Today it is a professionally led, highly organized force.[5]

The thrust of the marketplace performance issue has been to stimulate companies to improve the quality and price of products and services and the quality and integrity of merchandising practices. Yet, as the business community has improved its marketplace performance, many consumer leaders have come to view that accomplishment as less than full evidence of publicly acceptable corporate performance. Broad-based, multi-issue consumer organizations continue to espouse consumer-oriented practices; however, many of them have turned to advocating benefits to consumers by supporting such objectives as deregulation of some industries, environmental protection, and corporate governance reform. Also, some consumerists have formed advocacy groups concerned with aspects of energy, nutrition, health care, and other narrower issues.

The consumer movement is, thus, undergoing change. Whether advocating policies on broad or narrow issues, numerous consumer

[5]Richard Aszling, unpublished background paper for the Resource and Review Committee.

groups are coalescing with environmental, health, labor, and other groups. Much of the legislative and regulatory activity is shifting to state and local governments.

While these changes have broadened the range of pressures on corporate managements, some consumer leaders are showing interest in problem-solving dialogue with managements. Such dialogue has, in turn, resulted in some opportunities for ad hoc coalitions and agreement on significant issues.

# CHAPTER 4

# Profit

*The Issue* • To what extent does emphasis on profit as the corporate purpose exclude adequate management consideration of other societal interests, including legal and ethical behavior? What is the appropriate magnitude of profit? These concerns have provoked the related question of whether or to what extent government should control or limit profits.

*Importance* • While profit is the major driving force of the private enterprise system, profit motivation is commonly cited as a principal cause of most kinds of unacceptable corporate performance. Corporate critics charge that the professed corporate objective of profit maximization is the reason why some corporate executives engage in unethical or illegal behavior.

Public concerns about corporate profit are among the most important, persistent, and difficult problems confronting corporate management. Like corporate power, corporate profit is a highly emotional issue. It poses the continuing dilemma of reconciling the conflicting claims and expectations of shareholders on one hand and other corporate constituents on the other. Another factor in the importance of this issue is that government limitation or control of profits can dampen entrepreneurial initiative and adversely affect the economy.

*Causes* • While the vast majority of Americans agree that profit is essential to the functioning of the United States economy, there is continuing public criticism that large corporations emphasize profits to the detriment of other important considerations, make excessive profits, and make them in unacceptable ways. The issue is intensified by financial reporting practices, allegations of profiteering, and basic disagreement concerning the effects of the profit motive on corporate decisions, the appropriate magnitude of profit, and the question of whether government should limit profits.

Following are brief summaries of the three principal aspects of the debate concerning the public issue of corporate profit.

## THE PROFIT MOTIVE AND CORPORATE DECISIONS

Many corporate executives assert that the primary purpose of the corporation is to *maximize profits* for shareholders by providing goods and services to the public. They add that profit serves society in many ways. It is a measure of management performance and an incentive for corporate efficiency, growth, and continuity. It is also a prerequisite for sustaining or increasing a corporation's ability to provide future products and services and to compensate its shareholders with both income from and increased value in their investment. Executives also point out that profit is the basis for creating jobs and enhancing employment conditions; and, of course, profit is taxed to help finance the public sector. Finally, profits perform the important economic function of directing the flow of capital into new ventures in response to consumer demand.

Important as all those functions and benefits of profits are, there is a widespread belief among the American people that the primary purpose of the corporation is to *provide goods and services* to the public with profit being the result of doing so successfully. The subtle distinction is important. The public does not see profit maximization as the purpose of business but rather sees profit as a reward for good performance of a company's basic function. This difference in perception tends to sustain the popular notion that corporate executives are ruled primarily by the profit motive and, at best, have a secondary interest in consumer satisfaction and other aspects of the public interest.

Another factor in the debate on the profit motive concerns the time frame in which profits are viewed. An increasing number of observers have suggested that a general preoccupation by corporate management with short-range profit goals, for whatever reason, hampers long-term planning and investment, with adverse effects not only on the vitality of their companies and their shareholders' interests but on United States technological innovation, productivity, and ability to compete with foreign companies. They believe that this overemphasis is the result of management's desire to raise the price of its company's stock, either to avoid unfriendly takeovers or to facilitate acquisition of other companies. They also point out that in many large companies bonuses and other forms of incentive compensation for executives are based on present profits or are enhanced by stock appreciation rather than being based on headway toward longer-range profit objectives.

One company that by its policy and performance has successfully coped with the profit motive question is the Dayton Hudson Corporation. Kenneth N. Dayton, chairman of the Executive Committee, described the purpose of that company in this way:

> Fundamentally, we believe business exists for only one purpose: to serve society. Profit is our reward for serving society well. It is the means and measure of our service, but it is not the end. There's nothing wrong with profit. Dayton Hudson is just as anxious for profit as any company in the country. And by any standard used to measure profit we are a leader in our industry. But we view profit from a different perspective.
>
> From the very beginning, our business strategy recognized that serving society was our central goal. We identified four key publics we aim to serve: our customers, our employees, our shareholders, and the communities where we do business. Now some of you may argue that there's conflict in trying to serve all four. But once we examined what our obligations were to these four constituencies, we concluded there was absolutely no conflict whatsoever in serving them all. They all want the business to be successful over the long haul, because unless it is it can't serve any of them well. So, the means by which we serve them all is profit. And the means by which we serve them all well—is *maximum, long-range* profit. This subtle difference in the perception of the role of profit—as a means not an end—is crucial.[1]

Despite the fact that many corporate managements are concerned with all factors that can affect their companies' profitability over the longer term, a Lipset-Schneider study of contemporary opinion polls

---

[1]Kenneth N. Dayton, "The Case for Corporate Philanthropy," address to the Forum Club of Houston, June 25, 1980.

found that more than two-thirds of the respondents in each poll believe that corporate managements put profits ahead of such considerations as morality, public need, human values, and jobs and wages.[2]

Some social critics regard the pursuit of profit as a corrupting influence that causes business people to act unfairly or even dishonestly and to neglect or disregard the interests of consumers and other groups, resulting in such abuses as consumer deception, monopolistic practices, and environmental degradation. As mentioned in Chapter 14, many people point to examples of corporate executive compensation and prequisites as evidence that profits are too high. Lipset and Schneider found that about two-thirds of the respondents in contemporary public opinion studies concluded that profits are used to pay too much to top management.

Nevertheless, most people believe that the competitive enterprise system is fundamentally sound and that the profit motive is morally neutral. The profit motive is seen as immoral only if used in an illegal or unethical manner. Many business observers add that some people will be immoral whether in pursuit of profit, power, prestige, political influence, pleasure, or other purposes. They also recognize that corporate executives, in addition to discharging their obligation to shareholders for profitable performance, are also increasingly accountable to other constituent groups and to many levels and agencies of government for all aspects of their performance.

## THE APPROPRIATE MAGNITUDE OF PROFIT

Many surveys have shown that the public is misinformed about the actual size of corporate profits. This general overestimation of corporate profits, furthermore, is prevalent at all levels of society, even among those generally considered to be better informed than the rest of the population. One explanation may be that many people confuse profit with the seller's markup, which, of course, must include all the costs of distribution. Another is the prevalent belief that many legitimate expenses, such as wages and pollution controls, are paid for out of profit. Thus, some opinion experts, such as Lipset, have concluded that overestimating profit does not necessarily mean that the public feels such profits are unreasonable. This conclusion tends to be supported

[2]Seymour Martin Lipset and William Schneider, *The Confidence Gap: How Americans View Their Institutions,* Macmillan Publishing Co., Inc., New York, 1981. Copyright © 1981, The Trustees of Columbia University in the City of New York. Reprinted by permission of The Free Press.

by the fact that a large majority of people select as appropriate levels of profit amounts that are considerably higher than corporations actually achieve.

Although corporate profit represents a small—and, over the past decade, a declining—percentage of both corporate sales and national income, some corporations have succeeded in achieving extraordinarily high profits. Public concern is fed by such examples and by inflationary prices, allegations of profiteering, and unions citing high profits as a justification for their bargaining demands. Hostility to profits is, in part, an expression of concern about higher prices, again because profit is commonly confused with markup. Also, as discussed in Chapter 5, "Financial Reporting and Control," some financial practices magnify the stated size of profits. Another factor is that most managements understandably like to present their stockholders with the best possible financial report compatible with accepted accounting practice. Further, some corporate managements do not give adequate public prominence to the more meaningful trends in margins on sales or in returns on stockholders' equity.

As every executive knows, the competitive marketplace serves as a regulator of profit in our economic system; except for unusual short-term market situations, competition prevents the exercise of unrestrained power in pricing decisions and profit levels. Those who disagree with this interpretation allege that some large corporations have obtained "excessive" profits by dominating, or sharing in the domination of, a highly concentrated industry, enabling them to reduce or nullify the effects of competition on their prices and profits.

In addition to providing the motivation for potential rewards, the role of profit has a deeper economic significance: profit and loss, along with price, play dominant roles in coordinating and controlling activity in our economic system. J. Clayburn La Force, dean of the UCLA Graduate School of Management, has put it this way:

> When a company earns profits in a competitive market it has accomplished a significant and positive social service. By buying resources, producing a commodity, and then selling it for a gain, the company in effect has moved scarce resources from lower to higher valued uses. A net gain in consumer well-being has occurred. That is, the *costs* of a company represent the *value* to consumers of what could have been produced alternatively with the company's resources. And the revenues of the company represent the value to consumers of the resources in their present use. Profit means that the current use of resources has more value to people than alternative uses. Losses mean the opposite. It is not how large profits are or their importance to a company and its shareholders

that are most important—rather, it is their role in directing our scarce resources to their best uses that is of overriding importance.[3]

There is no simple or permanent benchmark to measure the reasonableness of profits. The question of what is reasonable profit in any industry is complicated by the wide spectrum of criteria used in measuring it, the diversity of accepted accounting standards, the impact of inflation, monetary fluctuations, and transient events such as "phantom" inventory profits. A. R. Marusi, the former chairman of Borden, Inc., defined "reasonable" as a competitive profit large enough for a company's stock to compete with alternatives such as savings accounts and government and corporate bonds, to pay competitive dividends, and to invest in growth and new jobs for the future. He added that the concept of reasonable profit varies from industry to industry and by the risk of a given venture.

## GOVERNMENTAL LIMITATION OF PROFIT

Apart from regulated utility industries, profit controls in the United States have generally been for broad public policy objectives such as controlling inflation or financing wars. An exception, however, is the windfall profits tax, an excise tax on gains resulting from domestic oil price deregulation. Proposals such as those to restrict mergers and require divestitures would also act to limit corporate profits. Profit can also be indirectly limited by government regulations whose primary purpose is to change corporate behavior; examples are health, safety, environmental, and consumer protection laws and regulations. Notwithstanding the fact that there are no specific laws to limit directly the profits of unregulated industries, Lipset and Schneider cite several opinion surveys of recent years that found that majority opinion favors government limitations on profits.[4]

## CORPORATE INITIATIVES AND ACTIONS

In addition to information in company annual reports, some corporate managements present their profit picture to employees by such means as special letters, reports, publications, and meetings that feature

[3]J. Clayburn La Force, correspondence with author.
[4]Lipset and Schneider, op. cit.

explanations of income and expenditures. They also communicate information on profits to the general public by advertisements, usually when their profits are too low to generate necessary capital or so high that they have generated criticism.

Prior to the Financial Accounting Standards Board's 1979 standard of reporting profits on an inflation-adjusted basis, several major companies voluntarily stated the effects of inflation on profits in their annual reports. Another action by many major companies has been to emphasize their profits as a percentage return on investment rather than on a quarter-to-quarter basis.

Many executives have found that creating public understanding about profits is a complex communication problem. Earle Birdzell, a business consultant, has pointed to difficulties in explaining profits, either in terms of the private enterprise system as a whole or on the basis of an individual company:

> The operation of all business organizations centers on the uncertainty of the relative size of planned revenues and planned expenditures, since the expenditures must almost always precede the revenues. Profits thus find their institutional origin in risk and uncertainty and not in fairness and equity—what happens to stockholders is often unfair and inequitable, in both directions. The substantive role of profits as a risk cushion is unpalatable to many people who have a strong aversion to gambling and do not like to think of a common stock investment in major corporations as speculative. Thus emphasis on the system's role of profit alienates some people.
>
> Explanation of profit on a single company level is equally difficult. What is "excessive" return to investors is akin to deciding what is excessive return to any other risk taker on the basis of the outcome of one event or results over a short period of time. For an individual company, profit simply has no "appropriate magnitude," except for the minimum that is necessary to sustain securities values/asset values relationships at non-takeover bid levels.[5]

Notwithstanding these difficulties, corporate executives frequently speak on the subject of profits. "Probably since the time of Adam Smith, we've been defending the profit motive," said Robert V. Krikorian, chief executive officer of Rexnord Inc., in an article on deadly speeches. Since most people overestimate the amount of profit that corporations make, Krikorian has advised that an executive who defends profits would seem to be defending excessive profits and thus could lose his or her audience from the start. Krikorian prescribes this approach:

[5]L. Earle Birdzell, Jr., correspondence with author.

The task for the business speaker, then, is twofold: first, to tell his or her audience how much profits really are and, second, to credibly define the role profit plays in business. I agree wholeheartedly with the former president of Quaker Oats, Kenneth Mason, when he said: "Making a profit is no more the purpose of a corporation than getting enough to eat is the purpose of life. Getting enough to eat is a requirement of life." Life's purpose, he hoped, as with business and profit, should be broader and more challenging.[6]

In writing or speaking about profits, corporate executives often do not deal directly with the public's questions about profits—their large size, how they are made, and how management decisions balance profit and other objectives. The defense of profits that some corporate executives make by blaming "public economic illiteracy" while avoiding the issues of public concern usually does their cause more harm than good. Irving Shapiro, when chairman of E. I. du Pont de Nemours & Co., cautioned that people are tired of executives pleading the case for corporate profits. In talking to a business group, Shapiro said:

> You and I care about profits. Most other people don't, least of all politicians, and lots of them think businessmen have calculators and computers instead of brains and hearts. The political nervous system is sensitized to people, so we have to talk in terms of proposals to create and preserve jobs, to improve products and services, to advance people's health or wealth or security.[7]

The corporate profit issue has evoked the same question by succeeding generations of corporate executives: "If we're so successful in selling our products, why can't we sell our ideas on profits and free enterprise?" Traditionally, many corporate executives believe that if people understood better how the business system operates, there would be fewer challenges to the size of corporate profit. While that may be true, it has not proved easy in practice to build such understanding. Perhaps the most visible single effort has been the one carried forward under the flag of economic education, and it has had mixed reviews. Over the past quarter century, corporations have spent many millions of dollars organizing and supporting various forms of economic education, ranging from accredited courses in economic principles to simplistic advertising.

Few people will deny that economic understanding is a necessary attribute of an informed citizen. Yet, many corporate executives and

---

[6]Robert V. Krikorian, "Avoid the Three Deadly Speeches: A Businessman's Advice to His Colleagues," *Enterprise*, December 1980, p. 19.

[7]Irving Shapiro, "The New Politics of Business," address to the American Textile Manufacturers Institute, Boca Raton, Fla., Apr. 15, 1977.

observers of the business scene now maintain that economic education will not in itself resolve the corporate profit issue. Another category of Robert Krikorian's deadly speeches is "If They Only Understood Economics!" On this subject he has provided this comment and advice:

> Every year, hundreds of speakers tell their audiences that if only the American people understood economics they would understand and approve of business. Business audiences are urged to go into the community and help teach economics in schools, to the clergy, to homemakers and, of course, to their own employees. As much as I endorse the idea of better education in economics—indeed, it is vital—I don't believe that there is necessarily any correlation between understanding and supporting business. Here again, a survey conducted for the Financial Executive Research Foundation clearly indicated that economic education programs, if designed solely to enlist support for business, are doomed to failure.[8]

Among the observers of corporate behavior, Lipset and Schneider have concluded that many economic education programs are of dubious value, because hostility to profit is attitudinal or ideological and is difficult to change by information or facts. Also, Irving Kristol, professor, editor, and *Wall Street Journal* contributor, pointed out in his essay "On Economic Education" that public attitudes toward business were more favorable 20 to 30 years ago and yet people knew less about economics then than they do now. Kristol concluded: "Clearly, public attitudes toward business are no more a function of their knowledge of economics than public attitudes toward government are a function of their knowledge of political science."[9]

Reliable financial accounting and reporting are basic to public understanding of the magnitude aspect of the profit issue. It follows, therefore, that for this as well as other important reasons discussed in Chapter 5, corporate managements should satisfy themselves and be prepared to satisfy their shareholders and others that their financial reports are a reliable portrayal of their companies' financial position.

The following management practices have proved successful in discussions of profits or losses in annual reports or other public statements:

• Discuss profit and other aspects of corporate performance in broad terms with reference to both financial and other corporate goals and results. Statements which convey the impression that profit is the only objective should be avoided.

[8]Krikorian, op. cit., p. 19.
[9]Irving Kristol, "On Economic Education," *The Wall Street Journal*, Feb. 18, 1976, p. 20.

- Report financial results with the same explanation to all constituents. Any implication of touting the significance of profit results to shareholders and the financial community while deprecating them to government regulators and labor unions is detrimental to management integrity.

- Be part of a concerted business effort to report financial results in ways that convey understanding to the media. Quarterly and annual reports and news releases should include not only clear and concise language but charts and graphs for use, as appropriate, in both print and television media. The eroding effect of inflation should be noted as long as this problem remains, and profit should be reported as a percentage return on investment and sales rather than by quarterly changes.

- Avoid advocating positions that appear to produce profit regardless of adverse effects.

- Provide shareholders, employees and families, and other constituents with descriptive information and explanatory illustrations on how their companies operate under the United States private enterprise system. This may be the best form of economic education that a company can provide.

In addition to their value in reporting on profits, the foregoing practices can, as well, help to convey that the profit motive does not run amok in management's thought and action. Following are two management practices that are specifically intended to assure that the profit motive is not the cause of corporate misconduct:

- Set realistic profit forecasts and performance goals that can be achieved by acceptable business practices. Unrealistic goals are a way to abuse the profit motive since they can induce otherwise responsible people to violate legal and ethical behavior, to make adverse short-term decisions, and to act in other ways that sustain public distrust of corporations and their executives.

- Give special consideration to policies and decisions in terms of their long-term versus short-term prospects. Recognize that short-term profit may be detrimental to the shareholders' interest and even be considered a management conflict of interest.

One final thought about corporate managements' posture in dealing with the profit issue: today there are a host of scholars—economists, political scientists, lawyers, and sociologists, to name a few—who are extolling market forces economics and calling for fewer government solutions. Their views are endorsed by the Reagan administration, and, in turn, the scholars have endorsed many of the administration's policies. Thus, for the first time in the careers of the current cohort of corporate executives, many members of the intellectual community and government are vigorously advocating the principles of private enterpise and the profit motive. This phenomenon means that executives do not always have to plead the case for bigger profits. They can discuss what many people want to hear: the benefits to the public that result from how well private enterprise and profit motivation work in their companies.

## THE OUTLOOK

The outlook for the profit issue differs somewhat according to its elements. The age-old mind-set that links the profit motive with business malpractices is not likely to change easily. Corporate misconduct for whatever reason is almost always ascribed to the pursuit of profit, even if the act was committed inadvertently or was a Hobson's choice. As a consequence, public concern about the profit motive, like concern about corporate governance, rises and falls in relation to the degree that the public is concerned about the other aspects of corporate performance. If several matters of corporate performance are concurrently subject to criticism, public concern about profit motivation will be amplified. Another factor that exacerbates this issue is the reporting of unusually high profits by some companies or industries in the context of general unemployment, high prices, and inflation.

With respect to the magnitude of profit, there is likely to be greater sympathy toward corporate profitability as the public recognizes the need for capital to revitalize our economy. The Reagan administration's policies are intended to provide incentives for corporations as an instrument to help abate inflation, foster productivity, and accomplish economic recovery without compromising such social goals as a clean and healthy environment. To the extent that the incentives increase their profits, corporations will be expected (even obligated in the public's mind) to help deliver the anticipated benefits. To the extent that corporate profits rise but the benefits not be delivered, both the magnitude of profits and the profit motive would become a joint target of public criticism. To an even greater degree, the Reagan administration and corporate leadership would then be blamed for a prescription that had failed.

# CHAPTER 5

# Financial Reporting
# and Control

***The Issue*** • The usefulness and validity of corporate financial reporting have been questioned by some government representatives and members of the financial community. The issue they have raised has drawn public attention to what can and should be done to improve the effectiveness of corporate accounting systems and to assure a reliable portrayal of the financial position of companies. The issue also concerns the independence of outside auditors and the adequacy of corporate internal controls. An integral question involved in the issue concerns the roles of corporate management, the accounting profession, and the federal government in determining what changes, if any, should be made in financial accounting and reporting and in internal accounting control systems.

***Importance*** • Reliable reporting and internal accounting controls are essential for public, investor, and governmental confidence in the corporation and the integrity of its management. These tasks are a prime responsibility of management. In response to past criticism, the Congress and the Securities and Exchange Commission (SEC) are regulating financial reporting and controls, and the Financial Accounting Standards Board (FASB) is setting accounting guidelines. As a result, the discretion of corporate management has become more limited, and the costs of compliance have increased. If public and government criticism of corporate accounting continues, even tighter controls may be imposed.

The issue of financial reporting and control is importantly related to proposals to regulate corporate governance.

*Causes* • Public concern with this issue has been largely based on company financial reporting that has not been useful to investors, has not revealed financial difficulties or even imminent company failures, has misrepresented profits on either the high or the low side, and, in rare cases, has proved to be fraudulent. Also, criticism of management for unsatisfactory corporate performance, including financial reporting, has focused government and public attention on the need for more effective internal control systems.

The FASB has identified a number of practices that have led to misunderstanding and weakened confidence in financial reporting. Among them are these: the existence of two or more acceptable methods to account for similar transactions by separate companies; changing to less conservative accounting methods; reporting income before it has been earned, such as franchising fees for a new venture; providing for future contingencies as a means of smoothing earnings artificially; deferring recognition of expenses to avoid reducing net income; estimating asset values, such as receivables and unrecovered costs, with unjustified optimism; improperly using materiality criteria to justify nondisclosure of unfavorable information; and using off-balance-sheet financing (e.g., leases). Some financial authorities say that not all these financial practices are unfair or misleading. Moreover, no one corporation is likely to use all of them, and many corporations use none. Nevertheless, the FASB concluded that such practices weaken confidence in all corporations and their credibility.

In addition to the demand for more useful financial information and a call for increased corporate accountability, accounting and financial control problems are aggravated by dynamic changes in the economic environment. For example, the impact of inflation makes profits appear unduly large; that perception has led to substantial public criticism of "excessive" corporate profits. Historical cost methods overstate the aftertax real profits of companies and their dividend-paying ability. Official corporate statements reporting high profits are compared by journalists with executive speeches that complain about low real profit and the need for tax changes. As a result,

> some people conclude that the financial reporting process is
> misleading or that corporate executives are deceptive or hypo-
> critical.

Three principal public policy concerns are involved in this issue: (1)
financial reporting, (2) the independence of outside auditors, and (3)
internal accounting controls. The following brief description of applicable laws, government regulation, and private standard setting is basic
to the discussion of the issue.

The Securities Acts of 1933 and 1934 gave the SEC the statutory authority to ensure "full and fair disclosure" with respect to the purchase and sale of securities. That authority includes the setting of financial accounting standards for purposes of reports filed with the SEC.
Shortly after its creation in 1934, however, the SEC delegated to the
public accounting profession responsibility for the setting of financial
accounting standards and has recognized two private-sector accounting
policy groups for that task: the American Institute of Certified Public
Accountants (AICPA) served as the primary authority from the mid-
1930s to 1972, when the FASB was established as an independent
private-sector agency to set accounting standards.

Although subcommittees of both the House of Representatives and
the Senate have criticized the SEC for its delegation of power to the
private sector, the SEC has continued to defend its position. Nonetheless, the SEC has taken a greater interest in financial accounting
standards and has become more active in exercising its oversight of the
FASB.

In several instances, the SEC has not supported the judgments of the
private-sector bodies: the investment credit controversy in the early
1960s, accounting for marketable equity securities, and inflation accounting are prominent examples. More recently, the SEC's refusal to
support the FASB statement on accounting standards for the oil and gas
industry caused that statement to be withdrawn. In effect, no private-
sector accounting standard can prevail unless it has SEC support.

## FINANCIAL ACCOUNTING AND REPORTING

The concerns about corporate financial reporting to a large extent are
based on the diversity of accepted accounting methods, the impact of
inflation on financial reports, and the existence of both tax and
financial accounting systems, often referred to as "two sets of books."

Many people who are unfamiliar with principles of financial management believe that financial reporting represents a precise and accurate statement—in effect, the single "truth." In fact, there are a number of acceptable accounting methods, and management must make choices concerning their use. For many significant transactions, there are two or more acceptable ways to record them. A few prominent examples are different methods for inventory valuation, depreciation, pension accounting, and accounting for business combinations. There are also forecasts inherently involved in selecting methods and in assessing the financial position or the earnings of a company. For example, the accrual process, that is, the identification of revenues and expenses with specific time periods, is at the heart of financial accounting, and yet some accruals are a type of forecast. Even accounting experts have been unable to reach a consensus as to which method is "best" in like circumstances or for all companies.

In illustrating how United States managements are to blame for many of the problems they now confront, Reginald H. Jones, chairman of the General Electric Company, spoke of the optional use of LIFO or FIFO accounting for inventories:

> When we use Last-In-First-Out accounting we keep phantom inventory profits out of our financial statements—a very important consideration in a period of inflation. We also retain the cash in our business that would have been used to pay taxes on those phantom inventory profits if we had been using FIFO accounting. Certainly LIFO makes sense in terms of the integrity of our financial reporting and also in terms of cash savings.
>
> Yet study after study shows that two thirds of the inventories in this nation are carried on a FIFO basis. We are not only misleading the public; we are misleading ourselves.[1]

As a result of the continued diversity of acceptable accounting methods and their use, some members of Congress and other critics have advocated changes. For instance, some critics have suggested that accounting flexibility is sinister in intent and results in misleading statements and misled investors. Leonard Spacek, former managing partner of Arthur Andersen & Co., also has been a vocal advocate of a single uniform set of accounting standards. The FASB has responded to such criticism by attempting to limit the methods of accounting, and this policy is likely to continue; examples include the FASB accounting standards on research and development expenditures, self-insurance and contingency reserves, foreign-currency translation, and leases.

Another area of criticism is the honesty and completeness of financial reporting, which, of course, involves the issues of ethical

[1]Reginald H. Jones, "Time to Break out of 'Management Malaise,'" address to the Economic Club of Chicago, reported in *Financier*, January 1981, p. 42.

behavior and public disclosure. Prominent corporate failures have also led to the erosion of credibility in financial statements. The failures of major corporations, such as Penn Central Transportation Company and W. T. Grant Co., have led to claims that their financial reporting did not reveal financial difficulties as soon as they could have. In franchising operations, "front-ending" was criticized when companies such as Career Academics and National Student Marketing Corp. used that method and experienced financial difficulties. Land development companies were also accused of front-ending and reporting optimistic estimates of the future realizable value of their assets. Highly publicized financial difficulties, such as those of GAC Corporation and U.S. Financial Inc., confirmed such criticism.

The reporting of inflationary impacts on profits also has been a subject of debate. The problem is basic. Under inflationary conditions, revenues and most operating expenses generally increase with inflation. However, depreciation expense does not increase with inflation when it is computed on the basis of the historical cost of acquisition of the asset. As a result, in the case of a company that is merely maintaining itself in real terms, the percentage increase in historical cost earnings may be greater than the inflation rate. Consequently, changes slowly began to take effect in this area. According to a May 1975 article in *Business Week*, Shell Oil Company was the only major United States corporation that included the effects of inflation in its 1974 annual report.[2] In 1979, the FASB issued a statement entitled *Financial Reporting and Changing Prices*, requiring supplemental disclosure of the effects of inflation, a provision that is more comprehensive than a 1976 SEC requirement that large companies disclose replacement costs in their filings with the commission.

Reginald Jones expressed this view of inflation-adjusted accounting:

We all know that our financial statements based on historical costs are not portraying with accuracy our profitability in these inflationary times. While we may argue that Statement No. 33 of the Financial Accounting Standards Board has many problems, and it does, at least it is an effort to achieve somewhat more reality in our reported figures.

More important, it provides a mechanism for displaying to the public the extraordinarily high tax burden loaded on American industry.

Yet most companies' annual reports treated this issue as the last in a long string of footnoted tabulations appended to the financial statements, gave the absolute minimum information required, and then commented on the inadequacy and misleading nature of the figures. How many of us internally measure each of our operations on an inflation-adjuted basis?[3]

2"How to Report Results in Real Dollars," *Business Week*, May 5, 1975, p. 72.
3Jones, loc. cit.

Discussions of "real" profitability impairment have also brought attention to the inequities of historical cost accounting for income tax purposes. Under inflation, a rate of return equal to the inflation rate is required merely to keep an initial corporate investment whole in real terms. Yet under historical-cost-based taxation, that component, which is actually a return of capital, is taxed rather than treated as a return on capital. As a result, the effective tax rate on "real earnings" (after adjusting for inflation) is considerably higher than the apparent rate. This naturally reduces the aftertax real profits of the corporate sector.

Historical cost accounting, with its serious impact on corporate taxation, is also seen as one aspect of a broader issue: the relationship between financial reporting and tax reporting. Corporations, in response to two different concepts, have long had different reporting systems for shareholders and for the Internal Revenue Service, for example, straight-line depreciation in financial reporting to reflect the cost over the useful life of plant and equipment but accelerated depreciation in accord with tax regulations that provide incentives to encourage capital formation. However, that practice often has been characterized by critics as a double set of books by which corporate managements attempt to manipulate accounting statements so as to avoid taxes and yet portray the financial status of their companies in the best possible light. The use of auxiliary accounting records for tax purposes, however, is an accepted practice that permits companies to respond to incentives provided by law to increase capital formation.

Nonetheless, Reginald Jones expresses this view on the disparity between book and tax accounting:

> We have been hitting Washington very hard for improved capital cost recovery allowances in our tax legislation, and I might add we have made a real impression.
>
> Supply-side economics are "in," and without question, 1981 tax legislation will provide for improved depreciation deductions from taxable income. We have successfully made the point that the very slow write-off of the historical cost of buildings and equipment does not provide adequate funds for replacement and modernization in an inflationary economy. Yet I cannot help but be disturbed that, even today, we do not deduct from our reported profits the amount of depreciation that we take for tax purposes. There is a big disparity between book and tax depreciation and it is indeed difficult to explain this to a Congressman when you're arguing for even higher tax-deductible depreciation.[4]

The argument over historical cost accounting and the 1979 FASB statement *Financial Reporting and Changing Prices* illuminates anoth-

[4]Ibid., pp. 42–43.

er major trend in corporate financial reporting: the use of supplemental disclosure. From the perspective of the FASB and the SEC, formal financial statements alone are becoming less important per se, and a total financial reporting system that includes both financial statements and supplemental disclosures is becoming necessary for a useful, timely, and valid portrayal of the financial position of a company.

One reason for this trend is an increasing realization that company financial statements cannot alone meet the increasing burden being placed upon them. Another is a growing recognition of the role that the professional investment community plays in the financial environment. Financial analysts and institutional investors are seen as having greater skill in interpreting financial disclosures than the mythical "average prudent investor," and they certainly have a greater demand for soft data such as supplemental interpretive information.

While increasing amounts of financial information are sought by professional investment specialists, some financial scholars argue that current regulations already require excessive information that is of little use to most investors and is costly to provide. These academic researchers present empirical evidence of the "efficient market hypothesis," which suggests that equity markets quickly and accurately adjust stock prices to reflect information that will affect the future of a company. They profess that their research indicates that sophisticated investors through their buying and selling cause stock prices to reflect existing information long before it reaches smaller shareholders through quarterly or annual reports.

## AUDITOR INDEPENDENCE

An important concept of financial management is that the public accounting firm, as the auditor, should be independent so that users of financial statements will have trust and confidence in its audit reports. The primary function of an audit is to determine the fairness of a company's financial statements, with detection of fraud occurring only incidentally. While the public and the government have come to expect more, auditors are confronted with the impossibility of verifying millions of transactions or discovering unrecorded ones. Yet in cases of alleged management fraud, such as those involving Equity Funding Corporation of America, Stirling Homex Corporation, National Student Marketing Corp., U.S. Financial Inc., and Continental Vending Machine Corp., the public accounting firm has been cited as either an unknowing or active accomplice. Such examples of alleged fraud or deception in financial statements both erode corporate management credibility and contribute to the perception that professional auditors are either unable or unwilling to detect fraud and can lead to even further erosion of confidence.

As a result, the role of the auditor and how to describe it have been matters of debate for some time. The Commission on Auditors' Responsibilities, known as the Cohen Commission, concluded that many shareholders lack understanding of the auditor's role and services. This and other developments resulted in the AICPA Auditing Standards Board's proposing the adoption of some of the Cohen Commission's recommendations to revise the auditor's letter, the traditional seal of approval on annual financial statements of publicly held corporations. In essence, the proposed revisions would have required explanation that the financial statement was prepared by the company and that the audit was "intended to provide reasonable, but not absolute, assurance" that the management's representations were free of "material misstatements." Formal comment both supported the proposal as necessary and opposed it as moving the concept of auditor independence to a point at which the public accounting firm would provide little assurance and bear even less responsibility for its services. After lengthy review and discussion, the Auditing Standards Board early in 1981 announced that the current auditor's letter could not be improved enough to warrant the cost of the proposed change.

Criticism of the auditor's function also has led to concern over the relationship of the public accounting firm and the corporation. Nonaudit services—executive search, computer services, and management consulting, for instance—provided by public accounting firms for companies they audit have come under fire. The Cohen Commission examined the activities of Yale Express System Inc., National Student Marketing, Westec Corp., and other companies in which the provision of nonaudit services by public accounting firms allegedly impaired the firms' ability to render independent opinions that could have resulted in an earlier reporting of the financial difficulties of those companies. The Cohen Commission concluded that there was no evidence, except possibly in the Westec case, to support the contention that such nonaudit services had in fact led to a lack of independence. However, the commission also concluded that a potential impairment of independence does exist and that public accounting firms and corporate managements must be aware of it.

In 1976, the Senate Subcommittee on Reports, Accounting, and Management expressed severe concern about the question of auditor independence and asked the SEC to explore it further. In June 1979, the SEC issued an accounting series release which, while not prohibiting any specific nonaudit services, listed examples that in its opinion would prove difficult to justify. In effect, the SEC held that the question of auditor independence is a matter of professional judgment.

The audit committee of the corporate board of directors serves several purposes, one of which is to enhance auditor independence. This is accomplished by direct communication between the auditing firm and the audit committee composed of outside directors. While this concept has developed over the last 50 years, the New York Stock Exchange since 1977 has required its listed companies to have a board audit committee. Experts credit the audit committee with satisfying a variety of needs, from management's desire for self-regulation to the public's expectation of corporate management control of financial integrity.

## INTERNAL ACCOUNTING CONTROLS

In the mid-1970s, government and corporate management attention was directed to corporate systems of internal accounting control. As an outgrowth of the Watergate disclosures and Senate hearings in 1975–1976, it became apparent that questionable and often illegal payments had been made. In some cases, the payments were unknown to top managements. In others, top executives were involved. As a result, the SEC invited voluntary disclosures concerning questionable payments that resulted in several hundred large companies reporting payments that varied from inconsequential to illegal. In reviewing the circumstances surrounding these payments, the SEC concluded that many of the payments occurred because of weak or nonexistent internal accounting controls. Frederick L. Neumann, Price Waterhouse Professor of Auditing at the University of Illinois, commented on the disclosures:

> Why did this happen? What made people believe that companies could, and would, investigate themselves and actually reveal such information to possibly indignant stockholders and potential court suits? To say that it was solely due to the latent power of the SEC would be to overlook the role of the fledgling audit committee. Many audit committees had been in existence for only a few years; yet as an independent group of outside directors, the audit committee in many companies was given the assignment of overseeing the investigation of questionable payments and, in general, performed with distinction. By so doing, they provided one of the more convincing demonstrations of responsibility in the private sector that has been seen in a long time.[5]

[5]Frederick L. Neumann, "Corporate Audit Committees and the Foreign Corrupt Practices Act," *Business Horizons*, June 1980, pp. 64–65.

The SEC, which had long espoused voluntary corporate audit committees, was pleased when the New York Stock Exchange required its listed companies to adopt such committees. Subsequently, however, the SEC introduced and Congress passed the Foreign Corrupt Practices Act (FCPA) of 1977, which many observers believe put the SEC in a position to influence the conduct of management as well as to specify its disclosure requirements.

In addition to the prohibitions which give the FCPA its title, the act contains certain accounting provisions. These provisions require the keeping of accurate books and records and devising and maintaining an adequate system of internal accounting control that will protect company assets and produce reliable financial statements. These requirements are not limited to foreign payments but apply to domestic transactions as well. While the SEC and Congress did not invent the concept of internal control or establish it as a management responsibility, greater emphasis has been placed on this important activity because it is no longer just a good business practice but the law of the land with substantial penalties for noncompliance. In this regard, Professor Neumann has pointed out:

> The [act's] provisions may be used to imply that . . . illegal acts often are the result of, or are accompanied by, deficiencies in a company's record keeping or controls. This Act exposes internal record keeping and control, previously in management's domain, to the SEC's qualitative judgment.[6]

Faced with the FCPA, corporate management, particularly financial and legal officers, began reviewing their systems of control to determine their adequacy. As a result, internal control systems and, in many cases, codes of business conduct have been established or reinforced as discussed in Chapter 7, "Legal and Ethical Behavior." Audit committees composed of outside directors, many already providing oversight in areas of accounting and internal accounting control, have added emphasis. On that subject, some commentators have suggested that the lack of an audit committee is in itself a weakness and may constitute a violation under the act.

## GOVERNMENT ACTIONS

The SEC's authority to ensure full and fair disclosure with respect to the purchase and sale of securities has been extended by its interest in

[6]Ibid., p. 65.

accounting standards and internal accounting control. In these matters, the SEC has proposed rules to help ensure conformity with its notions of desirable management behavior. This action represents a new regulatory effort by the SEC. In a similar vein, the SEC has been considering proposals that deal with the qualifications and accountability of members of boards of directors, an intimate aspect of the corporate governance issue. Although the SEC Advisory Committee on Corporate Disclosure, composed of public, professional accounting, and business representatives, some time ago suggested that the primary purpose of a disclosure regulation should *not* be to alter management behavior, the SEC pointed out that change in management behavior is often one of its intended effects.

When SEC chairman, Harold M. Williams publicly argued for improved performance and accountability by corporate boards of directors and managements and expressed his interest in an active SEC effort in that regard. If pursued by the current SEC chairman, John S. R. Shad, and other commissioners, the SEC could open a potentially large area for regulation that did not exist under the prior concept of disclosure of material information to help investors make decisions.

Some observers believe that in recent years the SEC began to view the setting of accounting standards as a political process, with the debate centering on who would be affected and in what ways rather than on technical accounting considerations. An example they cite was that in the SEC's public hearings the FASB statement on oil- and gas-producing activities was opposed because it was alleged that it would lead to greater concentration within the oil and gas industry.

The increase in the political nature of standards setting has been partly due to increased concern by Congress and the public at large as to whether standards should be set by a private-sector body such as the FASB. Some members of Congress, critical of the SEC delegation of the setting of financial accounting standards to the private sector, brought pressure on the SEC, and in turn the SEC brought pressure on the private sector to do a "better" job.

Both Congress and the SEC appear to have taken a wait-and-see attitude concerning proposals to regulate financial reporting, with the SEC reporting to Congress on an annual basis regarding the progress of the private sector. William Beaver, professor of accounting of the Stanford Graduate School of Business, has expressed the opinion, however, that the active interest Congress has shown in recent years, if continued, will be the most important development for the future of financial reporting, strongly influencing the role that the private sector plays in setting reporting standards. Similarly, Professor Neumann has pointed out that congressional interest in internal accounting controls has already significantly affected corporate practices.

In the SEC's 1980 report to Congress, *The Accounting Profession and the Commission's Oversight Role*, Chairman Williams noted that the relative roles of the private sector and government in the process of setting accounting principles and auditing standards have been long debated, and added:

> We continue to believe that the private sector, with Commission oversight, is the most effective and logical arena for those efforts. We are, however, at a critical period in assessing the ability of the private sector to move responsibly in addressing financial reporting issues. The FASB must, therefore, have the continued support and encouragement of the accounting profession and the corporate community.

Chairman Williams also advised Congress:

> The accounting profession is undergoing significant change and development. The Commission, while not fully satisfied with the profession's progress, nonetheless recognizes that important strides have been made and that the profession's leaders confront deep and sincere divisions among accountants concerning the wisdom and direction of future changes. The Commission will, of course, continue to monitor the profession and to offer our guidance and comments wherever appropriate.[7]

In May 1980, the SEC withdrew its proposed rule that would have required management to make a representation that its system of internal accounting control was, in effect, in compliance with the FCPA. In withdrawing the proposal, the commission agreed that the private sector had shown substantial initiative in developing improved internal control systems and that this process should be allowed to continue for 3 years, after which the need for a rule would be reconsidered.

In a reversal of previous commission policy, in mid-1981 Chairman Shad expressed basic support for several changes in the FCPA. He testified before Senate hearings that the law has created unintended problems for American businesses abroad and uncertainties concerning compliance with the provisions for accounting controls. With Reagan administration support and substantial congressional sentiment for changes, the FCPA is subject to revisions that would clarify or eliminate the accounting provisions, refine the definition of bribery, and specify the extent of corporate executive liability.

---

[7]Securities and Exchange Commission, *Report to Congress on the Accounting Profession and the Commission's Oversight Role*, 1979, pp. ix–x.

## CORPORATE AND OTHER PRIVATE-SECTOR
## INITIATIVES AND ACTIONS

Corporations, as the preparers of financial reports, and the public accounting profession, as attesters of such reports, have attempted to improve the quality and scope of financial reporting and control through a number of different efforts. Individually, corporations have attempted to deal with pressures created by changing economic conditions, such as inflation, and governmental requirements, such as the FCPA. In the absence of an FASB statement on how the effects of inflation should be reported, some corporations have experimented with reporting systems that reflect changing price levels. Companies began experimenting with various inflation accounting approaches in the early 1970s to test various measures of the impact of inflation. Corporate action has had an impact. For example, voluntary company reporting and corporate interest in experimenting with management reports were credited as key reasons that the SEC withdrew the proposed rule which would have required management to adopt costly and questionably effective representations that its system of internal accounting control was in compliance with the FCPA.[8]

Professional accounting associations, such as the AICPA, Financial Executives Institute (FEI), Institute of Internal Auditors (IIA), and National Association of Accountants (NAA), are firmly committed to private-sector setting of accounting standards. The FEI, AICPA, and NAA have representatives in the Financial Accounting Foundation, the parent body of the FASB. Representatives from the AICPA and FEI serve on committees that meet regularly with the SEC and FASB. These representatives also serve on the task forces which the FASB creates for each accounting issue that it studies.

An example of action taken by professional associations occurred in 1976, when the SEC issued a rule requiring many publicly held companies to disclose the current estimated replacement cost of inventories and plant as well as the approximate amount of cost of sales and depreciation based upon replacement costs. In 1977, an AICPA task force developed four accounting measurement models, and the FEI encouraged its member companies to field-test the models. The results of these tests were reported to the FASB. In 1979, the FASB issued the statement *Financial Reporting and Changing Prices*, which prescribed how publicly held companies must report the impact of inflation. As a result, the SEC withdrew its 1976 rule.

[8]Ibid., p. x.

After more than a decade of mounting government regulation, many observers—critics, government officials, and corporate executives alike —believe that it is impossible successfully to legislate and regulate many aspects of corporate performance, including accounting standards and internal controls. Corporate leaders, in reaffirming their strong support of the FASB and the retention of standards setting in the private sector, recognize that it behooves business to have an active interchange with the accounting profession. Thomas Murphy, when chairman of General Motors, gave as an example of such interchange these recommendations to improve the quality of accounting and financial reporting:

- The standards setters should clearly identify the problem before an attempt is made to write a standard or a rule. Contrary to a business executive's approach to problem solving, the standards setters too often fail to identify clearly the problem that caused the standard or rule to be proposed in the first place.
- The full role of financial *reporting* as a means of conveying needed data to the various users, including the nonfinancial statements, should be clearly explained and understood.
- Lines of communication among preparers (business), users (creditors, investors, and analysts), and standards setters (FASB, SEC, and Congress) should be broadened and regularly maintained.[9]

Boards of directors and their top managements are accountable for the validity and usefulness of financial reporting and the integrity of internal controls. Companies with boards that have an effective audit committee of outside directors, a management that has a professional and issue-alert financial accounting and auditing staff, and an independent outside auditing firm have found that such practices as these are effective:

- Giving careful consideration to accounting methods and other factors that may adversely affect the validity and usefulness of financial reports
- Avoiding legally correct but questionable financial statements, particularly regarding earnings
- Describing financial results to all constituents in a consistent and meaningful manner

[9]Thomas A. Murphy, "Setting Accounting Standards—A Suggestion from a Businessman," *Financial Executive*, August 1979, p. 52–57.

- Supporting the principle of private standards setting and the independence of the public auditing firm as bulwarks of the private enterprise system
- Improving rigorous internal accounting and other control systems and monitoring their effectiveness

## THE OUTLOOK

The outlook for this issue is that all its elements will continue to be important to the many interests involved. Corporate managements, the accounting profession, the SEC and Congress, the financial community, the business media, and the FASB, AICPA, FEI, and other relevant organizations will continue to interact in a public policy arena concerned with accounting standards and financial reporting and the crucial question of whether standards should be set by government or private-sector agencies.

Another stimulus to public interest in the validity of financial reporting is resulting from the Reagan administration's initiatives dealing with national economic recovery by tax incentives, lower costs of regulatory compliance, and other public policies that are beneficial to business. Such measures inevitably raise questions about the accuracy and usefulness of financial accounting and reporting in depicting the needs of large corporations for policies that aid in capital formation. Also, high rates of inflation, failures of large corporations, and illegal corporate behavior are circumstances that focus critical attention on the financial reporting and control aspects of corporate performance.

While most large companies have had internal control systems and some have had codes of business conduct for many years, the FCPA, even as amended by Congress, would likely continue to focus attention on the importance of internal accounting controls and legal and ethical behavior as important factors in corporate performance and governance.

Many of the observers who question the proliferation of regulation believe that effective company internal self-control systems are an important alternative to government intervention. Internal accounting control, like openness and the effective use of company public disclosure, is a management process that can disarm critics and serve as a deterrent to managerial misconduct or ineptitude. Both of these processes are important elements of the concept of voluntary corporate accountability discussed in Chapter 22 as an alternative to government-imposed accountability. The record of large corporations in establishing and using internal accounting controls will provide empirical evidence whether or not corporate managements can be accountable without government-imposed changes in their internal governance.

With Congress and the SEC allowing corporations time to improve both their financial reporting and control practices, they have posed a key question for the corporate community and the accounting profession: Will company managements act voluntarily, or will they be compelled to adopt government-prescribed accounting standards, financial reporting requirements, and internal accounting control systems?

# CHAPTER 6

# Public
# Disclosure

*The Issue* • To what extent should corporations publicly disclose information about company policies, activities, plans, and performance that they are not required by law to disclose?

*Importance* • The rise in public concern about corporate performance has created a desire among many segments of the public for more information about corporations. This has caused many corporations to disclose information previously considered proprietary to management or irrelevant to the public. Demand for public disclosure of relevant company information is usually the first response to suspected corporate misconduct. It is also a primary method used by those who seek to alter corporate performance.

Compulsory public disclosure is often a more practical way for government to monitor or influence corporate performance than is the adoption of detailed regulations. Disclosure of corporate information may serve to allay public mistrust or fear and thus reduce the rationale for additional regulation. Also, the value of disclosure is implicit in the concept that, for the marketplace to be a more effective regulator than government, people as voters and consumers need timely, relevant information on overall corporate performance as well as on products and prices.

Disclosure can benefit a corporation by defusing external

pressures; e.g., untrue allegations about corporate malpractices, such as the alleged energy crisis conspiracy among oil companies, are more likely to be dispelled by the disclosure of relevant information than by general denials. Indeed, some corporate managements regard their policies of public disclosure as an important deterrent to managerial misconduct or ineptitude.

On the other hand, excessive or ill-considered disclosure can aggravate other legitimate concerns, for example, by jeopardizing proprietary information or customers' and employees' rights to privacy. But there is a broad middle ground between secretiveness to hide poor performance and genuinely injurious disclosures. Many people believe that corporations can and should disclose much more information about themselves.

In the absence of voluntary disclosure that meets reasonable public expectations, both deepening public mistrust of corporate power and stringent legal requirements for compulsory corporate disclosure result. As a consequence, there has been a growing consensus among corporate leaders that voluntary corporate disclosure of nonproprietary information will help defuse the mistrust that breeds government intervention.

*Causes* • Government agencies, such as the Securities and Exchange Commission (SEC), Equal Employment Opportunity Commission, Occupational Safety and Health Administration, and Environmental Protection Agency, have required that they be given access to previously undisclosed information in order to monitor corporate performance. In addition, as part of the public expectation of greater openness by all institutions, the media and interest groups are also seeking greater corporate disclosure. Also, corporate employees have come to expect their management to inform them of factors involved in key management decisions, particularly when their company or industry is involved in public controversy. As a result, many questions have been raised concerning the categories, form, and timing of information which corporations should be willing or required to disclose.

The intensity and scope of the corporate disclosure issue has been increased by (1) public dissatisfaction with the leadership and performance of both corporations and government, (2) public interest in the social, political, and environmental impact of corporations, (3) the inquiries of a large number of public-interest groups, (4) public suspicion that secrecy is used as a cover for embarrassing, unethical, or even illegal activities, and (5) increased interest in corporate information among academic researchers, security analysts, and other individuals. Corporate management's response to inquiries often creates a dilemma: the disclosure of information may be costly and time-consuming, may lead to requests for more information, or may at times be damaging; yet the refusal to disclose often generates more distrust and increased pressures for mandatory disclosure. Interest groups often seek corporate disclosure because they lack confidence that the government will protect their interests. They also attempt to induce government to disclose more of the corporate information already in its possession.

## VOLUNTARY CORPORATE DISCLOSURE

Corporations voluntarily submit a substantial volume of information that is requested by government, the media, interest groups, and the public in addition to that required by law. The demands for greater disclosure place additional burdens on management to consider carefully the interests of shareholders, employees, and others affected by the information that would be disclosed. There is little public disagreement that managements should not disclose trade secrets and other sensitive commercial information that has proprietary value. Managements properly refuse to release information which would violate laws or abridge individual privacy, and they are reluctant to provide information that they feel would result in erroneous conclusions by the recipients. In addition, there is a tradition among some companies of avoiding disclosure because of a fear that information will be used in harmful ways. There is also a genuine concern for the cost of compiling, retrieving, and reporting information.

Large corporations receive thousands of requests for all sorts of information from sources ranging from students to reporters, adversarial interest groups, and numerous government officials and agencies. Information is rarely requested in a form that is readily available, and often it is unavailable without a major effort to develop it. In some cases, if data were provided as requested, they would be either misleading or meaningless. A further complication is that most requests express urgency in such ways as "My term paper is due next week" or "I need this for the morning edition."

## DISCLOSURE REQUIRED BY GOVERNMENT

The widespread notion that corporations should be required to make greater disclosures is often conceived without recognition of these developments, which are familiar to most corporate executives:

- *The Congress.* In addition to legislation such as the Freedom of Information Act (FOIA) and the Foreign Corrupt Practices Act (FCPA), Congress has sought greater corporate disclosure through committee hearings and requests by individual members. Not only has Congress increased the volume of its requests for corporate information, it also has expanded the scope of data sought.

- *The Securities and Exchange Commission.* In recent years the SEC has adopted more detailed disclosure rules which require corporations to disclose financial results by homogeneous geographical and industrial categories, noneconomic matters such as information on environmental pollution, compensation and perquisites of top executives, and some measures of the performance of outside directors.

  Under expanded disclosure requirements of the federal securities laws, corporate officers often face the threat of substantial liability if they fail, even inadvertently, to disclose material corporate information promptly and publicly.

- *The Federal Trade Commission.* To create a data bank for use in antitrust enforcement, the Federal Trade Commission (FTC) has adopted line-of-business reporting that requires certain large corporations to disclose to it financial performance in terms of a uniform set of market categories. The FTC has also initiated a corporate patterns reporting system under which certain corporations are required to report the "value of shipments" from their domestic manufacturing establishments in terms of product classifications. Each of these rules requires companies to report information to the FTC that many previously considered proprietary and that many others did not even compile.

- *The Administration.* Many executive departments request a good deal of corporate data. For example, reports such as environmental-impact statements have placed a substantial burden on companies in terms of the labor and costs required to produce them.

- *International Bodies.* Corporate public disclosure also involves foreign governments, regional organizations such as the European Economic Community (EEC), and international agencies such as the United Nations and the Organization for Economic Cooperation and Development (OECD). In 1976, several nations voluntarily adopted the OECD's guidelines, which were designed to specify information that multinational companies must disclose. While American corporations generally operate according to the guidelines, there have been efforts to make the codes mandatory. The EEC and the United Nations are interested in the issue of disclosure of key financial and nonfinancial data by multinational corporations.

Financial information is a complex aspect of corporate disclosure, particularly because of definitional problems, difficulty in identifying the expectations of its users, and significant variations in financial accounting and reporting practices. The Financial Accounting Standards Board (FASB), which establishes broad objectives and qualitative standards for financial accounting and reporting, has issued standards of supplemental disclosure whereby corporations are required to show the impact of inflation on financial results and the ways in which they translate foreign assets, liabilities, and earnings into dollars. As discussed in Chapter 5, "Financial Reporting and Control," formal corporate financial statements, from the perspective of the FASB and the SEC, are becoming less important per se than a total financial reporting scheme which includes such supplemental disclosures.

In addition to the foregoing types of corporate disclosure required by government, the Freedom of Information Act (FOIA) has been a major factor in reducing corporate privacy. Passed in 1966 and amended in 1974, the FOIA makes publicly available vast amounts of information collected by the departments and agencies of the executive branch of the federal government, including, of course, large quantities of information that companies are required or requested to submit. The 1974 amendments provide that agencies must generally respond to requests within 10 working days and charge no more than actual search and duplication costs.

As a result of expanded disclosure requirements, the federal government has become a central repository of information about a wide variety of corporate activities, both economic and noneconomic. To the general concern of corporate managements, the FOIA and related court interpretations have restricted the power of government agencies to withhold from the public the information that is submitted to them by corporations. One result is that many government agencies are besieged with requests from corporations, including foreign competitors, seeking agency-held data submitted by other corporations.

Since 1974, tens of thousands of requests have resulted in a massive revelation of information in federal files. Media and public-interest groups, which were the strongest advocates of the 1974 amendments, have not made as much use of them as expected. Corporations have used the law much more extensively than had been anticipated. For example, the FTC has found that requests from corporations exceed those of the media by several orders of magnitude.

Corporate requests are made to get a line on competitors' plans, to find sales leads, to help monitor the actions of regulatory agencies, and to bolster the corporate side in government and private litigation. Some companies have succeeded in learning what prosecutions federal agencies are planning and obtaining relevant information not attainable by pretrial discovery procedures. Moreover, the FOIA process is often quicker and less expensive. Yet, in some instances courts have narrowly defined the protection of trade secrets when corporations have sued to enjoin an agency from releasing information. Dangers to confidentiality are compounded when agencies receive so many requests that they cannot screen them carefully.

## DISCLOSURE TO THE MEDIA

The penetrating nature of investigative reporting has made the mass media a major force in the disclosure trend. Disclosure is intimately and inextricably related to the corporation's relationship with the media. This relationship has deteriorated over the past 20 years and is at best adversarial. As discussed in Chapter 21, the mutual hostility between corporation and press has had wellsprings in both camps. From the point of view of corporate experts on media relations, however, the primary corporate failings which detract from optimum media relations spring from these factors:

- The lack of a clear and well-thought-out disclosure policy on the part of most corporations
- The understandable but unfortunate unwillingness to face up to adverse situations which are of legitimate news interest
- The use of stilted, garbled, or pompous statements by some corporate spokespersons
- The lack of understanding among executives as to the nature and functioning of the news media

These factors are all within corporate control. The first, a well-thought-out and well-communicated disclosure policy, is basic. The second, facing up to bad news, is also of particular importance in establishing and maintaining credibility. A good example of this occurred in 1975, when internal auditors at Levi Strauss & Co. discovered an illegal overseas payment of $75,000. The company opted for a complete disclosure of the incident that included the amount involved, Levi Strauss's policy, steps taken to ensure that this breach of its policy was an isolated instance, and a tightening of controls to assure that there would be no repetition. This voluntary disclosure resulted in a sympathetic press treatment that stressed Levi Strauss's policy, its long-term sense of public responsibility, and the steps it had taken to prevent any recurrence.

## CORPORATE INITIATIVES AND ACTIONS

Despite the problems of public disclosure, there is growing recognition within the corporate community that a corporate management which conducts its affairs legally, ethically, and with sensitivity to reasonable public expectations can benefit by practicing openness and candor. An increasing number of corporate managements are concluding that they fare better when they are responsive to media inquiries than when they are secretive or reticent. They are reacting to the disclosure issue by regularly publishing more information on subjects of public interest and by responding more completely and rapidly to requests for information previously considered private. They also are taking the position that the burden of proof falls today on those who would withhold information rather than on those who want to make it known.

Beginning in the mid-1970s, large corporations began to define their stance on public disclosure. For example, Shell Oil Company established this policy in 1974:

> Beyond the many legal requirements to disclose corporate information, we voluntarily respond to government, media and bona fide public inquiries in a positive way and with a minimum of constraint. The principle of disclosure we follow is to provide requested information in a form, frequency, and amount practicable to assemble and which would not:

> 1. Lead to violation of any laws (e.g., antitrust) or proper contractual provision (e.g., secrecy agreements in negotiating documents).
> 2. Abridge individual privacy (e.g., employee health records, undocumented customer credit references).
> 3. Give competitors or others an unfair commercial or economic advantage (e.g., proprietary technical, trade secret, customer, or other sensitive financial or commercial information).
> 4. Be misleading in the absence of supplemental information not disclosed for the foregoing reasons.

If, in response to a specific request, disclosure involves "material information" (e.g., as contemplated by federal securities laws) such information is concurrently disclosed to the public at large.[1]

In 1974, during the national confusion about the reasons for oil shortages and price rises, the president of Shell Oil Company wrote the editors of many principal newspapers, advising them:

> I am personally convinced that this job of communications is as essential as finding more crude oil. The public has to know and appreciate the situation the U.S. faces, both today and long-term, if it is to respond intelligently to the social and political choices placed before it.
>
> Thus, it seems to me that Shell Oil Company has the responsibility to provide your editors and reporters with the information they need to give their readers as complete and objective a story as humanly possible. It accordingly seems incumbent upon us to adopt "openness" as a corporate policy. That we have done, and have so informed our managers.
>
> Let me be more precise about the import of our decision. It means essentially that we will try to do a better job of providing your staff with the information they need to do their job. If the information can be transmitted by a phone call, fine. If the subject is of such complexity that a face-to-face interview or briefing is required, we will make every effort to arrange a meeting either here in Houston or in your offices.

In 1976, BankAmerica published a comprehensive disclosure code with a policy statement and detailed information on what it would disclose on all aspects of its business. A. W. Clausen, president of the BankAmerica Corporation, explained in the preamble that the voluntary disclosure code was not simply a "code of conduct":

> BankAmerica, and Bank of America, have had strict ethical guidelines since their founding, and have taken swift action against employees who breached them. We are convinced that a far more powerful deterrent to wrongdoing is a code of disclosure. What better inhibitor to misconduct or ineptness than the certain knowledge that one's actions will become known? By the same token, the surest way to invite suspicion is to withhold information from individuals or groups who believe they are seeking it for good reason. In the absence of disclosure, it is human nature to suspect the worst.
>
> We are convinced that the marketplace can be a more effective regulator than excessive and often naive government restraints which dampen innovation and tend to constrict business. The marketplace can fulfill this role only when its participants have access to the timely information essential to any well-reasoned decision.

[1]*Social Performance Guidelines*, Shell Oil Company, Houston, 1974.

Voluntary disclosure going beyond the minimum requirements of the law seems to us to be the proper course.[2]

In 1977, Clausen headed a California Roundtable task force that studied corporate public disclosure. In reporting on the study, he stated:

The disclosure issue is controversial, mostly because management usually hears the word only when demands—often outrageous and unwarranted—are being made. Another reason why disclosure is a hard subject to come to grips with is that it is a relatively new concept, insofar as corporate practice and policy are concerned.[3]

In a survey of the 50 California Roundtable chief executive officers of corporations and more than 100 other large California corporations, a majority of chief executive officers indicated that they were receptive to new departures in this field. Most of them, for example, said that they did not think that limiting disclosure to matters required by law served either the best interests of the enterprise system or of their own companies. And a majority agreed that voluntary disclosure tended to forestall improper corporate behavior. However, an even stronger majority concluded that there was need to oppose proposals for wider disclosure of certain types of corporate information. In commenting on the survey, Mr. Clausen said:

I find no contradiction in these responses. To me they confirm what may be the principal contribution a consideration of disclosure policy can make to our goal of enhancing the credibility and strength of the enterprise system: Business needs to be assured that necessary constraints will be observed—that is, that the needs for privacy, confidentiality and the other important safeguards are not jeopardized, but rather protected, by a policy of voluntary corporate disclosure. With such assurances, most chief executive officers appear willing to consider voluntary disclosure policies which would make available, not only the information the company itself thinks should be available, but that information which its various constituencies say they need in order to judge the activities of the company.[4]

Corporate disclosure has proved to be an effective method in the creation and maintenance of public trust and a deterrent to government regulation of corporate performance and governance. Du Pont's Irving

---

[2]A. W. Clausen, "President's Preamble," *BankAmerica Corporation Voluntary Disclosure Code*, San Francisco, November 1976.

[3]Id., *Study on Corporate Disclosure*, California Roundtable Disclosure Task Force, Sept. 19, 1977.

[4]Ibid.

Shapiro has commented on the change in outlook of many corporate managements:

> For a long time, the operating principle on disclosure followed by most corporations was to let out what was required by law, and keep back everything else unless someone could show cause why it should be released. The familiar test question, well known to all who have served their time in the corporate interior was, "Have we ever said that before?" Today, the more appropriate disclosure principle would be the reverse: Whoever wants to hold back relevant material information should show cause why it should not be revealed.[5]

Differences in company tradition, management style, and the nature of businesses have precluded uniform disclosure practices. Variations are likely to continue. Nonetheless, companies that have had successful experience treat public disclosure as a function of their managing process with the underpinnings of a comprehensive disclosure policy and practical procedures. Some of the important considerations in formulating and using a company disclosure program are these:

- Consider the company's needs and objectives, for example, (1) to help regain or sustain public trust and confidence, including that of shareholders, employees, customers, government, or other constituents; (2) to help modify or eliminate the need for compulsory disclosure and command-and-control regulation; and (3) to help deter managerial misconduct or ineptitude.
- Analyze the company's present or likely involvement in public disclosure in these dimensions: (1) *sources of inquiry* such as government officials and agencies, customers, media, employees, public-interest groups, and professors and students; (2) *types of subject material requested*, both legally required and discretionary; (3) *routine or ad hoc inquiries*, differentiating between repetitive disclosures, such as regular reports to government and news releases, and random but predictable requests for specific information; (4) *functionally responsible company executives*, such as legal and financial officers with respect to material disclosures required by the SEC; (5) *top-management involvement*, i.e., disclosures that by sources, subject material, or disagreement among officers should be reviewed or approved by the chief executive and, in some cases, by the board of directors.
- Consider the types of company information that should not be disclosed, such as proprietary information or material that would

[5]Irving S. Shapiro, "Corporate Governance," Fairless Lecture Series, Carnegie-Mellon University, Pittsburgh, Pa., Oct. 24, 1979.

violate laws, abridge personal privacy, or adversely affect customers, suppliers, or others. Test each type that would be excluded by putting the burden of proof on those who would withhold it.

Some of the practices that have proved beneficial in managing the disclosure function are these:

- Assignment of a management coordinating function to an officer to help assure that (1) the disclosure policy and procedures are well communicated and understood by all concerned, (2) questions can be resolved by the officer or the chief executive in timely fashion, (3) disclosures are reviewed for consistency as to both information and disclosure policy, (4) coherent reasons are given for refusals to disclose, and (5) expert attention is given to the disclosure process as a management function.
- Audit the application of the disclosure policy and procedures for quality, consistency, and timeliness of response.
- Use the knowledge gained from inquiries to identify emerging problems or issues and to consider how to resolve or avoid them by voluntary disclosure, improvements in the disclosure policy or procedure, or changes in company performance.

## THE OUTLOOK

Both voluntary and compulsory public disclosure have become well-established processes. Overall, the extent and nature of their use will generally equilibrate with the degree and types of public concern about corporate performance and governance. In any event, corporate managements will continue to resist disclosure of information that would abridge personal privacy or jeopardize company or customer proprietary technical or trade information.

The willingness of corporate managements voluntarily to disclose relevant nonproprietary information will continue, and more companies are likely to follow the practices of companies that demonstrate beneficial results. The reasons for this growing acceptance are that voluntary disclosure has proved to be a means of management self-discipline in decision making and an alternative to compulsory disclosure and regulation. Also, voluntary corporate disclosure can be a means of achieving corporate credibility and public trust, but only if what is revealed is seen as publicly acceptable corporate performance.

Compulsory disclosure will continue as a government process for monitoring corporate performance. The Reagan administration's program of regulatory reform will affect compulsory disclosure in two ways. On one hand, disclosure requirements are to be minimized or withdrawn whenever practicable. On the other hand, when necessary to aid market forces or to encourage private initiatives and actions, disclosure may be used rather than command-and-control regulation. Therefore, some time will be needed to judge whether compulsory corporate disclosure is waxing or waning under the Reagan administration.

# CHAPTER 7

# Legal and
# Ethical Behavior

***The Issue*** • What can or should be done to assure that corporate performance complies with the law, that it satisfies general public expectations of fairness and ethical conduct, and that it minimizes pressures for illegal or unethical behavior by executives and managers on behalf of their companies? In what ways does the profit motive itself contribute to unethical or illegal corporate behavior?

***Importance*** • Legal and ethical behavior is at the foundation of the American society and private enterprise economy. Actual or perceived illegal or unethical corporate conduct lowers public trust in the business community and the private enterprise system, substantiates charges that corporate power is excessive and uncontrolled, and contributes to allegations and suspicions that other forms of misconduct remain undetected. Both illegal and unethical corporate actions are detrimental to the efficient functioning of the private enterprise system since business transactions depend upon honesty and trust. Illegal behavior can also result in the assessment of civil and criminal penalties against corporations and their executives.

Some critics who challenge the legitimacy of the private enterprise system and urge fundamental corporate reforms often cite examples of unethical or illegal behavior as evidence that the pursuit of profit is inherently unethical and thus contributes to immoral conduct by individuals. In countering this argument, corporate executives usually maintain that every organization and every segment of society have unscrupulous individuals and that there is nothing inherent in capitalism which causes unethical behavior.

When examples of unethical or illegal corporate conduct occur, they are used by critics to validate other charges of corporate misconduct. The result is increased pressure both for specific regulations governing corporate performance and for fundamental corporate reforms such as federal chartering and restrictions on mergers.

*Causes* • These issues are prominent because numerous examples of both unethical and illegal corporate actions have been disclosed in recent years. Among the reasons most commonly cited for corporate executives' violating laws and generally accepted ethical standards are personal weakness of individuals and corporate performance targets and evaluation systems that overemphasize bottom-line results. In addition, specific ethical issues arise because of reliance on legality as the predominant standard for corporate behavior, uncertainty concerning what constitutes ethical behavior, failure to establish or enforce company ethical standards, and inability to understand the changing ethical concerns of the public.

The distinction between legal and ethical standards of corporate behavior is important. Ethical standards are not codified; they are subject to changing social values and public concerns. Laws in our society proscribe intolerable conduct and prescribe the minimum obligation that is required by society. In general, law does not prescribe what society regards as *desirable* conduct by individuals or corporations. Furthermore, because law is stated in fixed language, it permits adherence to its "letter." Yet the "spirit" of the law incorporates some part of society's ethical standards. In short, compliance with legal requirements does not ensure corporate performance consistent with public expectations.

## ILLEGAL CORPORATE BEHAVIOR

Illegal corporate conduct generally is any action on behalf of a corporation by its officers, employees, or agents that results in adverse civil or criminal judicial decisions. To many people, however, noncompliance with voluntary standards, such as President Carter's wage-price guidelines, can create the impression of illegal corporate conduct. In addition, some questions of illegal corporate behavior may be obscured because they are resolved by *nolo contendere* and consent decrees and by private lawsuits without the degree of publicity usually accompanying civil or criminal prosecution of a large corporation and its executives.

Corporate executives obviously want their companies to be managed in accordance with applicable laws and regulations. Nonetheless, examples of corporate illegality in recent years that have caused closer scrutiny of all aspects of corporate performance include illegal foreign and domestic political payments, bribes, and kickbacks, illegal disposal of hazardous materials, price fixing, and fraudulent financial reporting practices and stock transactions.

### Reasons for Illegal Corporate Behavior

As with incidents of unethical corporate behavior, some corporate critics believe that incentive systems which are geared to profit encourage illegal behavior. In this regard, Courtney Brown, dean emeritus of the Columbia University Graduate School of Business, has observed:

> Loyalty to the bottom-line concept and to the company sometimes gets the corporate executive into serious trouble. Why should an executive risk a career, or even incarceration, by, for example, making illegal payments with no prospect of direct personal benefit? Yet it was done, and the cost in corporate image, as well as personal penalties, has been enormous. It has convinced many members of the public that deception is a normal practice among executives—that only one thing counts, the net profits of the enterprise.[1]

Other observers perceive a prevailing business morality that excuses illegal behavior as customary or necessary. The sheer volume, complexity, ambiguity, and conflicting requirements and interpretations of applicable laws make compliance difficult or, in some cases, impossible. As Prof. George A. Steiner of the UCLA Graduate School of

---

[1]Courtney Brown, unpublished background paper for the Resource and Review Committee.

Management has observed, "Regulations that are trivial, seemingly contrary to common sense, arbitrarily imposed and administered, and difficult to understand tend to erode respect for the law and willingness to comply with it."[2] Some observers also believe that vociferous grousing about the unreasonableness or inanity of laws and regulations or grudging compliance by senior managers has encouraged evasion of law by their subordinates.

In some cases, corporate illegality may occur because executives receive poor advice from their legal counsel or ignore advice that would have precluded illegal behavior. In other situations, managements may not have the effective internal controls necessary to assure legal compliance. In fact, some corporate compliance programs draw criticism because they are viewed by some people as window dressing rather than as serious efforts to ensure legal behavior by the corporation.

### Public Concern

The extensive use of legal resources by large corporations is among the most visible symbols of corporate power. Public reactions to real and alleged incidents of illegal corporate behavior contribute to public suspicions that corporate executives are above the law. Still others believe that corporations comply only with the letter and not with the spirit of the law.

Another factor that compounds this issue is a widespread public belief that two standards of justice exist in the United States: one for "common criminals" and one for "white-collar criminals," including high government officials and corporate executives. Many people are offended by examples of short sentences, modest fines, and special facilities and treatment given convicted government officials, corporate executives, and others while imprisoned. They also are galled by the attitudes of some convicted executives and their managements toward punishment for corporate crime.

Still another factor affecting public attitudes is that corporate executives are generally reluctant to condemn publicly the illegal conduct of other companies or their executives. That reluctance places corporate executives, their companies, and the business community in an unenviable position. As Irving Kristol has observed:

> Corporate executives almost never criticize other corporate executives, even when the latter are caught in *flagrante delicto*. No one seems to be

[2]George A. Steiner, "New Patterns in Government Regulation of Business," *MSU Business Topics*, autumn, 1978, pp. 53–61. Reprinted by permission of the publisher, Division of Research, Graduate School of Business Administration, Michigan State University.

"read out" of the corporate community, which inevitably leads the outsider to wonder whether this community has any standards of self-government at all. . . . [T]he business community as a whole remains strangely passive and quiet before this spectacle. This disquieting silence speaks far more eloquently to the American people than the most elaborate public relations campaign. And it conveys precisely the wrong message.[3]

Executives offer several reasons for their lack of comment. Most feel that they do not have adequate information about a case to make a reasonable judgment and, in any event, believe that legal questions are best resolved in the courts. And some executives feel that public criticism of another company's misfortune is a "cheap shot" or a holier-than-thou posture. Also, as Thomas Murphy of General Motors Corporation pointed out, "There would always be the suspicion of self-interest in any attempt by one competitor to police or censure another. And if a group of companies were to get together to censure another, there could be strong antitrust implications." Instead, he suggests, "We should continue to rely on the corrective forces already existing in our law enforcement and judicial systems, and rely as well on the basic integrity of the vast majority of business people."[4] In that spirit, some corporate executives believe that the best way to respond to public expectations and to reaffirm corporate integrity without condemning another corporation and its executives charged with legal violations is by speaking out against wrongdoing in principle.

## Government Actions

Corporate loss of public trust resulting from examples of illegal behavior has spurred new laws and stricter enforcement. As previously mentioned, in 1977 Congress enacted the Foreign Corrupt Practices Act (FCPA), which requires United States corporations, in both domestic and foreign operations, to provide "adequate" internal accounting controls to help prevent illegal or questionable payments.

A number of laws have significantly altered corporate legal obligations. The operation of health, safety, and environmental laws like the Toxic Substances Control Act and the Clean Air and Clean Water Acts is resulting in an extension of liability from the corporation to its

[3]Irving Kristol, "Ethics and the Corporation," The Wall Street Journal, Apr. 16, 1975, p. 18.

[4]Thomas A. Murphy, "Two Vital Issues: Business Ethics and National Planning," University of Michigan Business Review, The University of Michigan, Division of Research, Graduate School of Business Administration, Ann Arbor, Mich., July 1976, p. 2. Reprinted by permission of the publisher. Copyright © 1976 by The University of Michigan. All rights reserved.

managers. In some instances, that extension of liability does not require actual knowledge or personal involvement for an executive to be deemed responsible. Those laws can have the effect of shifting the standard for culpability from *mens rea,* or evil intent, to structural responsibility: an executive's criminal liability accrues solely from the fact he or she holds the responsible position in the company. The business community has opposed attempts to impose liability without knowledge or fault on higher management. Additionally, some laws assign the executive a responsibility to exercise an "affirmative duty" by notifying those persons adversely affected by the corporation's behavior once a potential harm has been discovered. Some lawyers look upon this provision as conscripting senior executives as law enforcement agents.

As discussed in Chapter 17, the Securities and Exchange Commission (SEC), the Federal Trade Commission, and Sen. Howard M. Metzenbaum are among those in government who have pressed for legal requirements that corporate boards of directors exercise greater accountability for the legal behavior of management. In addition, Congress has considered proposals that would increase the personal criminal liability of corporate executives. In a growing number of judicial decisions there is a tendency to hold executives accountable for failing to oversee compliance with a government regulation even though such a responsibility has been delegated.

The nature of punishment for illegal corporate behavior also has changed. Traditionally, punishment usually was levied against the corporation and seldom against its officers or managers. Prison terms were rarely imposed on convicted executives, and when executives were fined, the corporation routinely paid the fines. In recent years, larger fines have been assessed against corporations, corporate executives have become more vulnerable to criminal prosecution, and if convicted, they may personally face large fines and prison sentences.

The issue of legal behavior has raised questions about the role of the corporate attorney. For several years, the SEC and the corporate bar have been at odds over two interrelated questions. The first question is to whom is a corporate lawyer responsible: the board of directors, the officers, or the shareholders? If the answer is either to the board or to the officers, the second question arises: When is a corporate lawyer obliged to blow the whistle on his or her client? Both the SEC and the American Bar Association are confronted with the question of whether corporate lawyers, who now tend to act as confidential advisers to management, should be required to assume a more independent role like that of accountants.

## UNETHICAL CORPORATE BEHAVIOR

The distinction between legal and ethical norms does not render clear standards of corporate ethical behavior. The concept of corporate ethical behavior and its managerial application remain vague: many different standards or ideas are advocated by corporate executives and others. What is clear is that the public usually has higher expectations of corporate behavior than are codified in law. As a result, corporate executives must identify and be guided by standards of behavior that go beyond legal proscriptions. They must be continually concerned with what types of legally permitted behavior are unacceptable to the public.

Complicating this issue is the fact that our society does not apply a single ethical standard for business behavior but instead evaluates corporate ethical behavior on a spectrum extending from ruthlessness to the golden rule. As Irving Kristol has observed, the difficult ethical choices confronting business executives do not involve good opposing evil but instead "a collision between two goods." The problem for many corporate executives is that they have "come to think that the conduct of business is a purely 'economic' activity, to be judged only by economic criteria, and that moral and religious traditions exist in a world apart."[5]

Questions of unethical conduct also arise because of increasingly fragmented ethical and moral beliefs. Behavior considered permissible in one sector of society or at one time may be condemned in another sector or at another time. For example, the issues of equal opportunity and of environmental quality have created new questions of corporate ethical performance. When W. Michael Blumenthal was chairman of the Bendix Corporation, he pointed out, "Certain practices that were once acceptable are no longer considered proper because the rules and expectations of society have changed."[6]

Corporate managements recognize the importance of ethical behavior in their business operations, as Edson W. Spencer, chairman of Honeywell Inc., has emphasized: "The businessman who straddles a fine line between what is right and what is expedient should remember that it takes years to build a good business reputation, but one false move can destroy that reputation overnight."[7] Nobody would dare lend

---

[5]Irving Kristol, "Business Ethics and Economic Man," *The Wall Street Journal*, Mar. 20, 1979, p. 22.

[6]W. Michael Blumenthal, "Business Morality Has Not Deteriorated—Society Has Changed," *The New York Times*, Jan. 9, 1977, p. 28. © 1977 by The New York Times Company. Reprinted by permission.

[7]Edson W. Spencer, *The Week in Review*, newsletter published by Deloitte, Haskins & Sells, Sept. 14, 1979, p. 1.

money, start a business, or buy or sell goods in the absence of faith in the integrity of persons and the responsibility of the institutions concerned. Former Bank of America Chairman A. W. Clausen, now chairman of the International Bank for Reconstruction and Development (World Bank), put it this way: "Integrity is not some impractical notion dreamed up by naive do-gooders. Our integrity is the foundation for, the very basis of, our ability to do business.[8]

### Reasons for Unethical Corporate Behavior

To a greater extent than applies in strictly legal matters, competitive pressures and constraints involve ethical questions which are not always recognized or considered in management decisions. Business critics as well as corporate executives point to organizational reasons for what is, or is perceived as, unethical behavior. As with illegal corporate conduct, unethical conduct can be caused by:

- *Corporate objectives and evaluation systems that overemphasize profit.* No matter how strongly ethical standards are articulated, an overemphasis on production and sales quotas or profit targets can lead managers to believe that their top management places financial results above ethical considerations. Decisions concerning common business activities create ethical dilemmas that can result in unethical behavior.
- *Inadequate management controls to monitor and enforce compliance with company policies.* High ethical standards without management control systems can be ineffective and provide a false sense of security to top management.
- *Acceptance of legality as the standard for corporate behavior.* Since legal standards of behavior are more specific than ethical considerations, some executives, often by default, rely much more heavily on legality to evaluate and justify corporate behavior.
- *Ambiguous corporate policies.* Managers can err in interpreting general policy statements that do not differentiate unacceptable from acceptable conduct. They also may have difficulty in deciding whether policies are cosmetic or are actually to be observed.

There are two additional causes of unethical corporate behavior that can be differentiated from the foregoing causes of both illegal and unethical behavior:

[8]A. W. Clausen, "Voluntary Disclosure: Someone Has to Jump into the Icy Water First," *Financial Executive*, June 1976, p. 21.

- *Failure to understand changing ethical concerns of the public.* A particular issue, such as illegal campaign contributions, may raise public interest in corporate ethics and delineate unrelated areas of concern. For example, in the wake of the flurry of illegal contributions in 1975, some corporate practices that previously were not considered improper came to be labeled unethical.

- *Amoral decision making.* Some observers, including corporate executives, believe that decision making can produce unethical actions even though the moral integrity of the individual managers is unquestioned. Their reasoning goes like this: decisions based primarily on their effect on people are generally considered in a moral realm; those based primarily on their effect on profit are generally considered in an amoral context. The impacts on people of decisions made in the latter context often are not considered, except to the extent that they may affect profitability. In that impersonal context, it is said, ethical implications tend to be overlooked, or decisions involving questionable ethics are justified.

## Public Concern

Public concern about corporate ethical conduct has historically followed major incidents of illegal corporate activity. During the Watergate investigations, several prominent corporate executives were forced to admit making illegal contributions to the 1972 Nixon campaign fund. As discussed in Chapter 5, several hundred large corporations disclosed to the SEC that their managers had made questionable or illegal payments abroad. Those incidents, particularly the latter, stimulated government and media investigations of corporate practices involving questions of both legal and ethical conduct.

As a result of major incidents, quite a number of common corporate practices have been questioned, and some are now considered unethical. Among them are failure to disclose important information concerning the effects of industrial processes and products on human health, safety, and the environment and the unwillingness of corporate management to discipline executives convicted of illegal behavior. Other examples are deceptive marketing practices, such as confusing legal jargon in warranties, service contracts, and advertising, and managerial abuses of perquisites.

With the growth of investigative reporting and its role in disclosing some spectacular corporate malfeasances, the media are an important factor in identifying and defining issues of ethical behavior. Also, some activist church groups explicitly promote corporate ethical behavior, and they and other public-interest groups often cite examples of unethical corporate conduct to support their justification of corporate reforms they are advocating. For example, as soon as activists labeled the foreign marketing of infant formulas an ethical issue, they were able to defuse corporate responses.

Another exacerbating factor is that corporate executives are almost always portrayed in literature and the performing arts as ethically suspect or worse, no matter how unrealistic or unfair such portrayals may seem to members of the corporate community, their families, and others who know them. However, while many questions of unethical corporate behavior address issues of real concern, some charges are not accepted as factual by many people, particularly when the allegations are seen as a publicity device.

## CORPORATE INITIATIVES AND ACTIONS

Ethical behavior may well be the most difficult of the performance issues for corporate managements to deal with successfully. Executives must make many decisions involving ethical considerations which, regardless of the outcome, are subject to criticism, often by a public not fully informed about the subject. Compounding managerial difficulties are changing public views of what should constitute ethical behavior, the problems of clearly formulating and communicating ethical standards throughout a large organization, and the necessity of monitoring and assuring compliance with them and frequently changing legal standards and interpretations of them.

With corporate behavior under close scrutiny, even the appearance of unethical or illegal conduct can have an adverse impact on both an individual company and the corporate community as a whole. Some executives have suggested that corporate managements must therefore be concerned with three standards: the legality of an action, its ethical propriety, and how it will appear to people with widely differing values or to those with little understanding of business.

When corporate executives have recognized that unethical conduct which could affect their corporation's reputation has taken place, the most effective response has been to admit the breach, take immediate steps to repudiate the action, and assure that it will not recur. The most damaging corporate response in these circumstances has been to stonewall questions or criticisms, with the result that when malfeasance is ultimately disclosed, the public generally concludes that the actual situation is worse than has been revealed.

Corporate managements have responded to the contemporary issue of legal and ethical behavior in a variety of ways. As developed in Chapters 17 and 18, the performance by boards of directors has been improved, particularly with regard to their accountability for matters of legal and ethical behavior. Also, many company managements have developed compliance programs to educate managers and monitor their performance with respect to antitrust and other laws as well as internal codes of conduct. Others have established specific internal responsibilities by specifying compliance as a managerial duty and requiring employees to certify periodically that they have obeyed the law in the conduct of the business. As Robert S. Hatfield, when chairman of the Continental Group, Inc., observed:

> An effective compliance program can help prevent the enormous human suffering experienced by corporate managers charged with violations of criminal antitrust laws. They and their families live sometimes for years in fear of the ruin of their life's work. If a company's compliance program succeeds in saving some of its managers from this fear or this fate, it will accomplish an important social and human service.[9]

Beyond improving board performance and accountability and related compliance programs, many corporations have taken steps to assure that ethical as well as legal standards are observed. The most common actions are:

- *Periodic reaffirmation by corporate chief executives of the importance of legal and ethical behavior by example and statement.*
- *Codes of conduct, both on the corporate level and for specific business operations such as marketing, purchasing, overseas operations, and governmental relations.* Advocates of corporate conduct codes believe that well-written and effectively managed codes can substantially reduce the likelihood of illegal or unethical conduct throughout a corporation. Some advocates believe that codes of conduct can provide a firm stand against wrongdoing in an industry or for large corporations collectively. A 1975 Business Roundtable study on corporate codes of conduct concluded that a single code for all large corporations is impractical but encouraged member companies to establish, publish, and enforce their own codes of conduct.
- *Internal control systems to monitor areas of special concern.* Some companies have internal monitoring systems specifically concerned

---

[9]Robert Hatfield, "The Impact of Antitrust on the Large Corporation," address to the American Bar Association National Institute on Preventive Antitrust, New York, June 14, 1979.

with consumer and environmental protection. In others, managers must certify each year that they understand and have adhered to company policies or codes of conduct.

- *Realistic use of business targets and personnel reward criteria.* Some company managements are particularly conscious of the need to set sales, profit, production, and other business objectives that avoid pressures to meet them by illegal or unethical means. Similarly, they endeavor to administer compensation and promotion systems with criteria that do not invite inappropriate executive behavior.

- *Procedures for airing legal and ethical dilemmas.* Some companies have established procedures by which individual employees can get an independent hearing on legal and ethical dilemmas they encounter with assurance that questionable matters are brought to the attention of senior management.

- *Special investigations and audits.* Outside auditors and legal counsel are sometimes used to look for questionable behavior and to dramatize to company managers that illegal or unethical behavior will not be tolerated.

The managements of multinational companies are confronted with special problems because of the complex, diverse, and conflicting legal and ethical standards that exist throughout the world. Some United States multinational companies apply American ethical standards worldwide. Other companies operate in accord with the ethical practices in each country. Many large corporations, such as Exxon and Du Pont, have voluntarily exceeded United States legal requirements, such as those of the FCPA, by endorsing, in principle or in fact, either the Organization for Economic Cooperation and Development's declaration on business ethics or the International Chamber of Commerce's code of international conduct, or both.


## THE OUTLOOK

Examples of illegal and unethical behavior occur in the activity of every human institution. However, in the opinion of many people, the nature of economic activity, whether primitive bartering or modern commerce, produces greater temptations for wrongdoing than the activities of most other institutions. This factor, in addition to those previously discussed, means that legal and ethical business performance is a special and ongoing challenge to corporate managements. In a speech entitled "Managing in the 1980s," Reginald Jones, chairman of

General Electric Company, stressed the continuing importance of legal and ethical behavior:

> The people rightfully expect something more than technical competence in the managers of our large corporations. They look for a moral center—some evidence that we are operating from higher principles than expediency or narrow self interest.
>
> These are entirely reasonable expectations, and if they are ignored they quickly become a matter of law. So if the manager of the future wants to hold the respect of his peers and keep his company out of the toils of the law, he will be absolutely scrupulous in matters of law and ethics, and make sure that these same standards are upheld at all levels of the organization.[10]

Legal and ethical behavior is an integral factor in every aspect of corporate performance—a common denominator of all the performance issues as well as a key issue itself. The outlook for this issue, therefore, is that it will surface just about whenever malpractices in corporate performance occur. This reciprocal relationship is also a reason why corporate managements must assiduously manage the legal and ethical aspects of corporate performance and executive conduct. Because of the complexities of that task, corporate managements must use the best of today's policies and methods of organizational behavior and introduce other ones that may be necessary to establish the large corporation as an institution whose legal and ethical behavior is not a matter of public concern.

[10]Reginald H. Jones, "Managing in the 1980s," address to the Wharton School of Business, University of Pennsylvania, Philadelphia, Feb. 4, 1980.

# CHAPTER 8

# Quality of
# Working Life

***The Issue*** • There are a variety of well-known employee relations issues involving labor relations, wages, hours, employee benefits, and working conditions about which corporate managements have in-depth knowledge and experience. Quality of working life and the interrelated issue of employee citizenship rights, the subject of Chapter 9, are included in this book not only because they are relatively novel, their dimensions yet to be charted and their solutions yet to be found, but because they are particularly critical to the large corporation.

Quality-of-working-life issues in many ways are an extension of well-known employee relations issues. They include employee participation in decisions about job assignments, scheduling, and work-related activities; opportunities for employees' personal and occupational growth and development; and improvements in working conditions in terms of safety, health, variety, and sense of community. In a real sense, quality of working life also includes the issues of employee citizenship rights.

***Importance*** • Quality-of-working-life issues affect both the satisfaction that employees and managers derive from their work and, in turn, the productivity of large corporations. The pressures generated by these issues and the steps taken by corporate management or government to address them are having significant effects on corporate costs, operating efficiency, employee productivity, and management flexibility. At a minimum, the concept of quality of working life challenges some of the traditional behavior and prerogatives of both management and union leadership. And the lengthening list of employee expectations, if publicly endorsed, could result in a new set of employee-management relationships, extending to entitlements guaranteed by company policies, to rights specified in union contracts, and to both entitlements and rights established by law.

*Causes* • During the past 15 years people's expectations regarding careers and employment conditions have broadened and become more complex, and this trend shows no signs of abating. What often were regarded as pioneering steps or exemplary employee relations policies yesterday have in many cases become today's baseline standards.

According to the pollster Daniel Yankelovich, there is a "new breed" of Americans convinced that success as traditionally defined is not enough to satisfy their expectations in the workplace. A job and a fair paycheck are not enough, even when they come with fringe benefits (which in many cases are seen as entitlements) and considerable security against adverse economic conditions. Yankelovich maintains that tensions build in the new breed when jobs are unable to satisfy their deepest psychological needs or nourish their self-esteem. In other words, employees demand full enjoyment as well as full employment.[1]

This trend has stimulated management efforts to modify workplace environments by providing "quality" work calling for greater individual judgment and responsibility. These efforts are on behalf of white-collar and professional employees as well as production workers and are grounded in the idea that employee satisfaction and reduced employee relations problems (less absenteeism, lower turnover, and better attitudes) might go hand in hand with higher productivity.

[1]Daniel Yankelovich, "Work, Values, and the New Breed," in Clark Kerr and Jerome M. Rosow (eds.), *Work in America: The Decade Ahead,* Van Nostrand Reinhold Company, New York, 1979, pp. 3–26.

In many ways, the concept of quality of working life is merely the continuation of long-standing concerns about working conditions. The meaning of the term itself is still unclear, and while some corporate executives counsel caution to avoid faddish solutions, others see a need for prompt attention. Already, many companies have attached enough importance to the issue to establish trial projects or ongoing programs. Professors Leonard Schlesinger and Richard Walton of the Harvard Graduate School of Business Administration have estimated that at least one-third of the Fortune 500 companies have quality-of-working-life experiments under way.[2]

## EMPLOYEE WORK SATISFACTION AND PRODUCTIVITY

Stephen Fuller, General Motors vice president for personnel administration and development, sees quality of working life as an integral part of the job of building corporate organizations suited to the 1980s and beyond. James F. Bere, chairman of Borg-Warner Corporation, speaking about employee expectations for quality-of-working-life changes, has asked:

> Who, if anyone, is discussing such revolutionary ideas? Who recognizes the need for change? More persons than many of us in corporate management may think. Politicians know it; so do labor leaders. Anyone attuned to the thinking of working people has to be picking up the signs. We see them in the grievances and issues that come up in every work group, and they are obvious from the opinion polls. . . . For chief executives in particular, they [quality-of-working-life issues] must be at the top of our managerial agenda.[3]

A major problem in coming to grips with this issue is that there is a fuzziness about proposals for "workplace community" or "self-fulfillment." Such terms draw puzzled looks from managers used to equating work satisfaction with the hard coin of more pay. There is a suspicion that these may be substitutes for more individual and measurable indices of performance—that, for example, "participatory democracy" may really mean "participatory mediocrity" or that quality of working life is little more than job enrichment. There is, further,

---

[2]Leonard Schlesinger and Richard Walton, unpublished background paper for the Resource and Review Committee.
[3]James Bere, "A CEO Looks at Work: Why We Need a Second Industrial Revolution," MANAGEMENT REVIEW, July 1978, AMACOM, a division of American Management Associations, New York, 1978, p. 22.

something akin to impatience on the part of some managers who have been around long enough to compare today's plant and office conditions with those of a generation ago.

Those who say that the concept of quality of working life ought to be taken seriously give three main reasons for management to heed this issue:

- Observation and studies show substantial and increased job disaffection by employees of many types and levels that cannot be explained as routine grousing or escalation of the "gimme" complex.

- Demographic trends point toward a reduction in the number of new entrants to the labor force, indicating that it may become increasingly difficult in the mid- to late-1980s for corporations to attract, train, and retain enough skilled high-quality employees in many job categories. Moreover, with fewer people entering the workforce and the effect of inflation on pensions, more employees are electing to work until age 70.

- There may be enough substance to claims of higher productivity or greater creative output derived from quality-of-working-life programs to justify significant investment in experiments. Some failures can be expected; the track record to date assures that. It may also be that some quality-of-working-life advocates are waving the productivity banner to promote pet ideas for reforming corporations. However, with productivity an important national issue, an increasing number of corporate managements are making a stronger effort to couple quality of working life and productivity.

Pat formulas for improving employee work satisfaction and productivity are usually regarded with suspicion, but there is enough employee disaffection with jobs and management dissatisfaction with productivity in traditional workplace environments that strong pressure for change is resulting. Scholars, such as Prof. Rosabeth Kanter of Yale, who have explored the quality-of-working-life issue in depth, believe that pressures are building and that it is the work, not the workers, that will have to change.

Professor Kanter's conclusions were discussed by a group of senior managers from General Motors, Nabisco, Weyerhaeuser, and Xerox who attended a 1977 conference sponsored by the American Center for the Quality of Working Life. The conference ended with a general feeling that quality of working life was an urgent issue, one that faced the entire American economic system. Merrill Robison, a senior vice president of Weyerhaeuser Co., said that his discussion group "unanimously agreed that over time we in management had to do something. . . . We felt this was a real challenge, the biggest challenge of the 80's facing us all."[4]

In a *Fortune* magazine article, Charles G. Burck discussed the quality issue in terms of "a lesson from the Orient":

> The old-line manager may doubt that there is any positive correlation between job enrichment and higher productivity, particularly in such areas as middle management, where productivity is hard, if not impossible, to measure accurately. But the examples of success continue to multiply at a rate that makes a causal relationship almost impossible to doubt.
>
> The Japanese offer perhaps the most prominent body of evidence—and they have begun exporting their techniques to the plants they own in the U.S. They have run their enterprises with an almost intuitive understanding of the connection between employee satisfaction and enhanced productivity.[5]

Some American executives and observers, however, believe that the Japanese approach to employee productivity is largely based on distinctly different social and cultural systems, including an emphasis on paternalism within companies rather than the collaboration which is central to the concept of quality of working life. This belief is called to question by a method used by Japanese companies called "quality circles." This process is carried out by groups of coworkers who advise their supervisors of ways to improve quality and thus productivity. This successful bottom-up form of employee participation was generally regarded as a Japanese invention until Peter Drucker called attention to the fact that it and other productivity ideas had been borrowed from the United States and over the past 20 to 30 years had been forgotten by American management until they were applied by Japanese managements in their United States plants.[6]

## CORPORATE INITIATIVES AND ACTIONS

Whether or not higher productivity is a clear result, it is significant that the companies that have examined the quality-of-working-life concept most carefully continue to experiment with it and encourage other

[4]American Center for the Quality of Working Life, Management Conference, Leesburg, Va., Nov. 15–16, 1977.

[5]Charles G. Burck, "The Intricate Politics of the Corporation," *Fortune*, April 1975, p. 190.

[6]Peter F. Drucker, "Learning from Foreign Management," *The Wall Street Journal*, June 4, 1980, p. 20.

corporations to look at it with an open mind. General Motors, one of the pioneers, began with programs at assembly plants and has found the results valuable enough to launch related programs with its professional staff and dealers.

GM's best-known effort is the one at the Tarrytown, New York, assembly plant. Poor morale and low efficiency were leading to a plant shutdown until managers and union representatives began working together with assembly-line workers to resolve problems. With the workers treated as participants, not as passive subjects, motivation increased and grievances and absenteeism declined. In a 1980 feature article *Time* magazine reported that the Tarrytown factory had "earned the reputation of being [among] the giant automaker's most efficient assembly facilities" and that "Tarrytown's current renown is more surprising because in the early 1970s, the 55-year-old plant was infamous for having one of the worst labor-relations and poorest quality records at GM."[7] General Motors now ranks Tarrytown among its best locations. As Thomas A. Murphy as chairman of General Motors observed, "We've had great success with 'quality-of-work-life' programs. We've found they increase human satisfaction and performance, and we intend to continue them."[8]

TRW Inc. has also established quality-of-working-life projects in some of its manufacturing plants. One union plant started its project with a plantwide productivity bonus. That incentive created a favorable climate in which other activities could take place. Another project focused on the development of mutual trust and joint problem-solving techniques among union and management officials and followed with an open process of choosing ideas for quality-of-working-life and productivity improvement experiments.

Quality-of-working-life programs have been successfully adopted with employee groups in nonunion situtations. The Polaroid Corporation is a case in point. However, when companies have national unions, as in the GM example, a key to success has been full collaboration between managements and labor leaders. In both union and nonunion settings, the central factor in success appears to be a management attitude and willingness to bring workers into the process of searching for solutions.

For years, some companies have been following, at least in some of their facilities, certain of the policies and practices now being advocated. Those companies have wholeheartedly endorsed such ideas as scrupulous attention to safety, greater openness and disclosure of explanations about important management decisions and company

[7]"Stunning Turnaround at Tarrytown," *Time*, May 5, 1980, p. 87.
[8]"Hot UAW Issue: 'Quality of Work Life,'" *Business Week*, Sept. 17, 1979, p. 122.

plans to employees, efforts to elicit employees' suggestions, and employee participation in finding ways to make the work move more efficiently and the jobs be more worthwhile. What has occurred, other than the growth of quality-of-working-life programs, is the institutionalizing of the effort by more formal structures and procedures.

Union leaders have been ambivalent toward quality-of-working-life programs. The United Auto Workers (UAW) and General Motors, for example, have jointly designed and publicly endorsed such projects since 1973. Other unions besides the UAW have publicly endorsed such programs; however, many union leaders fear that corporate managements will use "quality" programs to undermine unions or increase worker productivity without improving job quality or wages.

To avoid a leap to the conclusion that some managements have found the answer to employee work satisfaction and productivity, several points need to be added. Most of the experiments and analyses of problems have related to work of the assembly-line type. However, most jobs in the United States today are not of that variety, and it should not be supposed that GM's Tarrytown success could serve as the model for projects applicable in office or laboratory settings, even in the same company.

A further reason is to be found in the nature and extent of the management commitment required. Collaboration, as opposed to paternalism, is a central requirement, and that is difficult if not impossible to prepackage. All the evidence suggests that quality-of-working-life projects are rarely transferable to other locations or companies. For example, GM and the UAW report that the approach that has worked at Tarrytown has not even been salable on a trial basis at some other GM assembly plants, despite backing from corporate and union headquarters. Inflexibility on the part of some local labor leaders and difference in management style have been cited as reasons for the transplant failure.

Experienced quality-of-working-life practitioners agree on several principles that should govern experiments:

- The corporate climate must encourage quality-of-working-life projects. Management must not only endorse some trials but must enter into the effort with the recognition that what may have to change is its own attitudes and behavior, fully as much as those of workers.
- Projects have the best chance of success if they build on basics that predate the quality-of-working-life label. Employees will be more generally satisfied when their work challenges their ability and knowledge, when they have opportunities for advancement, when they have some role in determining the way to go about their own

work, when they feel secure from health and safety hazards on the job, when their management is open and candid in disclosing information that affects them, when they have confidence in the integrity and good intentions of management, and when they believe that the output of the total effort is a product or service of some utility, such that providing it is a respectable way to make a living.

- Those experiments which carry a built-in way of measuring success or failure, in unambiguous terms and fairly rapidly, appear to be more readily accepted by management, workers, and union representatives than those which have more sweeping but abstract objectives.

- It is difficult if not impossible to separate the quality factors that employees associate with their work from the personal attitudes and feelings that they bring into the workplace from their life at home, in the community, and as citizens of a nation. Opinion research shows that people now give lower scores to their satisfaction with life in general than they did a few years ago. That perception of lost ground would be expected to carry over into the working environment to some degree, and it is a factor to be considered in management's evaluations of workplace quality projects.

## THE OUTLOOK

The performance of the economy has an important effect on employee and management attitudes toward quality-of-working-life factors. Normally, the expectations of employees shift to improvements in their working lives when they experience fair and regular compensation, reasonable working conditions, and benefit programs that help provide for emergencies and long-term security. On their part, managements are most likely to experiment or adopt quality-of-working-life programs when their businesses are prospering. However, with national attention directed at the country's need for economic recovery, employees, unions, and managements may well be more deeply interested in developing quality-of-working-life programs that have good prospects for achieving higher productivity. In addition, management attention is likely to be stimulated to the extent that foreign competitors achieve competitive advantages in productivity, quality assurance, or harmonious employee relations from quality-of-working-life programs.

Demographic factors are also likely to intensify management interest. If, as mentioned, serious shortages of qualified younger people occur in the late 1980s, competition for them will focus attention on quality-of-working-life features. The availability of older employees is another demographic factor. Many people have retired between ages 50 and 65 because of dissatisfaction with their jobs and the quality of their work environment. Managements, therefore, are likely to find that even employees whose working lives have been extended by the inflationary erosion of fixed incomes are interested in quality-of-working-life features. Furthermore, as serious inflation abates, managements are even more certain to find quality of working life a factor in keeping or attracting older employees.

# CHAPTER 9

# Employee Citizenship Rights

*The Issue* • The issue of employee citizenship rights relates to constitutionally asserted and, in some instances, legislatively mandated claims to protection of equal employment opportunity, personal privacy, freedom of expression and dissent, due process, and other rights. They are, like the quality-of-working-life issues discussed in Chapter 8, a series of nontraditional concepts of employee relations that have continued to emerge as critical matters for the large corporation.

*Importance* • Employee citizenship rights range from the long-standing and critically important issue of equal employment opportunity to the emerging concept of jobs as a property right. Like other employee relations issues, the employee rights issues affect employee workplace attitudes and productivity. They also have opened a new area of management-employee relationships that are affecting company policies, managing styles, and constitutional and labor law.

*Causes* • As in the case of the quality-of-working-life issues, employee citizenship rights result from the broader expectations that people have about careers and conditions of work. The rights and entitlements explosion of the last decade has helped to focus attention on the question of whether basic citizenship rights have been infringed by limitations placed on those rights in the workplace. As a result of changing social values and some real or presumed corporate violations of rights, many employees are interested in acquiring additional rights or entitlements. Among the exponents who are at the leading edge of this movement are those who advocate con-stitutional-type rights on the job. At the same time, some corporations, endeavoring to improve their employees' work satisfaction and productivity, are adopting or experimenting with policies and programs that recognize some types of citizenship rights on the job.

The issue of employee citizenship rights involves complex and subtle questions affecting the proper balance between protecting employees and efficiently managing business affairs. Complicating the issue are legal ambiguities and the absence of well-proven models of effective company policies and programs. There is a growing debate over the necessity for and nature of such new protection for employees and the extent of government involvement that may be required to assure it. Meanwhile, the managements of many of the largest corporations are endeavoring to develop new practices to deal with some of the questions of employee citizenship rights.

A wide variety of persons, ranging from corporate critics such as Ralph Nader to authors such as David W. Ewing, executive editor of the *Harvard Business Review,* and corporate leaders such as Frank T. Cary, former chairman of IBM, have advocated greater employee citizenship rights. Of course, such diverse advocates have different motivations. Nader, for example, included citizenship rights in his proposal for federal chartering as well as in his promotion of the proposed Corporate Democracy Act of 1980. Cary has been a strong advocate of protecting employees' personal privacy.

Some corporate executives and other observers reject the need for many of the proposed employee citizenship rights. They contend that most employees are not interested in such rights in the workplace, that providing them would impair management's ability to manage, and that most employees have access to grievance procedures or, in extreme cases, to the courts. Other executives believe that employee rights must be weighed against corporate responsibilities. For example, an employee's right to privacy must be balanced with a company's need for work-related information about both applicants and employees.

William I. Spencer, president of Citibank, has argued that recognizing individual rights is good business and that many of today's socially mandated and legally protected employee rights came about because corporations themselves are active agents of social change. In a 1980 address, Spencer stated:

> The modern trend is to view employment, or a series of employments, as one of many life interests—all serving the common purpose of self-fulfillment, which usually includes a sense of social purpose. Thus, workers are more determined than ever to bring into the workplace the same values they cherish outside the workplace.
>
> This includes such intangible values as self-respect, dignity, and individuality. It also includes the particular values enumerated in the Constitution. Workers no longer consider the "Bill of Rights" something to be stashed out of sight, like a wet umbrella, when they arrive at work. They expect such guarantees as "due process," "privacy," and "free speech" to follow them to their desks and work-stations. After all, a right that doesn't apply through much of your waking day and which you can be fired for exercising, isn't much of a right.
>
> Workers today not only claim the right to dissent from company policies and practices on Constitutional grounds, but to dissent publicly on grounds of personal conscience, if practices they perceive as unethical are not corrected through internal appeal mechanisms. Some old-line company managers shake their heads in dismay and ask "Whatever happened to the concept of employee loyalty?" The answer is: it's still around, but now a company must earn it through performance—not command it through a paycheck.[1]

Opinion research suggests that the issue of employee citizenship rights is a growing one among rank-and-file employees. In addition, a *Harvard Business Review* survey has shown substantial support among corporate managers for broader rights of privacy, dissent, and due process in the workplace.[2] Among the large corporations with programs to implement some of the citizenship rights proposals are IBM, Xerox, General Motors, Citibank, General Electric, and Bank of America.

In the following sections brief summaries of the employee rights issues are presented in the order of their maturity in the public policy process.

[1]William I. Spencer, "Recognizing Individual Rights Is Good Business," address delivered at the Third National Seminar on Individual Rights in the Corporation, Washington, June 12, 1980.

[2]David Ewing, "What Business Thinks about Employee Rights," *Harvard Business Review*, September–October 1977. Copyright © 1977 by the President and Fellows of Harvard College; all rights reserved. Reprinted by permission of the Harvard Business Review.

## EQUAL EMPLOYMENT OPPORTUNITY

Since 1964, equal employment opportunity has been a national goal prescribed by federal law. As corporate executives are well aware, all employers must take affirmative action to achieve and maintain a workforce having a minority and female composition at all levels that is reflective of individuals with appropriate skills in the applicable labor market. That goal includes, as well, qualified handicapped individuals and Vietnam-era and disabled veterans. While overshadowed by race- and sex-bias cases, age has also become an active equal-opportunity issue.

Both voluntarily and under the pressure of federal, state, and local agencies, corporations and all other employers have hired millions of minority-group members and women. The extent to which this record has helped achieve the national goal of equal employment opportunity has been the subject of much study. The conclusions are mixed and often are debated in terms of points of view, research methods, and assumptions used in the studies. In a summary of studies by government, academic, and public-interest-group representatives, *Dun's Review* reported that while educated blacks with a strong attachment to the labor force have moved ahead considerably, there remains an unskilled underclass, heavily concentrated among youth in the inner cities, that has actually fallen behind. *Dun's Review*, citing the National Organization of Women's estimate of a 50 percent increase in women workers in the 1970s, reported that despite the women's liberation movement, "Women have actually increased their concentration in clerical work, and their modest shifts into professional and technical jobs merely mirror the similar movement for men."[3]

Most experts agree that if there is an expansion of skilled, professional, and managerial positions, the significant decline in new candidates for employment that will occur in the 1980s should give women and members of minority groups more opportunities than in the 1970s. Just about everyone agrees that a growing economy is the key to their greater opportunities.

Confirmation of the right to equal opportunity has been followed by a growing number of nonracial groups seeking to abolish various forms of actual or perceived discrimination against their members. These groups include the aged, the physically or mentally handicapped, veterans, and various religious and ethnic groups. As a result, there have been continuing pressures by equal-rights groups and stronger enforcement of equal-opportunity laws and regulations, including

[3]"Equal Opportunity: A Scorecard," *Dun's Review*, November 1979, pp. 106–110.

guidelines concerned with sexual harassment, religious accommodation, and national-origin discrimination.

The growth of government involvement, including that of the courts, in equal-opportunity issues such as reverse discrimination has posed complex problems for all employers, particularly large corporations which have been brought into the public spotlight by enforcement agencies. The overall effect is that corporations, particularly large ones, are expected to achieve equal opportunity in all aspects of their business with fairness to all who are affected. That challenge to corporate management is compounded by advocates of a concept of egalitarianism that seeks equal results rather than just equal opportunity. Furthermore, enforcement of equal-opportunity statutes has often focused on actual results as a proxy for the illusive concept of opportunity.

## PERSONAL PRIVACY

The employee privacy issue involves corporate management's collection and use of personal information about employees and the right of employees to have access to information about themselves. Proponents of privacy protection for corporate employees favor corporate policies or government regulations which would (1) eliminate the covert collection of information, (2) guarantee individuals access to files that contain information about themselves in order to correct inaccuracies, and (3) provide individuals with some control over the dissemination of information about themselves. These rights now exist for federal employees and most public employees in several states. Nationwide surveys show substantial public support for extending them to all employees.

In 1974, Congress passed the Privacy Act, which applied employee privacy safeguards to federal agencies. The act and its application set an example that advocates of privacy protection felt the private sector should adopt. In 1978, the Privacy Protection Study Commission urged business and industry voluntarily to apply privacy and openness guidelines in order to preempt federal and/or state legislation. The privacy issue has been advanced at the state level of government. Several states have passed laws that establish personal privacy rights for private employees, and many more state legislatures have been considering such legislation.

In addition to information about employees that most company managements have come to believe is necessary for personnel administration, requests from government agencies and from insurance companies have led to the gathering of a good deal more. Some corporate managers have become concerned that the increasing computerization of personnel files would reduce the security of such records and make it difficult to provide privacy safeguards. Moreover, some personal information about employees required by the Equal Employment Opportunity Commission and the Occupational Safety and Health Administration conflicts with legal prohibitions on disclosure and the employees' rights to privacy that corporations are expected to protect.

Only a few years ago organized labor showed little interest in workplace privacy. Now, however, some union leaders are demanding privacy safeguards against lunch-box and locker searches, television surveillance, lie-detector tests, and other practices. With executives in some industries convinced that such forms of scrutiny are necessary to help prevent employee theft or to aid quality control, personal privacy is likely to become a sensitive subject of collective bargaining.

## FREEDOM OF EXPRESSION AND DISSENT

This issue involves the extent to which employees' rights to free expression and dissent are discouraged or prevented by corporate rules or management attitudes. Corollary issues are whether employees have rights to engage in public election campaign activity in the workplace, to assemble in the workplace for purposes of free expression or dissent, and to refuse to carry out management directives.

Employees have diverse external relationships, and their opinions on public issues tend to mirror those of the general public. However, since employees are often regarded as the number 1 constituency of the corporation, many managements encourage and listen to expressions of employee opinion. That relationship helps management respond to employee concerns and earn employee support on key issues.

But employee freedom of expression also involves stronger actions. In addition to registering criticism through supervisors, union, or company grievance processes and, sometimes more subtly, by their attitudes and work performance, some employees have been publicly critical of company policies and management decisions. A small number have used "whistle-blowing tactics" (such as public disclosure of alleged misdeeds of their managers), anonymous leaks of proprietary company information, and covert alliances with public-interest groups. Whistle blowers are outspoken employees who are usually motivated by moral, legal, or safety concerns, their views of the public interest, personal spite or frustration, or a belief that they have to go outside to be heard from within.

Some advocates of employee rights believe that all forms of expression and dissent should be guaranteed. There are, however, well-recognized limitations to what free speech deserves protection. For example, employees have no right to disclose trade secrets or to be parties to salary forecasts or other legitimate private corporate matters without management approval.

While corporate employees are not explicitly denied free speech and dissent, some people believe that they are subject to excessive managerial control in the exercise of those rights on the job. There have been several well-reported examples of company retaliation against employee whistle blowers who publicly disclosed alleged misdeeds of their managements. Such cases, despite a strong tradition of loyalty which generally recognizes that a company's legitimate private matters should not be disclosed by employees, have supported an emerging opinion that employees should be able to disagree publicly with the policies or actions of their employer. In the past there has been little basis in law for protection of employee whistle blowers; however, a step in that direction has been taken by provisions in the Mine Safety and Health Act, the Toxic Substances Control Act, the Occupational Safety and Health Act, and the Water Pollution Control Act which protect a worker who reports company violations to the government agency concerned. Also, in 1981 Michigan became the first state to provide protection for private-sector employees who report alleged company violations of law to public authorities. Under these circumstances, an employee can bring suit in state court for unjust reprisal.

## DUE PROCESS

This right is regarded by proponents as necessary to protect other rights as well as to assure the equitable administration of company personnel policies. David Ewing, in proposing a bill of rights for employees, has asserted that due process is needed to make all other employee rights operative. He has reasoned that ways must be found to put the employee on the same level as the boss whenever differences of opinion arise over the exercise of rights.[4]

Due process for employees may be provided by voluntary company

---

[4]David Ewing, Freedom inside the Organization, E. P. Dutton & Co., New York, 1977, pp. 155–156.

grievance procedures, union contract grievance procedures, or lawsuits brought by employees. As questions concerning rights of employees and other types of complaints have increased in recent years, all three ways of assuring due process have been increasingly used. Although union grievance procedures are usually related to disputes involving the application or interpretation of a contract, some arbitrators have reversed the discharges of employees by finding that an employer violated such citizenship rights as free expression, privacy, or due process. Even more convincing evidence of concern about due process and other employee rights has been provided by the growth of employee litigiousness. In reporting on that phenomenon, *Business Week* stated:

> Employee lawsuits have charged everything from invasion of privacy to breaking an implicit contract to provide a lifelong job, but the most common accusation is one of unlawful discrimination.
>
> Even if the company wins, it can be expensive. Investigating, planning legal strategy, and answering a complaint in court can cost thousands of dollars worth of executive time and law firm charges. But settling a case out of court inexpensively is dangerous.[5]

Expectations of some employees and demands by advocates of employee rights for a basic, uniform due process for resolving employee grievances are likely to grow. Increasingly, proposals have been made that would establish due process of law for employees to challenge changes in their job status, above and beyond any grievance procedures in union contracts or those provided by management policies. Some state legislatures are considering proposals for independent agencies that would establish and enforce rules for guaranteeing employees' due-process rights, particularly good-cause statutory job protection for employees not represented by unions.

## CORPORATE INITIATIVES AND ACTIONS

Corporate executives have differing views of the concept of employee citizenship rights. Some favor expansion of the concept; others believe that such rights should stand the test of public policymaking. They explain that if (as in the case of equal opportunity) laws are enacted to establish or recognize such rights in the workplace, they will comply with them. Beyond these generalized indications of executive attitudes

[5]"Coping with Employee Lawsuits," *Business Week*, Aug. 27, 1979, p. 66.

toward the overall issue of employee citizenship rights, corporate initiatives and actions are described below for each of the component issues in the order of their stages of maturity.

### Equal Employment Opportunity

With over a decade and a half of experience, corporate executives have become well informed about the importance of equal opportunity. In providing equal employment, they have had to comply with a comprehensive, complex, and, in some instances, conflicting system of regulations and administrative and judicial interpretations. This aspect of employee relations is an unusually challenging task for corporate managements, particularly in avoiding such pitfalls as reverse discrimination.

Virtually all large corporations have established equal-opportunity staffs whose purpose is to help organize and coordinate companywide affirmative-action programs. Those programs began in the mid-1960s with basic attention to hiring, but corporate managements soon realized that for progress to be made they must make intensive additional efforts within their companies, in schools and universities, and in the broader society. They found that sufficient qualified minority-group and women applicants were not available, particularly in skilled professional and management catagories. As a result, most large companies began providing financial and other types of support to help improve effectiveness in both teaching and learning in schools and colleges and to encourage women and members of minority groups to prepare for and succeed in technical and business-oriented vocational and college programs. These corporate outreach activities provide support for such purposes as teacher training, career counseling, scholarships, and student employment.

Within many companies, managements have developed special policies and programs to help create both a general atmosphere and specific conditions in which minority-group members and women can succeed and advance on their merits. In many cases, entry training and continuing education have been given special emphasis, with resulting benefits for all employees.

Some corporate managements have recognized the need for the advancement of equal opportunity beyond the corporation and the educational system. As a result they have made special efforts to purchase products and services from minority suppliers, to deal with minority-owned banks, and to recruit and develop minority-group distributors for their products. Some have supported equal-housing laws and have opened plants in disadvantaged areas. In addition, business philanthropy has been expanded to include grants to organizations concerned with the education and welfare of women, members of minority groups, and others who are seeking equal opportunity. Also, corporate managements have established programs to encourage their employees to serve in education, business, and social service organizations that further their goals of affirmative action.

Since equal opportunity is a citizenship right that transcends employment, corporate managements also administer their credit and advertising practices and all other aspects of their business on that basis.

### Personal Privacy

In the late 1960s and early 1970s, managements of such companies as IBM, the Bank of America, and the Prudential Insurance Company of America voluntarily decided to establish employee privacy protection programs. On the basis of their successful experience, the Business Roundtable, the Chamber of Commerce of the United States, the National Association of Manufacturers, and other business associations have urged companies to adopt the recommendations of the Privacy Protection Study Commission. The Business Roundtable, for example, called upon the chief executive officers of its member companies "to act promptly to devise new policies to protect employees' privacy." The Roundtable warned that "unless industry voluntarily takes a firm and decisive hand to insure the fair and proper use of employee records, legislators stand poised and in some states have already passed laws to limit and control this crucial area of private sector initiative and diversity."[6]

Although about 300 of the *Fortune* 500 industrials have employee privacy policies, advocates of privacy protection are concerned that sufficient progress has not been made in the business community as a whole. One of the foremost advocates of employee citizenship rights, Columbia University Law Professor Alan F. Westin, has noted:

> Even if *all* of the FORTUNE 500 industrial firms and their non-industrial counterparts were assumed to have privacy policies, this would cover only 20 million of the 70 million employees working for business firms. Many students of personnel administration argue that it is precisely the medium- and smaller-sized firm *outside* the FORTUNE 500 mold that are the slowest to recognize the rights defined by the Privacy Commission.

[6]*Fair Information Practices: A Time for Action*, Business Roundtable policy paper, New York, December 1978, p. 1.

Westin also has questioned the quality of some company employee privacy programs, commenting that much of what has been promulgated might be called "splendid but vague declarations of intent or a numbingly detailed code of procedures that contributes nothing to fair information practices."[7]

While Westin rejects any "full code" model of regulation, he argues for a "minimum rights" legislative approach with remedies by individual lawsuit.

## Freedom of Expression and Dissent

Many corporate managements encourage an upward flow of ideas and criticism as important to the vitality of their companies. At the same time, they have refrained from an unqualified endorsement of employee freedom of expression and dissent because of the adverse effects of unauthorized disclosure of proprietary information or whistle blowing for personal gain or spite.

Since disclosure of trade secrets and other proprietary information is generally recognized as outside the concept of free speech, most companies seek to prevent such employee disclosures either by written agreements or by internal security procedures that provide for legal recourse in the event of violation.

To avoid whistle blowing, many managements endeavor to create a climate in which their employees feel free to criticize or disagree within the organization and thus avoid adverse publicity for their company. Citibank President Spencer comments on the value of such a climate:

> If it is good business to set up internal procedures for recognizing and responding to individual rights, in general, that applies even more to conscience issues, in particular. An industrial worker's anxiety over a possible safety defect in a product, if raised early enough through internal channels, can prevent a costly recall later. A potential environmental hazard or discriminatory practice flagged by employee complaints can be corrected without the need for massive, costly regulatory agency intervention.
>
> Finally, a company's name and public image—its hard-won reputation earned by prior generations of employees and managements—have very real value. This intangible value is jeopardized when all internal dissent mechanisms have failed and a distraught employee feels there is no recourse but to express personal ethical reservations to a public that is often only too willing to hear and believe the worst.

[7]Alan F. Westin, "The Problem of Employee Privacy Still Troubles Management," *Fortune*, June 4, 1979, p. 126.

At this point the company incurs a very substantial loss—whether or not the employee's charge is verified by an impartial investigation of the facts.[8]

Citibank and other large companies, such as IBM and Bank of America, have voluntarily adopted internal methods that provide employees with both the right to express grievances and disagreements to company management and the protection of due-process procedures to help resolve them. Several of these dual-purpose methods are given as examples in the following discussion on corporate initiatives and actions concerning the issue of due process in the workplace.

## Due Process

Traditionally, many large corporations have had procedures for employees to discuss complaints or grievances with senior managers. These company methods of due process vary from statements to new employees that the chief executive's door is always open to formal grievance and complaint procedures. Since the early 1970s, many corporate managements have reinvigorated dormant grievance procedures or adopted new ones, to a large degree because of the federal government's greater presence in employee-management relationships. New laws and evolving regulations about equal employment, employee pensions, privacy, wage and price guidelines, occupational safety and health, and age discrimination have given rise to many novel questions, employee grievances, and judicial action. The regulations have also required regular monitoring of company performance in these regards, and employee grievance procedures have become an important part of the monitoring process.

In the preface to a *Harvard Business Review* interview with Bank-America's A. W. Clausen, David W. Ewing commended the bank on the quality of its relations with 77,000 employees. He also referred to the bank's unusual range of programs for encouraging and protecting the expression of employee complaints and concerns and providing access to due process at all levels. In the interview, Clausen described these forms of due process: (1) employee assistance officers who act as ombudspersons; (2) a formal problem-solving process that gives employees the right to discuss their concerns with several officers and obtain a review by impartial third parties; and (3) an open line by which employees, with anonymity, can address written questions to company officers and receive responses within 10 days. In the interview, Clausen testified that over 6000 employees used the formal

[8]Spencer, op. cit.

problem-solving process in one year and that these and other programs were effectively serving their "employees' need to be heard and management's need to listen."[9]

International Business Machines Corp. has long had a tradition of rapid and personal response to employee concerns; this has evolved into due-process procedures that are well used and respected within the company. These procedures are also a popular model for other companies that wish to emulate them. Beyond emphasis on individuals and their managers solving problems that arise, IBM has these programs to encourage employee freedom of expression and to assure that there is due process to help resolve questions, conflicts, or grievances:

• *Open door.* The right of any IBM employee to raise questions or register complaints with any level of senior management was recognized and practiced by Thomas Watson, Sr., the founder of IBM. While the right has continued for many years, the procedures for exercising it have been altered to meet the requirements of a worldwide company with over 325,000 employees. An employee may address to an executive of his or her choice any subject from a personal grievance to charges of publicly unacceptable company practices. The subject is investigated, and at the employee's request his or her anonymity is protected. An employee who is not satisfied with the response can select other doors to open, including that of the chief executive officer.

• *Executive interview.* This program encourages all employees, and managers as well, to have a confidential discussion at least once each year with a manager who is at least one level higher than their own manager. Some IBM units require all individuals to have executive interviews to help assure that employee concerns or criticisms can reach higher managers. Employees or managers who are not satisfied with their interview with an executive may use the open-door procedures with higher management.

• *Speak Up.* Since 1959, IBM has provided a means for employees to air company-related concerns and criticisms of a general nature. Throughout IBM there are coordinators of the Speak Up Program who are charged with seeing that employees get pertinent, candid answers to their questions and that the anonymity of each questioner is protected. IBM managers responded to over 17,000 Speak Ups

[9]"Listening and Responding to Employees' Concerns: An Interview with A. W. Clausen," *Harvard Business Review,* January–February 1980, p. 105. Copyright © 1980 by the President and Fellows of Harvard College; all rights reserved. Reprinted by permission of the Harvard Business Review.

worldwide in 1979 and to more than 200,000 in the 20 years since the program had begun.[10]

Citibank is another company that has emphasized upward communication and grievance resolution. Citibank's experience has resulted in this endorsement by its president, William Spencer:

> Today, an enlightened management recognizes that internal complaints and the procedures for addressing them offer positive benefits to both the individual and the company. This assumes, of course, that everyone understands that there are no rights without corresponding responsibilities. Any worker who assumes the right to disagree with company policy also assumes the responsibility to help improve that policy. . . . Put another way, the right to express dissent presumes the responsibility not to prejudge and not to make false, self-serving or unsupported charges.

Spencer is under no illusion that the Citibank processes will eliminate employee dissent, and he recognizes that an employee may go public with a complaint even after using them. He maintains that to get the greatest benefit,

> we must learn how to use dissent and ethical challenges to formulate policy from the employee upward—as well as from the Policy Committee downward. Doing so will improve the quality of life in the workplace, raise morale, motivate performance, and increase productivity. And that is not only good employee relations and socially progressive conduct for any company—it is also good business.[11]

### Other Employee Rights

Changing business conditions are a factor in the emergence of new employee rights. For example, the effects of plant closings by large corporations have led some employees, union leaders, and others to argue that employees are entitled to job rights much as all citizens have property rights. Partial support of this concept of job rights appears in proposed laws that would provide prenotification of plant closings, severance pay and relocation or reemployment costs for displaced workers, and compensation for affected communities. Those types of protection and compensation for lost jobs have in some cases already been provided voluntarily by company practices or union contracts.

Peter F. Drucker discussed the implications of the concept of the job

[10]Quoted in Harrison Kenney, "Speak Up Comes of Age," *Think*, November–December 1979, p. 45.

[11]Spencer, op. cit.

as a property right in a 1980 column in *The Wall Street Journal*. In noting recent United States legislation that provides equal opportunity and job security and protects pensions, Drucker wrote:

> Jobs, in effect, are being treated as a species of property rather than as contractual claims. Historically there have been three kinds of property: "real" property such as land, "personal" property such as money, tools, furnishings and personal possessions; and "intangible" property such as copyrights and patents. It is not too farfetched to speak of the emergence of a fourth—the "property in the job"—closely analogous to property in the land in premodern times.[12]

Another employee rights issue that has emerged is the concept of "equal pay for work of comparable value." This doctrine has been referred to as "the women's issue of the 1980s." It would provide comparable pay for jobs that involve unequal content but are of comparable value. Advocates of the comparable-worth approach say that such a practice would end pay discrimination against women and members of minority groups. In a compilation of papers on this subject, eight academic and legal authorities reached a central conclusion that an attempt to apply comparable worth would, because of the ambiguity of the term, encounter substantial difficulties and by substituting some undetermined form of bias-free job evaluation for traditional job evaluation and market rate standards would have disruptive, undesirable consequences.[13]

As new employee rights have been established or extended within the corporation, further pressures for changes in traditional business practices have appeared. With equal opportunity, for example, the practice of funding memberships for executives in clubs that admit no women or minority members has been attacked, demands for flexible work arrangements to help men and women to share family responsibilities have increased, and greater numbers of younger managers have refused promotions involving moves because of their spouses' careers.

## Additional Initiatives

In addition to the foregoing examples, here are some corporate practices that have proved helpful in dealing with the employee rights issue:

- Providing active and visible support for equal employment opportunity, the most mature of these rights. When practicable, show

[12]Peter F. Drucker, "The Job as Property Right," *The Wall Street Journal*, Mar. 5, 1980, p. 22.

[13]*Comparable Worth: Issues and Alternatives*, Equal Employment Advisory Council, Washington, 1981.

evidence of management support by promoting qualified women and minority-group members to senior management positions and electing them as board members. Another practice is to fund memberships and events only at private clubs which do not discriminate because of race, sex, or creed.

- Demonstrating active concern for employee privacy by promoting relevant policies and procedures.
- Providing a practical process for employees at all levels to raise difficult issues with company executives about company and personal ethics and propriety without threat of personal reprisal.
- Providing effective grievance procedures for employees to question decisions regarding changes in job status, work assignments, and other actions affecting the individual.
- Affirming publicly and within the company the company policies and practices that have been adopted to foster employee citizenship rights.
- Being sensitive to the range of issues of employee citizenship rights even if some may not be a matter of employee concern.

## THE OUTLOOK

Corporate initiatives and actions concerning issues of employee citizenship rights have varied according to the maturity of each in the public policy process, the nature of an industry and its employee composition, and the individual viewpoints of company managements concerning employee relations. On the basis of these variables, the outlook for the evolution of each employee right differs.

As the most advanced employee citizenship right, equal opportunity is subject to established laws and regulations and past and forthcoming judicial decisions. This momentum and the renewed energies of public-interest groups, spurred by their concerns about the Reagan administration, will sustain the importance of this issue. Privacy will be fostered by problem situations, such as those that arise when employee privacy and employee theft or quality control conflict. Freedom of expression and dissent will most likely be subject to test in hazardous industries in which technically qualified employees may disagree with management decisions on matters of health, safety, and the environment. Due process, provided by the company or by law, will be of most concern to employees who are insecure in their jobs, either because of adverse economic conditions or their own ability. Good-cause statutory job protection is likely to gain momentum in the 1980s since such a provision is routine for union-represented employees, has been increasingly supported by court cases in various states, and has precedents in many industrialized countries.

Advocates such as Alan Westin and David Ewing regard employee citizenship rights as one of the most important noneconomic issues facing large corporations in the 1980s. Other observers of the corporate scene believe that few employees are interested in the extension of employee rights beyond equal employment and personal privacy. Most of those observers recognize, however, that a small but vocal group of advocates has made progress in focusing attention on the broader concept of citizenship rights in the workplace. Meanwhile, corporate managements in some industries are responding to the employee rights issues in ways that they believe are important for the integrity and quality of their employee relationships and the productivity of their companies.

Given the concern in our society about work satisfaction and productivity, it seems inevitable that the issues of employee citizenship rights, together with the quality of working life, will command the attention of managements of large corporations throughout the 1980s.

# CHAPTER 10

# Health, Safety, and
# the Environment

*The Issue* • What can be done to assure effective and responsible management of the corporate impact on health, safety, and the environment? This issue involves what can be done to minimize or, wherever practicable, eliminate adverse effects of corporate technology on human health and safety and the environment. In addition, it is concerned with the question of the appropriate balance of health, safety, and environmental goals with other social and economic objectives.

*Importance* • In recent industrial history, few public policy issues have had the social, political, and economic impact that this one is having on many companies. The hitherto infrequently questioned benefits of technology are being seriously reassessed in light of actual or suspected costs such as environmental degradation and risks to human health and safety.

This issue is important to managements of many companies because it raises critical questions of corporate accountability and serves as a basic barometer of public trust. As long as public concern about it continues, the ability of corporations and other private-sector institutions to develop and apply technology will be subject to strict governmental control.

Together with technological innovation, this issue is of greatest importance in determining the balance point between corporate management and government control of technology.

*Causes* • This overall issue arises from public concern that corporate managements may lack sensitivity to adverse consequences that may result from their use of technology.

In large part, the health, safety, and environmental issue results from corporate processes and products that are alleged or demonstrated to be hazardous to human health and safety, contribute to the degradation of the physical environment, or promote wasteful use of natural resources. Government involvement in corporate decisions concerning technology is, in large part, a political manifestation of public concern both that managements have not given sufficient attention to the control of the adverse impacts of corporate technology and that market forces cannot do the job alone.

Since the 1960s, the public has become increasingly informed about effects of technology which threaten or harm people and the environment. People have been exposed to prolonged public debate over the carcinogenicity of industrial products and processes and the environmental impact of technological projects such as the supersonic transport, the Alaska pipeline, and nuclear power plants across the country. Public awareness of hazards has arisen, in part, because of tragedies such as Kepone dumping. These incidents, coupled with continuing disclosure of real or suspected health hazards such as air, noise, and water pollution and government attempts to ban products, have caused public concern. In addition, disclosures about products and wastes that have harmed people have helped to undermine public trust in the corporate management of technology.

Public concern has been stimulated by many national and local interest groups that actively advocate solutions to various health, safety, and environmental problems or issues. Many of these groups and other critics believe that there is a link between corporate technology and environmental deterioration. Another stimulus is disagreement among medical and other scientific experts on questions ranging from whether hazards exist to what are maximum safe human exposure levels. All of this activity underscores the dilemma confronting government, industry, and the scientific community in attempting to foresee and reduce or prevent hazards while at the same time trying to develop and use technology responsibly.

Corporate technology has profoundly shaped the nature and direction of life during the twentieth century. It has helped make possible unprecedented general prosperity and material security, and the American people have grown to expect it to provide continuing improvements in the quality of life. However, the belief that technology can be used to solve almost any problem has been seriously confronted by accumulating evidence of actual or suspected adverse effects of commercial products and industrial processes on people and the environment.

## THE PUBLIC'S CONCERN

To some observers, scientists seem to be uncovering more questions and problems than solutions to the adverse effects of technology. As this idea has received greater attention from the media, interest groups, Congress, and regulatory agencies, public concern about technology has grown. Although many people worry about the adverse effects of technology, most do not wish to sacrifice its benefits. Some people favor limiting economic expansion to control technological problems, but most believe that scientists and engineers eventually will be able to resolve or substantially control most health, safety, and environmental problems.

The general public appears ambivalent about risk because people freely accept some risks and reject others. In particular, the public disapproves of risks that it must assume involuntarily, such as air and water pollution. As John W. Hanley, chairman of Monsanto Company, has pointed out, "Americans desire industrial products and jobs, but also want thoughtful disposal of industrial wastes so that toxic substances do not come bubbling up in somebody's basement."[1]

The disposal of chemical wastes and pollution of surface and underground water in numerous parts of the country, as well as concern about the safety of nuclear power plants, have stimulated concern in many communities over known or potential health and environmental hazards. Like hazards to worker health, such cases have prompted widespread state and local efforts to regulate industrial activity that affects human health and safety and the environment. Some communities have attempted to limit industrial development, some have imposed strict air and water pollution standards, and others have adopted limited or no-growth policies that effectively preclude industrial development.

[1] John W. Hanley, "The Price of Hysteria," address to the annual meeting of the American Textile Manufacturers Institute, White Sulphur Springs, W. Va., Apr. 13, 1979.

An area of specific concern is the safety and health of employees. In recent years, industries such as mining, agriculture, and manufacturing have been identified as posing serious risks to employees' health. Risks that were previously unknown or undetectable have caused critical attention by governments, industry, and labor unions at national and local levels. That situation, in turn, has contributed to a rapid proliferation of laws and regulations. Government controls, in turn, have caused corporate managers to devote greater attention and more resources to their management of technology.

Some critics maintain that corporate managements will not adopt effective self-control of technology because that would impair profit. From that assumption, they conclude that only the federal government can assure that corporate technology will be used safely.

## GOVERNMENT ACTIONS

Rising public concern in the 1970s resulted in extensive federal regulation of health, safety, and the environment, particularly in the areas of air and water pollution, control and disposal of hazardous substances, resource conservation, solid-waste disposal, nuclear safety, occupational safety and health, and drug safety and efficacy. Congress also created the Occupational Safety and Health Administration, Environmental Protection Agency (EPA), Consumer Product Safety Commission, and Nuclear Regulatory Commission and greatly expanded the authority of existing agencies such as the Food and Drug Administration.

The scope and nature of that regulation have expanded, and its administrators have been granted greater authority. Regulators have been empowered, for example, to determine the efficacy as well as safety of new drugs before they are marketed. Workers in the chemical industry are required to report what appear to them to be dangerous materials. Federal regulators of toxic substances require extensive analyses of proprietary chemical materials.

Regulations issued by the EPA in 1980 established procedures for the handling and disposal of hazardous wastes, including 400 chemicals that were specifically identified. In addition, Congress passed legislation that gave the EPA authority to clean up existing hazardous-waste disposal sites and finance the efforts through a superfund underwritten largely by the chemical industry.

As discussed in Chapter 7, "Legal and Ethical Behavior," the interpretation and enforcement of health, safety, and environmental laws have extended liability from the corporation to its managers, and corporate executives have become more vulnerable to criminal prosecution and prison sentences.

Pressures to minimize or eliminate product hazards also have been increased by a reversal of the traditional concept of "buyer beware" to "seller beware." For example, many state governments have adopted the concept of liability without fault. Such "strict liability" shifts the burden of loss occasioned by a product that is "inherently" dangerous or poses unusual risk to the manufacturer, even though the company may have formulated and marketed the product by using every precaution known at the time.

The process of developing and implementing regulatory standards for health, safety, and environmental protection has resulted in especially difficult problems. Overlapping regulatory responsibilities have created jurisdictional enforcement disputes among federal agencies as well as between state and federal regulators. A particular dilemma is that while scientific methods now can detect chemicals and radiation with extraordinary sensitivity, science cannot yet quantify the potential impact of an alleged effect on humans and thus often cannot predict hazardous levels and durations of exposure. In these and other cases, federal agencies have had no reliable guidelines for assessing the risks. Confronted with legal mandates and without useful scientific criteria, some agencies have issued inappropriate or unenforceable regulatory standards that corporate managers feel are inconsistent, unnecessary, and inefficient.

Those problems have been particularly acute in the development of a federal carcinogen policy. One approach, labeled "zero risk," is the prevailing concept in federal regulation on food additives. According to the 1958 Delaney amendment to the Food, Drug, and Cosmetic Act, any food additive shown to cause cancer in reasonably conducted tests on animals must be removed from the market. Critics of this zero-risk standard have countered that humankind cannot and should not eliminate all risk but must relate risk to benefit and cost. Although many federal regulators concede the impracticality of the Delaney standard, federal agencies that administer the Food, Drug, and Cosmetic Act are legally bound to set and enforce regulations based upon zero-risk criteria.

When zero-risk is not the basis for regulation, government regulators are confronted with other intractable problems. For example, some are expected to balance risks and benefits while also measuring the economic and social value of a product compared with the health and life expectancy of an indeterminate number of people. This is a difficult and subjective task, and regulators are not comfortable in making such decisions, particularly when they must defend their actions before Congress as well as contending interest groups. As a result, they have a quite natural tendency to play it safe.

Authorities on risk-benefit determination point out that efforts to play it safe have resulted in serious misallocations of resources from productive uses. To help avoid that error, they recommend a process that involves these three discrete steps: (1) develop the scientific conclusions, including a statement of the uncertainties; (2) array the relevant societal considerations; and (3) incorporate the scientific conclusion and the societal considerations in making the necessary regulatory decisions. While this process is easier to describe than to apply, its virtue is in the rigorous development of the scientific conclusions without bias in either direction, whether that be to play it safe or to take a chance. The social considerations are thus not applied both in reaching the scientific conclusions and in melding the scientific conclusions and societal considerations into regulations. Not only are better decisions reached, but when people are given unbiased scientific conclusions, they are better able to evaluate social regulatory decisions and either to accept or to reject them. Even though the recommended separation process is not always achieved, society has already demonstrated that it will make the ultimate decision. In the case of the government's banning of cyclamates, for example, most people approved; when saccharin was banned, however, many people objected, and their objections were influential.

## CORPORATE INITIATIVES AND ACTIONS

Corporate managements face the same types of dilemmas as government officials. One special complication for industrial scientists is that their findings and recommendations are often challenged on the ground that such individuals are too closely linked to corporate interests to be objective and candid. Except as required by such laws as the Toxic Substances Control Act and the Consumer Product Safety Act, there is also the concern that corporate findings of potential hazards will not be disclosed in timely fashion. Monsanto's John Hanley stated in 1979 that some companies must "quit hiding behind the excuse that broader disclosure would only confuse the laity. This approach only increases our credibility problem by encouraging the public, government and our own employees to assume the worst."[2]

2Ibid.

As federal regulation of health, safety, and the environment has increased, many corporations concerned with this issue have found that they lack sufficient scientific expertise to participate effectively in the public policy process. As a result, they are acquiring the necessary technical competence and establishing departments to deal with health, safety, and environmental problems as a new function of corporate management. The staff members of that function provide expertise to help (1) comply with existing regulations, (2) act to minimize or avoid adverse technological consequences, and (3) participate in the public policy process on relevant questions.

For decades some corporations have conducted or contracted for toxicologic research to identify threats to human health, and in recent years many have increased their commitments. Many corporations with exposure to health and safety problems have formed organizations to work with government and the scientific community to devise practical, effective, and less costly alternatives to proposed government regulations. One such organization, the American Industrial Health Council, formed in 1977, has about 200 companies and trade associations as members, including producers of steel, aluminum, textiles, pharmaceutical products, oil, and consumer goods. The council, with and on behalf of its members, develops, reviews, and critiques methods for dealing with long-term industrial health hazards, particularly cancer.

Another group, the Chemical Industry Institute of Toxicology, with about thirty chemical companies as its members, does basic toxicology research and tests widely used chemicals that were introduced into commerce before there was scientific or extensive public concern over toxic substances. The institute, which operates independently of member companies and is free to publish its research findings, is emphasizing the development of faster, more reliable testing methods.

In promoting employee health protection, however, not all corporate efforts have met with general approval. Several chemical companies have been criticized because of genetic screening designed to identify individuals, particularly women and blacks, with particular susceptibility to certain toxic substances. The companies maintain that such tests can be used to protect workers from needless hazards. Critics contend that the tests are inherently discriminatory and that, rather than protect the worker, their purposes are to save the company from possible litigation, avoid liability, and reduce the cost of safeguards in the workplace.

Serious, intractable problems confront all parties concerned with minimizing the adverse effects of technology. Relevant scientific evidence is often unavailable, in dispute, or applied retroactively. In many cases it is difficult, if not impossible, to predict the consequences of new or existing technologies, particularly the indirect, secondary effects. In addition, regulatory dilemmas involving risk-benefit assessments and the effects on social and economic growth will continue to confound government, corporate management, and interest groups.

The experiences of leading corporations in this field and the American Industrial Health Council and similar groups suggest these elements as factors that will contribute to a successful strategy for companies that significantly affect human health and safety and the environment:

- A senior staff function of technically qualified people to assist company management to deal with matters of health, safety, and the environment
- A close and ongoing relationship with a body of respected scientific experts; in effect, deferring to scientific judgment in scientific matters
- A recognition that managers, professional staff, and relevant employees must be made fully aware of this issue and its importance
- An awareness that a company's closest constituents—employees, customers, neighbors, and suppliers—are those who are most deeply affected by adverse impacts and, thus, are particularly sensitive to health, safety, and environmental problems
- An awareness that the health, safety, and environmental issue interacts with other corporate performance issues, such as corporate marketplace performance, legal and ethical behavior, quality of working life, public disclosure, and social performance and that they must be dealt with together
- A recognition of the public and political realities surrounding technology issues, coupled with a sensitivity to potential compromises
- An understanding that a large part of the public and political concern in this area is emotional and in many cases cannot be resolved simply by facts and opinions presented by contending parties

## THE OUTLOOK

Corporations will require continuing, in many cases greater, efforts to help assure that the production, distribution, and consumption of products will be accomplished without harmful effects on people and the environment.

In the area of the environment, solutions to hazardous-waste disposal, underground-water contamination, and the large-scale burning of coal in lieu of oil and gas are expected to be of particular importance. In industries in which employee health protection is important, there will be more employee medical examination programs and an increase in workplace monitoring activities. In the area of consumer protection, individual awareness and public concern about the harmful effects of some chemicals, drugs, and food additives are likely to continue to be of key importance. Despite the safety record of nuclear energy, the safe operation of nuclear plants and the disposal of nuclear wastes will be continuing matters of public concern.

While most of the foreseeable major environmental laws are in place, under the Reagan administration amendments and implementing standards will feature greater attention to specifying ends rather than prescribing means and leaving it to those regulated to make cost-benefit comparisons in determining the optimum way to achieve the ends. Also, regulatory decisions will involve greater consideration of their impacts on inflation, economic growth, employment, energy requirements, and other economic and social considerations. The concept of risk-benefit assessment, however, is a long way from being broadly understood; it is difficult to implement and, therefore, will be applied slowly.

In anticipation of a possible public backlash, leaders of health, safety, and environmental interest groups are coalescing in an effort to become stronger than ever. A common effort of these coalitions is to provide extensive educational materials and to sponsor activities that are designed to maintain and develop public awareness. Many groups, however, are showing a greater willingness to meet with corporate managements to resolve differences.

To the extent that the regulation of health, safety, and the environment are eased under the Reagan administration, corporate managements will be in the public spotlight to prove that they can conduct their businesses without the need for reinstituting the trend of the past 10 years toward greater health, safety, and environmental regulation.

# CHAPTER 11

# Technological
# Innovation

***The Issue*** • What can be done to assure effective and responsible corporate management of technological innovation? To what extent have corporate managements contributed to a decline in the technological progress of the United States and the productivity of the United States economy? Do corporate managements use technological innovation for anticompetitive and antisocial purposes?

***Importance*** • There is serious public concern about the nature and pace of corporate innovation, the insufficient amount of problem-solving technology, and the social value of some products and processes.

Corporate technological innovation is essential for United States productivity, economic growth, and quality of life. It is emotionally linked in the minds of many people with national pride in world leadership and individual entrepreneurial activity. To the extent that United States technological innovation and its commercial application are found to be serious and continuing problems, corporate managements will be blamed and the management of technology will likely be subject to greater government control. To the extent that corporate technological innovation leads to more jobs, increased productivity, and a higher standard of living, the companies responsible will help generate public trust in the large corporation and private enterprise system.

Together with the corporate impact on health, safety, and the environment, this issue is of greatest importance in determining the balance point between corporate management and government control of technology.

*Causes* • This issue has arisen from public concern that corporate managements may have been misusing their resources in the development and use of technology. The principal driving forces that have contributed to the development of this issue are evidence of a slippage in the United States world position in technological innovation and public concern over the adverse impact of corporate technology on health, safety, and the environment. These developments have given urgency to questions of whether the corporate community has the ability to develop and apply technology safely, creatively, and usefully. In question are government and corporate policies and procedures affecting technological innovation and its commercial application.

In addition, some critics assert that large corporations misuse their market power to inhibit innovation by others. That criticism includes the charge that corporate managements use technology in antisocial ways such as planned obsolescence of products and reliance upon "hard" rather than "soft" technological projects and systems, e.g., massive pollution-prone systems to generate electricity rather than small pollution-free solar units.

United States technological superiority in the postwar world was taken for granted until the late 1950s, when Soviet achievements in missile and space technology shook American confidence. Subsequently, the strides of some foreign companies in technological innovation, economic productivity, and product quality, particularly that of the Japanese, caused the American public to question the relative performance of United States companies and the competitiveness of their executives.

# STATUS OF UNITED STATES TECHNOLOGICAL INNOVATION

A key point of debate on corporate technology has centered in evidence of a consistent decline in United States technological innovation over the last 15 to 20 years. The predominant view expressed by government, business, and scientific leaders has been that the United States overall has experienced decreasing rates of innovation and application of new technology to products, processes, and services.

Since the mid-1960s, corporations have tended to increase R&D funds at less than the inflation rate and to allocate the funds differently. There has been a relative decline in basic industrial research and a relative increase in corporate research and development expenditures applied to technological development to meet regulatory standards and to existing technologies for product improvement and other low-risk projects.

Government funds devoted to R&D began to decrease in the late 1960s, partly owing to reduction in the space effort. In addition, the government, like industry, has been giving priority to applied-research projects with specific objectives. In some cases, government has even stipulated design and production details, thereby limiting the opportunity for innovation.

Corporate and government officials generally disagree about the causes of declining innovation. In the late 1970s, Carter administration officials, members of Congress, and science authorities publicly acknowledged the need to consider modifications to government policies which inhibit private technological innovation. However, they pointed out that new and existing products, processes, and services must be evaluated for their effects on human health and safety and the environment. They also contended that declining innovation might have been due more to corporate research and development strategies than to government policies. When Dr. Frank Press was President Carter's science adviser, he cited corporate strategy as emphasizing short-range profit goals and applied research while minimizing basic and exploratory research. Charles Kindleburger, an MIT economist, has likened the response of American corporations to that of British firms when confronted with declining innovation and stiff foreign competition: instead of redoubling efforts at innovation, British companies became defensive, curtailing investments and soliciting government protection from imports.[1] Some observers have also charged that United States

[1]Charles Kindleburger, conversation with the author.

corporations have not effectively adapted either United States or foreign technological innovations to commercial uses.

Professor William J. Abernathy of the Harvard Graduate School of Business Administration believes that innovation and productivity may inherently contradict each other regardless of government or corporate policies: there may be no virtue to innovation when only marginal improvements are possible in an established cost-effective product. Striving for productivity can be a barrier to product innovation. Novelty, according to Abernathy, often serves to clog the efficiency of many production processes that depend on the repetition of identical tasks.[2] Other experts add that as an industry matures, it becomes more resistant to new technology and to related innovations because of its financial commitments to present facilities and processes.

Corporate managers have long regarded the root cause of the problem of declining innovation as a set of tax, antitrust, foreign trade, and regulatory policies that reduce the incentive for research and development and for the commercialization of results. They have contended that the development of new products and processes has been impeded by the problems of inflation and capital formation and by the need to use much of their research funds to ensure that existing products and services comply with regulations.

In addition to citing government policies as the basic cause of declining innovation, corporate executives point to instances in which Western European and Japanese companies have successfully innovated through cooperative ventures with their respective governments, in contrast to United States government policy that either discourages or prohibits such activity. However, most corporate research officers also caution that collaborative industry-government research and development efforts can result in government domination of the research process.

Many corporate managements believe that federal research and development funding determines the nature and rate of a large share of United States technological innovation, as when the government has stipulated design and production details for the products it purchases. Many corporate R&D officers have concluded that the role of the government in technological research has been counterproductive because it has tended to replace rather than augment private investment in basic research. A related criticism is that federal research

[2]William J. Abernathy, *The Productivity Dilemma,* The Johns Hopkins Press, Baltimore, 1978. Copyright © 1978 by William J. Abernathy.

program administrators are more responsive to short-term political pressures than they are to long-term United States economic or scientific needs.

Federal patent policy has also been cited as an impediment to sustained, successful innovation. Du Pont's Irving Shapiro has charged that judicial decisions in patent cases are weakening incentives for innovation and stimulating a decline in new technology. He has contended that the problem is exacerbated by the deleterious effects of Supreme Court patent rulings since 1940, the great difficulty that judges and juries have in resolving complex issues in patent cases, and the relative legal advantages accorded patent holders in other countries. Compounding the patent problem are restrictions on private interests that wish to acquire patent rights for technological innovations developed with government funding.[3]

In speaking on the United States "management malaise," General Electric's Reginald Jones commented:

> In one industry after another, foreign competitors have already surpassed us in productivity. Where once the Japanese and Europeans came to America to study productivity techniques, now we are sending teams over there—and finding that the students have surpassed the teachers.
>
> The evidence is that our foreign competitors are moving quickly to adopt the new technologies that will dominate the factories and offices of tomorrow—microelectronics, interactive graphics, computer-assisted design and manufacture, robotics, specialty materials, and others.
>
> Companies that are trying to make do with old products and processes are in for big trouble in the 1980's. Service businesses are in just as much danger of obsolescence as manufacturing.
>
> It is my feeling that any company which is not already engaged in an internal revolution in product design, production, and distribution could well find itself assigned to the dustbin of history by 1990.[4]

A 1980 Yankelovich study of executive opinion on technological innovation confirmed the view of the adverse United States climate for innovation. However, according to the study, "a surprising number of executives are critical of business's own efforts to encourage innovation and agree that corporate policies often act to discourage innovation." They cited such corporate inhibitors of innovation as short-term incentive plans for executives, pressures for short-term profit perform-

---

[3]Irving Shapiro, "Technology's Decline: America's Self-Made Paradox," address to the Economic Club of Detroit, Jan. 22, 1979.

[4]Reginald H. Jones, "Time to Break out of 'Management Malaise,'" address to the Economic Club of Chicago, reported in *Financier*, January 1981.

ance, reluctance to replace costly technologies, and senior executives who are not thoroughly conversant with technological concepts.[5]

These concerns are held even more intensely by Abernathy and his colleague, Prof. Robert H. Hayes. In a 1980 *Harvard Business Review* article they cite evidence of "broad managerial failure—a failure of both vision and leadership—that over time has eroded both the inclination and the capacity of U.S. companies to innovate." In their judgment, the causes of marked deterioration in United States competitive vigor cannot be attributed solely to such economic and political factors as the Organization of Petroleum Exporting Countries, excessive regulation, and government tax and monetary policies. Abernathy and Hayes believe that the responsibility also rests with the failure of American managers to keep their companies technologically competitive.

In advancing their controversial diagnosis, Hayes and Abernathy stated:

> American managers have increasingly relied on principles which prize analytical detachment and methodological elegance over insight, based on experience, into the subtleties and complexities of strategic decisions. As a result, maximum short-term financial returns have become the overriding criteria for many companies.

In explaining this belief they cite (1) the substantial increase in the percentage of new company presidents whose primary interest and expertise are in the financial and legal areas, (2) the increasing number of top-management positions filled from outside company ranks, and (3) a preoccupation, in the business community as in academia, with a "false and shallow concept of the professional manager"—i.e., an individual having no special expertise who can step into an unfamiliar company and run it successfully through "strict application of financial controls, portfolio concepts and a market-driven strategy."[6]

The only factors that were frequently noted in the Yankelovich survey as having encouraged some industries to innovate were rising energy costs and foreign competition. The executives pointed out that higher energy costs have provided faster paybacks from conservation measures and a market for new energy-saving products, while foreign

[5] *A Business Perspective on Technological Innovation,* survey conducted by Yankelovich, Skelly and White, Inc., for the Sperry Corp., New York, August 1980.

[6] William J. Abernathy and Robert H. Hayes, "Managing Our Way to Economic Decline," *Harvard Business Review,* July–August 1980, pp. 67–77. Copyright © 1980 by the President and Fellows of Harvard College; all rights reserved. Reprinted by permission of the Harvard Business Review.

competition for some industries has provided the incentive to innovate or withdraw from some markets.[7]

With respect to the impact of government regulation on innovation, Harold M. Williams, when chairman of the U.S. Securities and Exchange Commission, made this point:

> When business is required to operate in a regulatory environment— and, when it is concerned that any misstep which it may make will be used to justify even more regulation—business is compelled to become more and more attentive to its regulators and, consequently, becomes less rather than more responsive to the needs and expectations of the market and the public. Correspondingly, business's unique entrepreneurial ability to create and innovate—the ultimate justification for an independent private sector—tends to atrophy.[8]

Because of mounting public concern about declining innovation and productivity, a Presidential Commission on Industrial Innovation was formed in 1978 to study and recommend solutions. The commission's report, issued in 1980, featured proposals that would facilitate the transfer of scientific and technical information among business, government, universities, and private research organizations; modifications in antitrust, patent, environmental, and federal procurement policies; financial support for small companies engaged in developing new technologies; and facilities for broad efforts at technology development by private corporations, universities, and government agencies.

In 1980, the Committee for Economic Development, a private research group of corporate executives and scholars, published a study concluding that "inflation, low productivity, trade deficits and job loss are all linked to inadequate technological growth and innovation."[9] The study by the committee reached the same general conclusions and made proposals similar to those of the presidential commission. However, experts familiar with both studies said that President Carter was unwilling to consider tax incentives to spur innovation.

Nonetheless, late in 1980 Congress began to show unusual interest in technological innovation. In addition to the enactment of legislation that makes it easier for small companies to raise capital, dozens of bills that recognized the national need to spur technological advances were

[7]Yankelovich survey, op. cit.

[8]Harold M. Williams, "Professionalism and the Corporate Bar," address to the annual meeting of the American Bar Association, Honolulu, Aug. 5, 1980; reprinted in *Vital Speeches of the Day*, Oct. 1, 1980.

[9]*Stimulating Technological Progress*, Committee for Economic Development, New York, January 1980.

introduced. Also, at the end of 1980 the U.S. Department of Justice issued a book of guidelines whose objective is to encourage companies to conduct joint research without incurring antitrust violations. Although the guidelines represent progress toward removing some legal uncertainties about joint corporate research, most observers believe that they fall short of what really would be helpful in meeting Japanese competition.

## ANTICOMPETITIVE AND ANTISOCIAL USES OF TECHNOLOGY

The second dimension of this issue concerns charges that large corporations dampen competition in technological innovation, dominate the development and application of technology through their market power, and use their technology for anticompetitive purposes. Among the specific charges leveled are that large corporations:

- Use their market and technological power in a reinforcing manner: market power gives them the economic resources to dominate the R&D process, and the resulting technological power enables them to control or limit new entries into the market, e.g., through the patent process.
- Use their economic resources to purchase the innovations of small companies or lone inventors.
- Withhold products and services that might disrupt or threaten their market position.
- Receive a dominant share of federal R&D contracts, and use know-how gained at public expense to strengthen their position as a supplier of both the public and the private sectors.

Charges of anticompetitive use of technology are often based on questionable statistical analyses and the assumption that corporate managements are more deeply interested in profits than in the public interest.

Large corporations have also been criticized for allegedly using technological innovations for antisocial purposes, specifically to:

- Achieve higher profits and build market power by a considered policy of technological obsolescence, building "self-destruct" features into some products, and changing models in minor ways and then promoting sales by massive advertising. That strategy is seen as contributing to the waste in resources and the creation of a throw-away economy.

- Promote the development of massive or hard technological projects and systems with inadequate attention to possible social and environmental consequences.
- Eliminate or downgrade jobs, lay off or demote employees, and destroy or weaken labor unions.

While these and similar charges may be viewed as based largely on value judgments inimical to large corporations and private enterprise, they have entered the public consciousness and have joined the debate about large corporations. Corporate managements generally respond to the charges by citing the record of corporate technological contributions to the development of new products and jobs and to the development of innumerable small businesses that provide essential services to consumers and the nation's basic industries. These developments have sparked economic growth for the past half century and have contributed substantially to improving the standard of living. Nonetheless, corporate managements have been looking more carefully at the consequences of how they manage their technology, particularly with respect to possible future shortages of important natural resources.

Allegations that corporations dominate the R&D process or gain an unfair share of federal contracts are derived from the simple fact that large companies, by their size, statistically account for a large percentage of research expenditures, personnel, and facilities. That fact is then frequently linked with the "bigness is bad" argument to arrive at a conclusion that corporate management of technology has undesirable consequences. Other observers stress that such criticisms are based on limited statistical analyses and overgeneralizations.

## CORPORATE INITIATIVES AND ACTIONS

Notwithstanding concern about federal policies that have discouraged technological innovation, the managements of large corporations in most industries have been committed to innovation and development of new products and services. Over 80 percent of the executives in the Yankelovich survey see innovation as central to their companies' growth in the 1980s.[10]

A slowdown in United States innovation has not been an across-the-board phenomenon. For example, in the field of chemistry, while not subject to headlines, there has been a steady stream of new plastics,

[10]Yankelovich survey, op. cit.

fibers, agricultural chemicals, and other families of products. Then, too, there were key breakthroughs in the 1970s, such as in microelectronics technology and genetic engineering. Innovation has flourished in industries that have led in the use of microelectronics technology, such as information processing, telecommunications, semiconductors, and instruments. The spread of microelectronic technology from those industries into customer industries is an example of technology-driven innovation that is certain to have significant effects on economic growth and productivity.

Genetic engineering became another landmark example of technological innovation when scientists learned to splice genes from one organism to another. Although dramatic developments in genetic engineering are expected to appear in the late 1980s, insulin and interferon have already been produced by genetic engineering processes. The prospects for the future include such products as cheap, plentiful antibiotics and plastics tailored from chemical waste.

Recognition that there has been a lag in corporate technological innovation has spurred many ideas of what corporate managements should do about it. The suggestions range from research management techniques to the corporate governance proposal for independent boards of directors that would insist that management decisions, including R&D, be made with a longer focal length than short-range profits.

One approach that avoids for the moment the argument of whether government policies or corporate decisions are to blame for the technology slowdown is to consider this question: How do some companies regularly develop innovations while others, with equal or greater technological resources, innovate little of value?

*Dun's Review* addressed this question and, on the basis of the findings of "a handful of management consultants working in relative obscurity," reported these clues on how certain companies consistently develop innovations—"one of the least understood aspects of corporate management":[11]

- *Technological forecasting.* Evaluating the state of the art of a variety of technologies in an effort to spot changes likely to provide a jump on competition.
- *Strategic business planning.* Joining technological forecasting and longer-range planning with the objective of achieving a balanced group of products or businesses whereby the cash generation of the older ones supports the capital needed by the newer.

[11]"Putting Innovation to Work," *Dun's Review*, October 1980, pp. 72–81.

- *Creative tolerance.* Assuring an environment in which novel ideas are welcomed and nurtured and in which "the creative fanatic" is tolerated as "the driving force behind most major inventions."
- *Entrepreneurial freedom.* Recognizing that insistence on systematic progress toward a specific completion date can be as abortive for some projects as overspending can be when used to try to break a logjam.
- *Research freedom.* Providing for a small part of a research program to be free from profit center control and for a modest amount of a researcher's time to be available to develop ideas that he or she believes would be in the company's interest.
- *Joint venturing.* Providing a small technology company with capital and access to a large company's distribution, sales, and service facilities in exchange for a share of the potential profits.

## THE OUTLOOK

The outlook for progress toward resolving this issue appears promising. The interest shown by the Ninety-sixth Congress toward its end, the guidelines of the Department of Justice to encourage joint company research and sharing of results, and examples of cooperative efforts, such as those in microelectronic research by universities and competitor companies to help meet the "Japan, Inc." type of competition, have been encouraging developments. Perhaps the most important element in the momentum to resolve this issue is the growing public realization that technological innovation is the fulcrum of badly needed productivity and economic growth.

These developments have contributed support to President Reagan's policies for dealing with the economic and social woes of unemployment and inflation. As the administration and Congress lower or remove government policy barriers to technological innovation, corporate managements will have the opportunity to prove that they can further advance United States technological innovation in responsible ways. The result of that test will help resolve the question of whether government policies or management decisions, or both, have been a significant deterrent to United States technological innovation.

# CHAPTER 12

# Political
# Participation

***The Issue*** • What is the proper role of the large corporation in
the electoral and public policy processes? The public debate
involves the socially and politically acceptable limits of such
corporate political participation and centers on corporate actions to increase participation and efforts of other interests to
limit or curtail it.

***Importance*** • A 1978 U.S. Supreme Court decision that
upheld corporate freedom of speech on political issues
and the recent growth in the extent and success of corporate
political participation have created counterpressures to limit
corporate political activism. Some critics characterize the
growth of corporate political participation as a "corporate
grab for political power." Other observers regard that
growth as a natural response to the increased activity of other
groups.

    The extent to which corporations may participate in electo-
ral and public policy processes will have a profound impact on
the future role of the large corporation. Most corporate executives believe that without active political participation the large
corporation will be adversely affected by government decisions
and that greater efforts are needed. Other executives are concerned that the growing trend toward greater corporate politi-

cal participation, together with other public concerns about corporate performance, may convince public and government leaders that large corporations must be further controlled, if necessary by extreme means.

L. William Seidman, vice chairman of the Phelps Dodge Corporation and former assistant to President Ford for economic affairs, has considered this issue from both corporate and governmental perspectives and has concluded:

> Today's political activism is changing the attitude of the business world. Corporate political activity is more than accepted: it is required.
>
> Any group which disdains to rise to the defense of its interests in the U.S. Congress, the statehouse, and the county building will soon lose each contest vitally affecting its future. Business interests are not different from other private-sector interests in this respect.[1]

*Causes* • Corporate political participation is not a new issue. Corporate executives are alleged to have exercised awesome political power, extending back to the era when it was claimed that the Robber Barons had "the best legislatures money could buy." Incidents that reinvigorated that long-standing concern were the illegal corporate campaign contributions in the 1972 presidential election and cases of corporate interference with foreign and domestic government operations. Also, the growth of corporate political action committees (PACs) and media coverage of corporate lobbying have been factors attracting public attention to this issue.

The surge in corporate political participation in recent years has been fueled by corporate managements' needs to compete with labor union PACs and a growing number of influential interest groups that support candidates in the electoral process and participate in the public policy process. Other reasons are that the larger number of congressional committees and subcommittees requires more extensive lobbying and that a greater number of state initiative and referendum propositions of concern to corporations has involved corporate managements in more numerous election campaigns.

[1]L. William Seidman, "Corporate Political Responsibility," in Thornton Bradshaw and David Vogel, *Corporations and Their Critics*, McGraw-Hill Book Company, New York, 1981, pp. 73–74.

While corporate lobbying, election campaign contributions, advocacy advertising, and political communication with shareholders and employees have long been recognized as separate issues, the Supreme Court decision in the *Bellotti* case has had the effect of consolidating them into the collective issue of corporate political participation.[2] By a 5-4 decision, the Court declared unconstitutional a Massachusetts prohibition on corporate spending in certain referendum campaigns. The case, although narrow in its focus, has broadened the rights of corporations to take part in open debate on issues including ones that affect their interests only indirectly. The case has also raised basic questions about corporate political activity in both the electoral and the public policy processes.

Some business leaders hailed the *Bellotti* decision as a "corporate Magna Charta" that would free coporate managements to engage in all forms of political activity. On the other hand, most critics of the decision contended that *Bellotti* would lead to massive corporate expenditures and activities that could undermine those political processes.

Corporate political participation has been a factor in focusing public attention on groups advocating narrow interests, whether they are corporate, labor, environmental, consumer, or any other groups. However, proposed legislation that would restrict legitimate attempts to communicate with government officials raises significant constitutional questions and would reduce the information available to legislators and other government officials. Nonetheless, proposals which would limit corporate political activity have continued to emerge. Some of them relate this issue to other corporate public policy issues. For example, as discussed in Chapter 16 on the corporate governance issue of shareholder rights, critics have proposed that the Securities and Exchange Commission (SEC) require disclosure or shareholder approval of various kinds of political activity. One corporate governance proposal would require shareholder approval before a corporation's management could make any aftertax expenditures for political participation. Another would require approval of a company's shareholders for any public position its management proposed to take on public policy issues.

Against this background, here are brief summaries of both types of corporate political participation and the public issues these activities have raised.

[2]*Bank of Boston v. Bellotti*, 435 U.S. 765 (1978).

## PARTICIPATION IN THE ELECTORAL PROCESS

### Political Action Committees

Since early in this century, corporations have been forbidden to contribute to federal election campaigns, although there has been no such prohibition on individual executives, companies, or other groups such as trade associations. The Federal Election Campaign Act (FECA) of 1971 provided that corporations, unions, and other groups could finance the costs of administering PACs and soliciting contributions for them. In addition, the 1974 amendments to the act created the Federal Election Commission (FEC) and established limits on individual, group, and political party contributions made directly to presidential candidates and their campaign organizations. The act and its 1974 and 1976 amendments also authorized creation of PACs as vehicles for employees and shareholders of corporations and for members of unions, trade associations, and other interest groups to contribute to political parties and candidates for federal and state elective office. Between 1974 and July 1981, the number of PACs increased from 608 to 2678. Of those, 1251 were sponsored by corporations, including corporations with multiple PACs, 1124 by trade, membership, and other organizations, and 303 by labor organizations.

At the state level, the laws of nineteen states provide that corporations may make contributions to state and local candidates and for the support of or opposition to state and local referenda. In eight other states and the District of Columbia, corporate contributions can be made but with various specific limitations. The fact that some of these laws were passed in recent years is evidence of public approval of corporate contributions. That evidence is, however, countered by the concern of others about the trend toward greater corporate political influence and the desire to help strengthen the political system by requiring PAC contributions to be given to parties, not candidates. This difference of opinion is one reason that the public debate includes proposals to limit or prohibit direct corporate contributions to state and local campaigns.

The proliferation of corporate PACs has led to criticism of this method of financing electoral politics. Popular opinion equates PACs with actual corporate contributions since PAC contributions are usually referred to in the media as "corporate money," despite the extreme care most large companies take in conforming with all legal requirements. Some observers believe that corporate PACs will dominate election campaigns within a few years, primarily because there are many more corporations than labor unions. Others maintain that labor unions and public-interest groups, with their ability to provide members for work on election campaigns, compete successfully with the financial resources of corporate PACs. Although corporate PACs have a variety of criteria for selecting candidates to receive contributions, some critics, including leading Republicans, have contended that corporate PAC contributions have been used to help assure access to legislators rather than to help elect candidates who favor policies that support private enterprise. In the 1980 congressional elections, corporate PACs gave about 62 percent of their funds to Republican candidates and about 28 percent of their support to candidates challenging incumbents.

Continuing concern about PACs and about the influence of money in politics has resulted in congressional proposals to curb campaign spending or replace private with public campaign financing for congressional elections. In 1979, the House of Representatives passed the Obey-Railsback bill, which would reduce the contribution limit from $5000 to $3000 per election and would prohibit candidates from accepting more than $70,000 in PAC donations. However, the Senate did not act on the bill prior to adjournment of the Ninety-sixth Congress in January 1981. Other proposed reforms would create stricter standards for PACs, establish public financing in all federal elections, or require shareholder approval of company political expenditures, including the costs of establishing and maintaining PACs.

Labor unions are concerned about corporate PACs. An extreme example was a brief filed by the International Association of Machinists and Aerospace Workers with the FEC which charged that eleven major corporate PACs were using intimidation to obtain employee contributions, in violation of the law. The brief also contended that the administrative costs of PACs borne by the corporations violated the constitutional rights of shareholders. The FEC dismissed the complaint, but subsequently the union filed suit in court.

A 1980 shareholder resolution brought by a public-interest group called for General Motors to disclose its PAC activities in its annual report. In response to that resolution, General Motors agreed, prior to its submittal to a shareholder vote, to disclose to its shareholders information about its PAC operations. The rules of the General Motors PAC were described in a published report.[3] Although most of the information requested was available through the FEC, as it is for all PACs, the public-interest group stated that it planned to use the General Motors disclosure in an effort to get other corporations to provide the information in their annual reports. The group also petitioned the SEC to require all corporations to reveal certain information about PACs not

[3]*General Motors Public Interest Report,* General Motors Corporation, New York, 1980.

included in the GM disclosures, namely, how members of candidate selection committees are chosen and how much money a company spends in administering its PACs.

## Communication with Shareholders and Employees about Election Campaigns

The 1976 amendments to the FECA permit unlimited corporate management communication with shareholders and also with executive and administrative personnel and their families. Such communication may contain partisan information, including the endorsement of federal candidates or national political parties. In contrast, communications between corporate management and all nonmanagement employees must be nonpartisan in nature. Generally, that provision of the act has been interpreted to apply primarily to voter registration and get-out-the-vote drives. Corporations may permit candidates or representatives of political parties to address or meet employees, shareholders, and executive or administrative personnel as long as all candidates for a given office or representatives of all eligible political parties are invited. Also permitted is the distribution of nonpartisan information brochures to employees, shareholders, and executive personnel. In addition, corporations may, through a third-party civic or nonprofit organization such as the League of Women Voters, distribute a voting guide describing the candidates and their positions or offer a public forum where candidates may present their views to employees. While expenditures for internal corporate electoral communication are not tax-deductible, some lawyers believe that the *Bellotti* decision justifies their deductibility.

## PARTICIPATION IN THE PUBLIC POLICY PROCESS

### Lobbying

Lobbying is the constitutionally protected process by which individuals and groups attempt to influence the formulation of laws and regulations. To many people, however, lobbying is often perceived as a sinister activity by which some special interests unduly influence or at times even corrupt the public policy process.

In recent years, there has been a substantial growth in both direct corporate lobbying and indirect, or "grass-roots," lobbying which encourages citizen support of business interests. The only specific limitation on corporate grass-roots lobbying is an Internal Revenue Service rule which prohibits tax deductions for the expenses of such activities. The growth of lobbying has resulted from the need for corporations to be well represented in the competition among an increasing number of interest groups, the need of legislators and other government officials in many cases for hands-on information that can be provided in many cases only by corporate managements, and a willingness of corporate managements to commit greater resources to government relations.

The current federal lobbying law, enacted in 1946, is generally regarded as ineffective, largely because its reporting requirements are not observed and not enforced. After years of inaction, both the House and the Senate have seriously considered tough lobbying reform bills each year since 1976. Although business and a diverse group of interests have supported various aspects of lobbying reform, Congress has not enacted lobbying legislation. Congress's inability to pass a reform bill has largely reflected broad-based opposition to proposed requirements for identifying individual contributors to lobbying organizations, burdensome reporting, disclosure requirements on grass-roots lobbying, disagreement concerning the definition of thresholds for compliance, and questions concerning freedom of speech. Lobbying reform, however, is a continuing issue.

In 1978, corporations and trade associations played a significant part in the outcome of several controversial congressional decisions including the Tax Reform Act and defeat of the proposed consumer protection agency, the common-situs picketing bill, and the labor law reform bill. Business spokespersons, advocates of defeated bills, and political commentators generally attributed those results to direct and grass-roots lobbying by representatives of both large corporations and small-business groups. Some corporate spokesmen and political commentators acknowledged that the defeated legislation did not command sufficient popular support. Nonetheless, bolstered by self-congratulatory public statements made by corporate and business association executives, many opinion leaders interpreted the results as evidence of strong corporate political power.

### Advocacy Advertising

Advocacy advertising has generally been viewed by government officials, the courts, and Congress as a form of corporate grass-roots lobbying. Some critics believe that corporate advocacy advertising should be prohibited because it distorts complex political, economic, and social issues through oversimplification, slogans, and appeals to emotion rather than reason. Others debunk that criticism by arguing that simple and emotional messages are the nature of political expression and that such techniques are used by most candidates and advocacy groups. Critics also allege that corporations, with their vast financial resources, can dominate public discussion of issues, even those not germane to corporate economic goals. Other commentators counter by pointing to the ability of government officials and interest-group representatives to obtain broad media coverage of their viewpoints.

Several congressional committees have been concerned with various aspects of corporate advocacy advertising, including its tax treatment. In testifying before a House Commerce subcommittee, Mobil Public Affairs Vice President Herbert Schmertz maintained that since the *Bellotti* decision clarified the rights of corporations to engage in political activity, corporations should receive the same tax deductibility for their advocacy advertising as do those corporations that are in the media business and also have economic interests in nonmedia subsidiaries. In contrast, some state regulatory commissions have directed public utilities to charge the costs of advocacy advertising to their shareholders rather than to customers, in the belief that political advertising is not a relevant business expense.

The advocacy advertising issue is focused at present on the print media because television broadcasting companies believe that the Federal Communications Commission's "fairness doctrine" effectively precludes advocacy ads. Mobil Oil Corporation offered to pay for equal time for rebuttal by opposing interests as a means of satisfying the fairness doctrine, but its offer was refused. One proposal would permit televised corporate advocacy advertising provided that corporations would fund an independent institution which would make advertising space or time available to groups that wished to counter corporate advocacy advertising but could not afford to do so.

### Communication with Shareholders and Employees on Public Policy Issues

Many company managements inform their shareholders, managers, and employees about relevant public policy issues and their positions concerning them. This information is communicated via networks that include company publications, bulletin boards, letters to homes, announcements over plant intercoms, and shareholder and employee meetings. By implication or specific request, shareholders and employees are encouraged to support their managements' position on key issues by writing letters to legislators and by discussions with friends and neighbors. In an article on various techniques used by several companies to encourage employees to write letters to their legislators, *Business Week* reported, "Predictably, the practice has inspired employee grumbling that 'managed' letter-writing is not part of their jobs, complaints from civil libertarians that it invades the writer's privacy, and attempts by political theorists, in and out of Congress, to curb the trend."[4] The article pointed out, however, that company attempts to inspire employee lobbying do not violate personal privacy if the requests are truly voluntary.

## CORPORATE INITIATIVES AND ACTIONS

In addition to references in the preceding sections to corporate initiatives and actions concerning the elements of this issue, several other observations are provided in this section.

Some corporate executives are concerned that the rapid and potential growth of PACs and their possible impact on election campaigns will invite restrictive legislation or public financing. Others believe that successful influence on the formation of laws and regulations is earned by the quality of corporate representatives and their presentation of facts and opinions. And, of course, many executives believe that both PAC and effective corporate lobbying are essential. In any event, the managements of some large corporations have not formed PACs, while others have generated only modest PAC activity. As of January 1981, about 55 percent of the nation's 500 largest companies had formed PACs, an increase from 45 percent in 1978.

Some observers, such as Louis M. Kohlmeier, Washington editor of *Financier,* have expressed the view that corporate outspokenness on social and political issues is leading to public demands for higher levels of corporate participation in social problem solving and public accountability; that is, if corporate managements are to have a broader right to influence legislation, they should also have an expanded responsibility for the consequences of such legislation on the well-being of society.[5]

Most large corporations are managing the various elements of their

---

[4]"Browbeating Employees into Lobbyists," *Business Week,* Mar. 10, 1980, p. 132.

[5]Louis M. Kohlmeier, "Corporate Free Speech Ruling Widens Political Exposure," *Financier,* June 1978.

political participation as an integral part of their business. Some preferred practices and attitudes followed by companies that are successfully managing their participation in the public policy and electoral processes are these:

- Company policies or guidelines are established with internal controls and provisions for monitoring and reporting performance to top management.
- Public policy positions or recommendations include recognition of management's view of its constituents' interests as well as those of its shareholders. William S. Sneath, chairman of Union Carbide Corporation, has emphasized this point with this advice:

  Corporate participation in the public policy process requires conduct which engenders credibility and trust, and recognition that there is no perfect public policy. The process works by balancing interests and the corporate goal must be to strengthen—not dominate—the system.[6]

- Information provided to support company positions or recommendations is factual, reliable, and useful to the recipients.
- Political participation is open to public view to help dispel the traditional public distrust of corporate political power.
- Administration of PACs defuses criticism by such means as these:

  1. Diminish any imputation of coercion by refraining from solicitation of subordinates by supervisors and by accounting and record-keeping arrangements designed to protect employee privacy. A number of corporations retain outside administrators to serve as repositories and to maintain confidential PAC records. Importantly, many corporate executives have been forceful in communicating the voluntary nature of their PAC programs to their organizations. In one such communication, the Continental Group's Robert S. Hatfield said: "Any violations of this policy should be reported directly to my office, and the parties involved will be subjected to severe disciplinary actions. This may include termination."[7]
  2. Encourage employee participation in the selection of recipients. This is done directly by allowing contributors to designate recipi-

---

[6]William S. Sneath, "Private Enterprise and Public Business," address to the annual meeting of the Compressed Gas Association, Jan. 29, 1979.

[7] Robert S. Hatfield, More Than a Vote, report of the Continental Group Civic Association, February 1978.

ents or by welcoming employee suggestions for the disbursement of PAC funds as well as by providing for employee involvement in PAC management.

3. Feature PACs as one of a number of activities to encourage employees to participate in both the electoral and the public policy processes.

## THE OUTLOOK

Corporate political participation is certain to continue as a sensitive and controversial public issue. The growth in corporate PACs and their effectiveness, support of state and local candidates, and participation in initiatives and referenda are factors that are maintaining corporate political influence as a major public concern. Examples of public policies that benefit business—even incentives to spur economic recovery in the overall public interest—usually are alleged to result from undue corporate influence in lobbying or other aspects of the public policy process. Also, as cable television and other channels of communication (that may bypass the television networks' present interpretation of the fairness doctrine) become more generally available, their use for advocacy advertising and communication with employees, shareholders, and other constituents will raise further questions about corporate political influence.

These and other factors and events will provide further tests of the Supreme Court's rationale in the *Bellotti* case that corporate free speech is protected by the First Amendment. Undoubtedly litigation will be concerned with various aspects of corporate free speech, and the judicial decisions will have important implications for corporate participation in the electoral and public policy processes in the 1980s and beyond.

In anticipation of such developments, Herbert E. Alexander, director of the Citizens' Research Foundation, has suggested that the corporate community establish a "corporate bill of political rights." Alexander, who is recognized as a leading nonpartisan observer and interpreter of political finance, believes that the corporate community should enunciate the recognized constitutional and legal rights which enable companies to engage in all aspects of the electoral and public policy processes. In the form of a corporate bill of political rights, the statement would stake out the parameters of presently allowable behavior and would endeavor to envision constitutional interpretations. The bill's purpose would be to provide guidance to corporate managements in making their own decisions as to the nature and extent of their company's political participation. It would also be intended to help improve public understanding and lessen public apprehension about corporate political participation.[8]

[8]Herbert E. Alexander, "Political Action Committees and Their Corporate Sponsors in the 1980s," *Public Affairs Review*, vol. II, 1981. Published by the Public Affairs Council, Washington, D.C.

# CHAPTER 13

# Social
# Performance

***The Issue*** • The widespread recognition that some aspects of corporate performance may have an adverse impact on people and their interests has inevitably involved the managements of large corporations in a range of problems commonly characterized as "social." The problems, which range from consumer protection to equal opportunity, have created the issue of corporate social performance. This issue is highlighted by the continuing question: What can and should the large corporation do to help prevent or solve problems in these two categories:

- Social problems in which corporate policies and operations are significant factors, such as damage to the environment and occupational safety and health hazards
- Social problems in which corporate policies and operations are not significant factors, such as community needs for public services and education and broad national questions such as welfare reform

***Importance*** • In the last decade, large corporations have become more active than ever before in helping to preclude and solve problems in the first category. In addition, they are expected to satisfy public standards of good citizenship and to support the efforts of both public-sector and private-sector agencies to solve problems of the second category. Successful efforts in both of these categories can contribute to public trust in the corporate community and a satisfactory business environment.

The credibility and legitimacy of the large corporation are significantly influenced by the willingness of their managements to help solve problems in both categories. Company managements are expected to conduct their business operations in a manner that avoids the creation of new social problems and contributes to the solution of existing ones. In this regard, a Business Roundtable statement quoted James L. Ferguson, chairman of General Foods Corporation:

> On the one hand, managers must work far harder than ever before to make sure that the business decisions they make each day are not contributing to the alienation (of social institutions) we're talking about. And on the other hand, as leaders of society in general, they must do far more to help address some of the social ills that are feeding this alienation.[1]

**Causes** • In the last 15 years, the large corporation has been identified as one of the significant factors in causing or significantly contributing to a number of major social problems, such as air and water pollution, discriminatory employment practices, and products and processes that adversely affect human health. These developments have, in turn, stimulated the public policy debate concerning what corporations and other nongovernmental institutions can and should do to help solve social problems of all types.

The traditional role of the corporation in social problem solving has largely involved corporate philanthropy and employee voluntarism in local communities that are characterized as "corporate good citizenship." That role has involved financial contributions to selected educational, cultural, and welfare organizations, top-executive leadership in headquarters cities, and the development of benefit plans for the protection of employees, pensioners, and their families.

Corporate good citizenship and certain aspects of corporate performance, such as environmental protection, safety and health, and equal opportunity, have come to be categorized as "social" and are variously referred to as matters of "corporate social responsibility," "corporate social performance," and "corporate social responsiveness." This classification persists notwithstanding the fact that almost all such

---

[1]*Yes, Business Has an Agenda*, Business Roundtable report of Mar. 17, 1980, p. 9.

social problems are also economic, political, and technological to varying degrees.

Comprehensive attention of corporate managements to the social performance of their businesses has been generated by the consumer, environmental, civil rights, and other advocacy movements and by a great volume of social legislation affecting business performance. The managements of many large corporations have responded by conducting their business operations in ways that endeavor to avoid or minimize adverse impacts on people. Many also have made special efforts toward dealing with broader social problems, including some unrelated to their businesses.

## THE CORPORATE SOCIAL DIMENSION

Corporate management response to both categories of social problems has been debated under the rubric of corporate social responsibility for over a decade. The fact that the concept of corporate social responsibility has acquired no common definition has led to a good deal of confusion, as illustrated by the following strange alliances:

- Those who have stated that corporations have no social responsibility include both conservatives (such as Nobel Laureate Milton Friedman) who maintain that the only responsibility of business is to maximize profits and radicals (such as Michael Harrington, national chairman of the Democratic Socialist Organizing Committee) who regard corporate social responsibility as a tactic to extend corporate power further in the government domain and to delay the demise of private enterprise.

- Those who have stated that business corporations have a social responsibility include corporate critics (such as Ralph Nader) who see corporate failure to deal with the concept as a justification for corporate governance reforms and corporate leaders (such as Du Pont's Irving Shapiro) who believe that socially responsible performance is necessary to assure a viable environment in which large corporations may prosper and survive.

Thus, people with conservative and radical ideologies and those with antibusiness and probusiness convictions both advocate and oppose the exercise of corporate social responsibility. This paradox has been caused, in large part, by failure to differentiate between societal problems in which corporations are cited as factors in their cause and the many broader societal problems that are not significantly the result of corporate performance.

The corporate community continues to debate the existence and nature of the large corporation's social dimension, still with little differentiation between the two categories of social problems. The four principal concepts debated are these:

- *The corporation is an economic institution.* Some corporate executives rely on Milton Friedman's admonition that spending corporate funds on social problems is non-profit-maximizing behavior. They maintain that corporations, as private economic organizations, are accountable only to their shareholders, the marketplace, and applicable laws and regulations. The opposing executive viewpoint is that because of the pervasive impact of corporate operations on people and their interests large corporations are a party to certain social problems and must help solve them.

- *The term "social" is a misnomer.* As mentioned earlier, many issues popularly labeled social are equally—or to an even greater degree—economic, technological, financial, and political. For example, environmental health problems usually involve complex technology, difficult economic trade-offs, large financial expenditures, and conflicting political pressures. Yet, some executives have found that when their positions on a social issue reflect such considerations, they are accused of being antisocial. Other executives accept the social classification as a fait accompli and believe that it has the beneficial effect of emphasizing the social content of business problems to executives whose principal focus is on economic, technological, and financial factors.

- *Only government has a mandate to deal with social problems.* Some executives maintain that the government's social role should be supported only by the corporation's economic role, particularly that of creating jobs and paying taxes. Others cite many social impacts of corporate performance and maintain that to ignore nonshareholder interests invites public and government retribution.

- *Corporations are not qualified to help solve social problems and fail when they attempt to do so.* This position evolved from the experience of some corporate executives who in the late 1960s committed their corporations to solve problems such as the deterioration of inner cities and found that corporate resources and skills were inadequate to do so. While some executives use this "lesson" as a rationale to avoid any significant involvement with social problems, others point to examples of successful corporate participation in the amelioration of broad social problems.

The merit of this continuing debate among corporate executives, as well as among corporate friends and critics, is the reminder that the market system and the role of government place limits on what a corporation can do to help solve social problems. Because public expectations for corporations to participate in social problem solving far exceed the ability or resources of any corporation, managements usually find it necessary to delineate the social dimensions of their business and establish priorities for both categories of social problems.

Out of the debate and the trial and error of corporate experience, the managements of many large corporations have concluded that they must conduct their businesses in a manner which contributes to both the avoidance and the amelioration of social problems, particularly those that their companies may have helped to create. To that end, they are endeavoring to manage their social performance as they do the traditional aspects of their businesses.

## CORPORATE INITIATIVES AND ACTIONS

### Social Problems in Which Corporate Policies and Operations Are Significant Factors

Social problems in this category include those involved in such issues as environmental protection, occupational safety and health, equal opportunity, protection of personal privacy, legal and ethical behavior, and consumer protection. Those problems and corporation initiatives and actions concerning them are discussed in several of the preceding chapters on corporate performance. They have provoked a large amount of legislation whose purpose is to require changes in corporate performance and executive behavior. Initially, most corporate managements believed that abiding by the provisions of the laws would constitute publicly acceptable performance. But because the laws specify minimum rather than optimum standards of conduct, there are in many cases broad areas of discretion beyond legal obligation, and in those areas there have proved to be a variety of motivations for publicly acceptable corporate performance that are also consistent with the profit motive.

An important motive for publicly acceptable performance is that profit objectives are furthered by corporate goals such as these: (1) products and services that meet the needs and wants of people; (2) merchandising practices that respond to such consumer expectations as reliable service, informative advertising, and responsive complaint handling; (3) innovative technology and operating methods that achieve competitive advantages in resolving such problems as environmental pollution and product safety; and (4) a work environment that encourages productive performance by employees and managers.

Another motive for publicly desirable performance that is important for longer-term profitability is to help create and maintain a viable business and social environment, including corporate behavior that minimizes the need for government regulation of business. An overall motive that permeates and reinforces all others is to meet public standards of what is regarded as right and morally sound. Many consumers, employees, investors, shareholders, and dealers are drawn to a company whose management, in addition to its other attributes, expresses high standards in every aspect of its business performance.

These examples join private motivation and public need. In doing so, they create a synergistic effect, since they apply the reliable and consistent motive of self-interest to achieving matters of public interest.

## Social Problems in Which Corporate Policies and Operations Are Not Significant Factors

The same motivations for publicly acceptable performance in the first category have also influenced corporate managements in dealing with problems in the second. Examples of corporate activities that are representative of contemporary standards of good corporate citizenship are reviewed in the following three aspects of company performance.

- *Corporate community outreach activities.* Comprehensive community relations programs are expected of business and particularly of a large company that is a significant factor in a community. The traditional forms of this participation include philanthropic contributions, the provision of some leadership and personnel, and the encouragement of employees to be active in community service on their own time. Some companies also actively cooperate with local political structures on priority community problems.

  Large corporations have a particular stake in helping make their headquarters cities and other locations with concentrations of employees viable places both for the conduct of their business and for their employees to live and work in. The goal of community relations activities is to help to produce an environment wherein a company can conduct its operations efficiently and in harmony with the needs and safety of the community. To accomplish this objective it is often important to work with local community leaders prior to the opening of a new location. Also it is vital to consult and cooperate with community leaders when a management must close a plant or a facility.

  Many large corporations deal with business-related social problems by identifying the coincidence of social and business needs when initiatives by managements can help satisfy both. Among the examples are purchasing and banking programs to encourage minority business ventures and promote economic development in the minority community. Cooperating with the National Minority Purchasing Council, hundreds of corporations have achieved large increases in their purchasing and banking relationships with minority-owned companies. Another example is the National Alliance of Business, a joint business-government program whose purpose is to provide training for the hard-core unemployed and jobs in the private sector.

State and local government officials, constrained by tighter budgets and conflicting political pressures, are relying more directly on corporate assistance in helping to solve a variety of community problems. Many corporations have developed community relations programs designed to work on pressing social needs with civic leaders. They are often motivated by the importance of a good community environment and services to their business operations and the quality of life of their employees. Priority community needs often include the quality of public education, housing, economic development, public transportation, neighborhood redevelopment, job training for the unemployed, cultural and recreational programs, police and fire services, and training for community leadership. In some major cities, corporate outreach activities have taken the form of action coalitions such as Chicago United, New Detroit, and the Allegheny Conference. A few companies are involving employee committees in decisions on which community problems to address.

Corporate community involvement was traditionally focused in the company's headquarters city and was often an extension of the commitment of top executives. Some corporations are, however, becoming involved in problem solving in other communities where they have significant operations. City officials and newspaper editorials praise company leaders who are involved and sometimes chide companies whose executives are not.

Although corporate community social problem-solving assistance is still voluntary, there is some evidence of legislation to compel it in certain circumstances. Congress has enacted the Community Reinvestment Act to encourage banks to meet the credit needs of the entire community; a related law, the Home Mortgage Disclosure Act, requires financial institutions to provide citizens and public officials with information to judge whether they are redlining or are providing financing to all qualified applicants in the geographical areas they serve. While some companies have softened the impact of a plant closing on the affected employees and the community, there have been proposals in Congress and several state legislatures that would require all companies to provide up to 24 months of advance notice, assistance to employees including severance pay and continuation of health and welfare benefits, and compensation to the community for lost taxes for one taxable year.

- *Corporate philanthropy.* Contributions to civic, educational, health, social welfare, and arts and cultural organizations are a traditional way for corporations to help improve the quality of life in communities where they have significant interests. An important objective of corporate giving is to encourage other private-sector institutions and individuals to serve social, educational, and cultural needs. Federal tax policy permits corporate contributions of up to 5 percent of corporate pretax earnings. In recent years corporate philanthropic contributions have increased, yet as a percentage of profit they have declined. Large company and corporate foundation giving exceeds $2 billion yearly, yet it averages slightly less than 1 percent of pretax earnings. Some corporate executives are encouraging corporations to contribute more and to improve the management of their philanthropic activities. An oft-cited statement to support this peer pressure is the comment of President Lyndon Johnson when he chided a group of national business leaders in these words:

> In spite of the fact your federal government has seen fit to allow a charitable deduction of five percent of your profits, the record is quite clear that you businessmen still feel that the federal government can spend this money more wisely than you can.[2]

Increasingly, company managements are applying a sound business approach to philanthropic decision making, setting priorities based on community and corporate needs, improving the process of screening and selecting grant recipients, and monitoring and evaluating recipient performance. Greater numbers of companies are encouraging employee participation in the social or civic work of the recipients; some require that prospective recipient agencies shall have attracted the participation of employees, and others are targeting grants to be used as leverage in securing other funds or volunteers.

For many years some shareholders have expressed opposition to corporations' spending what they consider to be shareholders' money. Others believe that their company's management should make grants only to educators and institutions with similar ideologi-

---

[2]Lyndon B. Johnson, quoted in Kenneth N. Dayton, "The Case for Corporate Philanthropy," address to the Forum Club of Houston, June 25, 1980.

cal positions. However, the relatively few shareholder proposals that would have curtailed or prohibited philanthropy by their companies have fallen far short of a majority vote.

An objection voiced by some people is that about 46 percent of corporate philanthropic contributions (representing the business tax rate) are financed by taxpayers. Another concern sometimes expressed is that corporate managements may acquire undue social influence by contributions that they make on behalf of their companies.

A related question involves the persons who should make corporate philanthropic decisions. In many companies, whether or not they have a philanthropic foundation, those decisions have traditionally been made by the chief executive or a few top executives. Increasingly, though, decisions are being made by committees of executives or even by committees involving employees.

In 1981, the Business Roundtable published a statement urging the business community to increase contributions for educational, health, welfare, and cultural activities.[3] Recognizing the Reagan administration's emphasis on private-sector initiatives, the statement said:

> If the business community is serious in seeking to stem over-dependence on government, and still allow the not-for-profit sector to make the same contributions to society that it has in the past, business must itself increase its level of commitment.

The statement included recommendations that companies manage philanthropic activities in a businesslike way with quality staff and top-management involvement, make an effort to maintain support of their most important philanthropic programs even during economic turndowns, and disclose in an appropriate way their philanthropic programs in order to increase public awareness of the involvement of business in improving the quality of American life.

- *Corporate participation in formulation of broad public policy.* In a political environment characterized by many special-interest groups, the task of developing a general agreement on broad national problems is difficult. Government officials often need corporate expertise to help formulate policy on complex issues and testimonial support to help attain a consensus. As a result, mayors, governors, and even presidents seek the participation of corporate leaders in the public policy process of resolving broad public policy issues.

Broad matters of public policy in which corporate managements

---

[3]"Business Should Increase and Sustain Philanthropy, Give It Greater Importance," *Roundtable Report*, no. 81-3, April 1981, p. 1.

are most often interested are such subjects as productivity, energy resources, unemployment, inflation, and international trade. Beyond those types of problems, some corporate leaders invest their time in helping to resolve national problems quite unrelated to their businesses. Irving Shapiro has commented on this aspect of corporate performance as follows:

> Thus you will find chief executives today working with government on some matters far removed from their own corporate interests—the Panama Canal Treaty for example, . . . or the problems of minority unemployment in urban centers where their corporations do not have any plants. . . . Unless they are careful, executives can get sucked into controversial areas where they don't have any particular competence, and in extreme cases their efforts to help could amount to unwarranted meddling. Yet at the same time, executives cannot walk away from national and community problems on the grounds that they don't have all the answers. Who does?[4]

In some large corporations, the chief executive identifies an upcoming issue, and he and other executives prepare themselves to speak authoritatively on it. Chairman William S. Sneath of the Union Carbide Corporation is one who follows that practice. In preparation for the subject "economic growth" in 1980, Union Carbide commissioned a survey of public attitudes and special studies on that subject as a basis for national advertising, special publications, and speeches and testimony.

There is evidence that corporate chief executives in some other countries are more active than their American counterparts in the formulation of broad public policy. In a June 1980 *Wall Street Journal* column, Peter Drucker described an occasion when a group of chief executives of large Japanese companies discussed with him how Japan should adjust to demographic changes resulting from the fact that the official retirement age was still 55, while life expectancy was closer to 80. Drucker quoted the leader of the group as follows:

> We don't want to discuss with you what we in Japanese business should be doing. Our agenda is what Japan should be doing and what the best policies are in the national interest. Only after we have thought through the right national policies, and have defined and publicized them, are we going to think about the implications for business and for our companies. Indeed, we should postpone discussing economics altogether until we have understood what the right social policies are and what is best for the individual Japanese and for the country altogether. Who else besides the

---

[4]Irving Shapiro, "Business and the Public Policy Process," address to Symposium on Business and Government, Harvard University, Cambridge, Mass., May 9, 1979.

heads of Japan's large companies can really look at such a problem from all aspects? To whom else can the country really look for guidance and leadership in such a tremendous change as that of the age structure of our population?[5]

## Managing Corporate Social Performance

As discussed in Chapter 22, many corporate executives who have been conditioned in a system of profit maximizing have found it difficult to accept the idea that corporations have a social dimension. This is particularly the case when they consider the problems involved as primarily economic, technical, and political. Nonetheless, most corporate managements have recognized the need to understand and to manage deliberately the increasingly important social factors in their businesses. Reginald H. Jones, when chairman of the General Electric Company, commented on that phenomenon:

> It almost goes without saying that managers are going to be much more sensitive to their social responsibilities. What is not understood is that this requires work and preparation, like any other aspect of management. Management time spent in community affairs, or in learning what motivates the activists who have such powerful effect on public policy, is not time wasted. Unless we understand these powerful social forces, and learn to respond to changing public expectations, corporations are going to become an endangered species.[6]

While the organization and managerial styles of large companies vary, most managements are endeavoring to integrate social as well as economic, political, and technical factors into their processes of planning, operating, and evaluating results. Since the early 1970s, most large corporations have established or have used existing staff departments to help identify and deal with the aspects of their businesses that have sensitive social implications. These include environmental, consumer, equal-opportunity, occupational safety and health, energy conservation, government affairs, and community relations departments as well as staff members concerned with employee, legal, philanthropic, shareholder, supplier-contractor, and public affairs matters.

While the chief executive officer and senior executives are responsible for their company's overall performance, including its social impact, managers down the line are expected to develop their ability to assess the social impact of their business decisions and to choose

[5]Peter Drucker, "Learning from Foreign Management," The Wall Street Journal, June 4, 1980, p. 20.
[6]Reginald H. Jones, "Managing in the 1980s," address to the Wharton School of Business, University of Pennsylvania, Philadelphia, Feb. 4, 1980.

socially beneficial alternatives within their delegated authority. Since, however, social factors are often difficult to assess and their impact may be extensive, managers are responsible for seeking advice from their higher management when corporatewide perspective is needed to resolve problems such as incurring significant added costs, foregoing short-term profitability, and resolving conflicting ethical considerations.

Some managements have concluded that social performance must be assessed on a companywide basis to provide an overview of the impact of a business on people and their interests and to evaluate the extent to which a company's efforts produce beneficial results. Just as the large corporation is judged in part by its social performance, some corporate managements are endeavoring to evaluate their senior executives and managers in terms of their handling of the aspects of their company's social performance for which they are accountable. This type of assessment has been difficult to achieve and awaits further development in the art of managing corporate social performance.

As public interest in the corporate social impact developed in the early 1970s, many large companies began to report on their social role, policies, or examples of their performance to their shareholders, employees, and other constituents. A few companies even attempted to provide a "social audit" but found that quantification of direct and indirect expenditures and tangible and intangible returns was overly subjective in the financial accounting mode. The social performance statements of some companies have given mixed signals to shareholders, employees, customers, neighbors, and other affected parties. At one extreme some managements have overcommitted their companies in promising to help solve social problems, and when they have not been able to perform, they have dashed the public expectations they had raised. At another, some managements whose operations have caused or exacerbated adverse social impacts have proclaimed the singularity of the economic role of the large corporation. Another confusing signal has been given by corporate managements that have been effusive about "corporate social responsibility" but have dealt with social performance by publicizing cosmetic activities.

Most company managements report on at least one or more aspects of their social performance in their annual reports to shareholders. The public accounting firm of Ernst and Whinney, in an analysis of social performance disclosure in corporate annual reports, has found that 85 to 90 percent of the *Fortune* 500 companies include some relevant information. Because some managements have concluded that appropriate coverage of social performance would require a substantial addition to what is fundamentally a financial report, they publish a separate social performance report. For example, Standard Oil Co. (Indiana) has issued a social performance report with a readership life of 2 or 3 years, while Atlantic Richfield Company publishes a social report each year. The first annual report of this kind was published by General Motors in 1971. In each succeeding year the General Motors *Public Interest Report* has supplemented the annual report to GM shareholders and the public as an account of the company's "goals, programs, and progress in areas of public concern." Thomas A. Murphy, then chairman of General Motors, introduced the tenth-anniversary *Public Interest Report* with this comment:

> If business people have learned one overriding lesson from the '70s, it is that economic success alone is not enough. Important as they are, superior products are not enough; nor are innovations in manufacturing, marketing or service. And certainly, returning a profit on our stockholders' investment, although absolutely necessary, is no longer sufficient by itself to ensure a firm's acceptance. All of these traditional marketplace measures of success fall short of fully explaining General Motors to the public at large.[7]

The most extensive industry social performance report is the magazine *Response*, which is composed of articles, news, and speeches concerning social policies and programs of the life and health insurance business. Its purposes are to encourage beneficial social performance by insurance companies and to report progress to various constituent interests.[8]

Among the factors that distinguish companies for their social performance are managements that act in these ways:

- They consider their social role in terms of social problems in which their operations are a factor and, separately, of those in which their operations are not.

- If they recognize a social role, they explain it for all their constituents, neither overpromising nor understating their commitment.

- They demonstrate publicly and within the company an active concern for the impact of corporate decisions on people. One clear signal of this concern within the company is to include discussion of social impact and performance in the planning and evaluation of operations, technology, employee relations, and particularly profit generation. A proof of this concern is effective self-regulation, particularly on matters in which management's policy favors deregulation.

[7]*General Motors Public Interest Report,* General Motors Corporation, New York, 1980.
[8]*Response,* Clearinghouse on Corporate Social Responsibility, Washington, bi-monthly.

- They include social performance as an integral part of the company's managing process. They manage community relations and philanthropy as well as acute problems such as environmental protection and legal and ethical behavior.
- In social problem solving in which the company is not a causal factor, they have followed some or all of these practices:

    1. Community involvement is an integral responsibility of each local manager, and plans and performance are monitored at each company location.
    2. Public stands are taken on some general public issues, particularly those most crucial to the welfare of surrounding communities and in which the company management has applicable expertise.
    3. Active programs of employee voluntarism are sponsored.
    4. Corporate philanthropy is managed by evaluating potential recipients, monitoring the performance of recipients, and promoting the leveraging of volunteer time and company support.

## THE OUTLOOK

The prospects for the social performance issues in which corporations are a causal factor are discussed in the chapters "Marketplace Performance," "Legal and Ethical Behavior," "Quality of Working Life," "Employee Citizenship Rights," "Health, Safety, and the Environment," and "Technological Innovation." Overall, the obligation of managements to avoid or mitigate adverse social impacts of their companies will continue, and the ability of corporations to meet public expectations will determine whether deregulation continues or reregulation becomes a political necessity. Meanwhile, although federal and regulatory action may be lessened somewhat in the Reagan administration, state and local governments are poised to take up the slack. Also, company causality will be penalized, often by judicial rather than regulatory action.

The outlook for company performance on social problems in which corporate policies and operations are not significant factors is summarized here. The concept of corporate community relations began to broaden in recent years as some local and state citizen groups focused on such issues as environmental protection, equal rights, and consumer protection. Other socioeconomic issues are regional. In the snow belt, for example, community development problems are associated with the loss of industry and jobs. In the sun belt, two basic problems are whether community infrastructures and public services can assimilate citizen migrants as well as undocumented aliens and their families. The incidence of the interaction of citizen groups with corporations on such issues is increasing and varies from simple inquiry to picketing and boycotts. Whereas the initiative is often taken by citizen groups, some corporate managements are seeking the understanding and support of such groups prior to the occurrence of problems.

There are two other factors which are likely to spur this broader and more controversial type of corporate-community relationship: the frustration that many people experience in trying to advocate or protect specific local interests at the state and federal levels and the growing stake that corporate managements have in communities where their companies are a significant factor.

In the longer term, there is emerging evidence that socioeconomic-issue groups will form coalitions to support their nominees for local office and to challenge the actions and influence of businesses with which they disagree. Meanwhile, there will be a modest but continuing increase in the traditional community citizenship activities of large corporations.

With the financial problems of higher education and cultural institutions, the impact of inflation on local and state public services in the face of voter demands for tax reductions, and the federal government's reduction of expenditures for certain social services, the traditional beneficiaries of corporate philanthropy are expecting corporations to make up from some to a sizable part of their shortfalls. This will become a recriminatory issue if corporations are seen to prosper from national policies for economic recovery and yet do not help to strengthen the nonprofit institutions of the private sector.

While some corporate top executives have taken part in the debate on broad public policies, this aspect of corporate social performance is not likely to mature rapidly. First, corporate executives must reach a point at which they feel less deeply embattled with the vital issues directly affecting their companies and industries. Second, as discussed in Chapter 22, there is need for the development of more numerous corporate executives who are as effective in managing the public policy dimension of business as they must be in managing the traditional aspects of their work.

# CHAPTER 14

# Executive Compensation
# and Perquisites

***The Issue*** • To what extent do the types and levels of compensation and perquisites for top corporate executives stimulate public concern and criticism?

***Importance*** • Public trust in large corporations and their top executives is significantly influenced by perceptions of corporate policies and practices concerning executive compensation and perquisites. When executive compensation is perceived to be too high or to bear little relation to the performance of the company or the individual executive, many people conclude that top executives have too much power to set their own compensation. Corporate perquisites, when misused, raise the same concerns.

Another factor is the belief that high compensation and extensive perquisites insulate top executives from the concerns of the typical American, with the result that the executives become insensitive to important public problems and needs. Corporate boards have responded to these public perceptions by exercising greater control in setting the amounts and types of compensation and perquisites. The public concerns, however, have led to proposals for elimination of tax preferences on any type of compensation and for requirements that independent directors have complete control over executive compensation and perquisites.

The most important public policy impact of this issue may not be direct attacks on compensation or perquisites but a more punitive climate in which government officials make and enforce regulations controlling other aspects of the performance of corporations and their executives.

***Causes*** • As a result of corporate disclosures required by the Securities and Exchange Commission (SEC) and articles in newspapers and business journals, there has been increased public information about executive compensation and perquisites. Some of that information has triggered criticism of large corporations and their top executives. Compounding this issue is a public awareness that there have been examples in which corporate chief executives either appeared to have determined or actually determined their own compensation and perquisites. Public attention has also been directed to perquisites that are or appear to be emoluments to enhance executives' status rather than services and facilities that they need to do their jobs better.

The slow growth of real incomes since the late 1960s has caused some workers to resent executive compensation that appears to keep pace with inflation better than their own wages. That sentiment is heightened by the citing of examples of increases in the total compensation of executives that exceed or appear to exceed those of wages alone. Studies have also shown that unusual forms of compensation and perquisites have become a significant part of total executive remuneration, particularly when they provide personal tax advantages. Other studies and publicized cases have indicated that compensation of top corporate executives does not always correspond to various standards that corporate executives themselves use to judge the performance of their companies. Finally, some experts on executive compensation believe that many incentive and bonus plans tend to influence executive behavior toward short-term decisions at the expense of the long-term health of their companies and the United States economy.[1]

---

[1]Edward Meadows, "New Targeting for Executive Pay," *Fortune*, May 4, 1981, p. 176.

While corporate executive compensation and perquisites are not paramount among public concerns, this issue flares up from time to time and weakens the contention of executives that their power is exaggerated. Published examples of what many people believe are unusual executive compensation and corporate perquisites reinforce a belief among some government officials, shareholders, and even some members of the financial community that the managements of some corporations have not been properly accountable.

## EXECUTIVE COMPENSATION

While Americans have always questioned how the wealthy get and use their money, the compensation of top corporate executives has generally been subject to even more intense public scrutiny than the income of well-to-do owner-managers. As professional managers, top executives are expected to receive justifiable compensation that is related to performance and is not out of proportion with the salaries of other employees. There is also the expectation that the compensation of all employees, including top executives, will be set by others and not by the executives themselves. When examples have been reported of top executives who set or appear to set their own compensation, the public tends to conclude that top executives are primarily motivated by a desire for personal wealth and power. Irving Kristol has agreed with those concerned about the personal cupidity of some executives. Writing in *The Wall Street Journal*, he stated that "many corporate executives . . . think they have the right to become wealthy . . . not simply to be well paid. . . . [C]onfusion between entrepreneurial rewards and management rewards . . . establishes salary levels for executives which, in the eyes of the public, are indecently high."[2] John C. Baker, a corporate director and former president of Ohio University who has written widely on executive compensation, adds that executive self-seeking may diminish public trust to the point that "capitalists themselves will become a major force undermining capitalism."[3]

While executive compensation is generally thought of by the public as consisting of salary, stock options, and perhaps a bonus, it may also include more than one of the following types of income: profit sharing

[2]Irving Kristol, "The Credibility of Corporations," *The Wall Street Journal*, Jan. 17, 1974, p. 16.

[3]John C. Baker, "Are Executives Overpaid?" *Harvard Business Review*, July–August 1977, p. 52. Copyright © 1977 by the President and Fellows of Harvard College; all rights reserved. Reprinted by permission of the Harvard Business Review.

plans, long-term incentive plans, performance shares, deferred compensation, special pension provisions, low-interest personal loans, and consulting contracts after retirement. The proliferation of these types of executive compensation from the 1960s on was partly motivated by efforts to protect the incentive concept and to shield executives from inflation and progressively higher tax brackets. However, to many people those efforts appeared to be attempts to hide the size of executive compensation and to beat the tax laws. As a result, some observers have predicted that excessive compensation will itself become a critical issue. While this has not yet occurred, criticisms have been heard from some shareholders and activist groups as well as from government officials.

In recent years, when a number of chief executives began receiving annual compensation exceeding $1 million, many people concluded that corporate profits and executive salaries were excessive. In an opinion survey on economic growth sponsored by Union Carbide Corporation, two-thirds of the respondents agreed with this statement: "When the economy is booming, most of the increase is kept by business in the form of higher profits, higher executive salaries, and fat expense accounts. The average person doesn't benefit very much."[4]

In contrast to the public's view, the perspective of a corporate board of directors is quite different. When a board has an urgent need to obtain a qualified chief executive officer, compensation is secondary. Often boards of directors have found it necessary to pay competitive prices for superior management talent in the context of a widespread public belief that such prices are too high. They generally recognize that the difference between merely good and outstanding talent is off-scale in relation to compensation differences. A dramatic example of facing up to the executive compensation dilemma occurred in early 1980, when British Prime Minister Margaret Thatcher chose Ian MacGregor, the retired chairman of AMAX Inc., to head the British Steel Corporation with an incentive compensation package that created intense criticism.

Criticism of the level of executive compensation has generally focused on extraordinary examples that have attracted widespread media attention. Peter Drucker has commented on the impact of such exceptionally high executive compensation on public attitudes in this way: "Economically, these few very large executive salaries are quite unimportant. Socially, they do enormous damage. They are highly visible and highly publicized. And they are therefore taken as typical,

---

[4]*The Vital Consensus: American Attitudes on Economic Growth,* survey conducted by Roger Seasonwein Associates, Inc., for Union Carbide Corporation, 1980.

rather than as the extreme exceptions they are."[5] Shareholders of several companies have addressed the excessive-compensation issue; in the cases of Rapid-American Corporation and Norton Simon, Inc., executives were forced to return portions of salaries previously awarded.

Some corporate managements contend that exceptionally high compensation is necessary to attract the very best talent to top corporate positions, to motivate promotable managers, and to establish the apex of a company salary structure. Critics argue that compensation is not the top priority of most exceptional executives and point to supporting studies as evidence. Others defend top executives' compensation by noting the high earnings of top television journalists, entertainers, and athletes. Numerous television journalists and entertainers have high earnings that span careers of two or more decades, a period which exceeds the typical tenure of chief executives of large corporations. Most top athletes have relatively short-lived high-income careers, yet there is considerable public resentment of the high compensation and collateral income received by them.

Some observers have called public attention to examples of executive compensation that appear to be unrelated to executive or company performance, and the media are quick to point out occasions when executive salaries rise while company earnings fall. The level of executive salaries has also provoked debate over the appropriate ratio of top-executive salaries to middle- and lower-level salaries. Some compensation authorities and social critics have recommended a fixed ratio of the highest to the lowest full-time salaries in a corporation. This concept, however, is regarded by compensation authorities as arbitrary and subject to manipulation.

Some financial and compensation authorities maintain that when executive compensation plans are based on short-range profitability or are enhanced by stock appreciation, such incentives can create personal conflicts of interest for executives in making short-range versus longer-range decisions. In mid-1981, a *Fortune* article commented on this point:

> There does appear to be a short-term bias in American management. Management consultants shake their heads over clients—no names mentioned, of course—who are hurting their companies' future prospects to beef up quarterly earnings. Dividends are paid out even when doing so eats capital that will have to be replaced. Companies neglect research and development, new technology, and advertising because these costs would drag down quarterly income. A great many U.S. corporations still

[5]Peter Drucker, "Is Executive Pay Excessive?" *The Wall Street Journal*, May 23, 1977, p. 20.

haven't switched from the FIFO inventory-valuation system to the tax-reducing LIFO system because the changeover would lower reported earnings.

The article explained that to overcome the perverse effects of conventional incentive plans, a number of corporations are making such changes as lengthening their executives' perspectives by stretching incentive plans over several years, correcting for the effect of inflation by setting real-growth goals, adopting plans that measure performance against comparable companies in similar businesses, and using strategic goals in incentive plans. These changes reflect the responsibility of corporate boards for the use of executive compensation to help assure both the long- and the short-range success of their companies.[6]

## EXECUTIVE PERQUISITES

Executive perquisites are generally regarded as services and facilities provided to allow executives to work efficiently and to protect them from unnecessary risks to health and security caused by working conditions. Perquisites vary but may include such items as these: company automobile and chauffeur services, special transportation and lodgings, club memberships, special expense accounts, special physical examinations, special disability protection, educational benefit trusts, financial, tax, and legal counseling, and special recreation facilities.

The current attention to executive perquisites has its origins in the scandals of the 1970s concerning questionable payments. Personal use of corporate apartments and hunting lodges and forgivable personal loans were among the examples that led to tighter scrutiny of top-executive practices.

Despite the legitimate business needs for most perquisites, the media have questioned the use of company planes, country club memberships, recreational facilities, and lump-sum entertainment allowances. There has also been criticism that the diversity of perquisites represents an attempt to provide executives with compensation that is untaxed.

To encourage changes, the SEC, beginning in 1978, required companies to report the total cash compensation of their top five executives plus a cash equivalent value for perquisites provided them. New tax laws have sought to close existing loopholes, sparking a back-to-cash movement. As a result, the Internal Revenue Service has been seeking a

[6]Meadows, op. cit.

workable and equitable means of taxing those executive perquisites which it deems to have no legitimate business purpose.

## CORPORATE INITIATIVES AND ACTIONS

Business observers have noted a number of measures that corporations are using to help restore and sustain shareholder confidence and public trust in the process of determining executive compensation. Among the most common are the following:

- *Board compensation committees composed of outside directors.* The slightest hint that top executives set their own salaries can destroy the credibility of a compensation program. A strong board compensation committee with a well-defined, independent process has become more commonplace and appears to be dispelling some concerns about the fairness and propriety of executive compensation and perquisites.
- *Proper levels of compensation.* Potential salary ranges should reflect competitive levels of compensation as determined by independent surveys.
- *Linking compensation to performance.* Year-to-year and executive-to-executive compensation levels should reflect actual short- and long-term performance. Undue reliance on short-term measures of profitability and growth can impede the achievement of longer-term company goals and divert management attention from political and social as well as economic considerations.
- *Essential perquisites.* So that perquisites are not and do not appear to be forms of nontaxable income, only those perquisites that are essential to the conduct of business should be provided.
- *Communication about compensation and perquisite practices.* To allay questions about the integrity of compensation and perquisite administration, corporate managements are offering more open and complete explanations of their practices than in the past.
- *Establishing effective control systems.* The use of corporate perquisites such as planes, facilities, and limousines should be controlled, and executives should be charged for their personal use. Shareholders, the public, and employees must be assured that corporate resources are used for legitimate business purposes only.

An example of both corporate self-restraint and accountability is illustrated by the response of IBM Chairman Frank T. Cary when asked at the company's annual meeting in 1978: "What is IBM's policy toward perquisites for officers and directors?" Mr. Cary replied:

> We do not have any hunting lodges or yachts or vacation homes. We have airplanes and some automobiles that are used for business purposes. In rare instances when those are used for personal business, they are charged for at cost. When one of our executives takes some member of the family along on an IBM airplane for something that is not business-related, the executive is billed at commercial rates.[7]

## THE OUTLOOK

Privilege and inequality by rank are generally accepted as a characteristic of most institutions, including corporations. Thus, sizable differentials in compensation and perquisites are generally accepted in our society if they are realistically related to the value and performance of the individual. However, public concern about compensation that is excessive or is unrelated to company and individual performance appears to be stimulated by a few conspicuous examples each year that reflect adversely on corporations as a whole.

As we look ahead, serious criticism of executive compensation and perquisites is most likely to occur in the context of plant closings, layoffs, extensive unemployment, serious inflation, and other factors that contrast the fortunate with the unfortunate. However, this issue is likely to have the most serious consequences for an individual company if the determination of its chief executive's compensation involves any conflict of interest or if perquisites are seen as unessential or abused.

Advocates of federal regulation of corporate governance are particularly alert to document examples of extraordinary compensation, executive self-determination of compensation, and perquisite malpractices to substantiate their proposals.

[7]Frank T. Cary, *Report to Stockholders*, IBM annual meeting, Apr. 24, 1978.

# PART THREE

# The Corporate Governance Issues

As documented in the previous chapters, public concern about corporate performance and executive conduct has contributed to the prodigious growth of government regulation of business and the economy. Yet, many people who favor such government intervention are dissatisfied because the additonal laws and their intensive enforcement have not changed corporate performance or the United States economic system as they had expected. As a result, corporate critics in and outside government have directed public attention to the "government" of internal corporate affairs as the basic cause and cure of corporate malpractices. They have alleged that the present governance system has failed to hold company boards and managements accountable for their use of corporate power and that boards and managements can best be made accountable by imposing external controls on the corporate governance process. This line of reasoning has such startling implications for the future of private enterprise that the ensuing debate quickly placed the generally unfamiliar term "corporate governance" on the corporate public policy agenda.

Corporate governance is concerned with the structure, the participants, and the processes by which corporations are managed. The governance of a company is based on a charter issued under the provisions of state law and involves the roles and relationships of the shareholders, the board of directors, and the management. For the purpose of differentiation, the term "management" refers collectively to the company chief executive officer and other full-time officers, some of whom may be members of the board of directors.

An important manifestation of the common view that the large corporation, despite its private ownership, is a quasi-public institution is that company managements should be more broadly accountable not just to shareholders, the laws, and the competitive marketplace, but to the constituents and interests they affect. While corporate managements are vastly more accountable today, both legally and voluntarily, than even a few years ago, some corporate critics charge that managements can be made fully accountable only by reform of corporate governance. In essence, the critics' three categories of alleged deficiencies and proposed reforms are these:

- *Corporate chartering.* Management is not accountable to state government because state charters are overly permissive; therefore, the large corporation must be chartered by the federal government.

- *Shareholder rights.* Management is not accountable to shareholders because management has preempted control; therefore, shareholders must have the right to participate in important management decisions.

- *Boards of directors.* Management is not accountable to the board of directors because board members are too subservient to management and the chief executive officer; therefore, the board must be restructured by replacing company officers and experienced corporate executives with representatives of a variety of interest groups.

Each of these contentions is subject to serious question, particularly in light of the substantial progress made by company managements in improving the process of corporate governance. Nonetheless, critics assert the existence of the deficiencies and contend that governance must be reformed.

Proposals for changes in corporate governance come from adversaries, dispassionate observers, and corporate executives. Their ideas range from radical measures that would be tantamount to the nationalization of large corporations to wider adoption of voluntary changes that have already proved successful. The three principal categories of criticism are discussed in the ensuing Chapter 15, "Corporate Chartering," Chapter 16, "Shareholder Rights," and Chapter 17, "Boards of Directors." In each of these chapters, the issue, principal proposals, government initiatives, and pro and con positions are summarized.

Chapter 18, "The Corporate Governance Issues in Context," deals with four related subjects. The first is concerned with the relationship of the corporate performance and governance issues and the reasons for directing management attention to corporate performance as a basis for resolving both sets of issues. The second describes the substantial progress that has been made in strengthening corporate accountability through such means as increased reliance upon independent directors, effective board committees, corporate codes of conduct, emphasis upon internal controls, and more extensive corporate disclosure. The third section recounts other private-sector steps to help improve the corporate governance process. The final section concerns the outlook for the governance issues.

# CHAPTER 15

# Corporate Chartering

United States corporations, with the exception of special cases such as the Communications Satellite Corp. (COMSAT) and national banks, are chartered by state governments. Each state and the District of Columbia have corporation laws which are enabling acts, authorizing the formation and management of businesses, large and small. Those state corporation laws provide a legal framework by which an entrepreneur can bring together capital, labor, plant and equipment, and management to carry out the business purpose stated in the charter. Each state law specifies requirements concerning the management of the internal affairs of the corporation, including the rights of shareholders, the holding of meetings of shareholders and directors, the powers and liabilities of directors and officers, and the financial structure. These laws authorize organic changes such as amendments to the charter, sale of entire assets, merger, and dissolution. They provide for limited liability for owners, perpetual life of the corporation, separate legal-entity status, and centralized management, all of which distinguish the corporation from other forms of business enterprise.

The primary purpose of state corporation laws thus is not to regulate the external conduct of corporations in matters such as antitrust, securities transactions, safety and health, and countless other aspects of corporate performance. However, some of the laws have regulatory provisions which are intended to prevent abuses by management and to protect minority shareholders and creditors.

States which have chartered the largest number of companies are alleged to have the least restrictive charter requirements. Delaware is

171

cited most often as an example. That state has more than 110,000 corporations under charter, including at least 40 percent of those listed on the New York Stock Exchange, and derives a significant portion of its state revenue from corporate franchise taxes and related income. Some observers have concluded that states compete in lowering their charter requirements in order to garner charter revenues, and they use that conclusion as an argument to justify federal chartering or federal legislation that would provide minimum standards for the internal governance of large corporations. According to other authorities, how-ever, that argument ignores important considerations that exist in states like Delaware. Companies incorporate in Delaware because they know where they stand. What makes Delaware attractive is not the permis-siveness of its laws but rather the fact that its corporate law is evenhanded, consistent, predictable, and equitable. Delaware's basic incorporation act is an enabling vehicle. Most of the limits to corporate behavior are contained in the case law, and that is quite restrictive and specific. Advocates of state chartering often point out that if charters from states like Delaware did not adequately protect shareholders, few people or investment funds would buy or retain shares of Delaware companies.

Some chartering advocates believe that federal chartering should provide both uniform standards for corporate governance and regulato-ry law to control the external conduct of large corporations. Thus, Ralph Nader's original scheme included antitrust law amendments, and the proposed Corporate Democracy Act of 1980 included amend-ments to the National Labor Relations Act and the criminal codes as well as plant-closing regulations. In addition, the advocates argue that the internal changes they propose would indirectly control the external conduct of large corporations. They assert that management's misuse of corporate power has caused harm externally to human health and safety, to the environment, to the political process, and indeed to the corporation's overall performance. Others advocate that management's power be internally checked as a substitute for or complement to external regulation, which they see as failing because it is overly complex and costly to both consumer and taxpayer.

For many years, one of Ralph Nader's numerous interests has been to advocate multiple-purpose federal chartering. Until 1976, he had neither significant support nor opposition. However, that year Nader proposed legislation which would have required several hundred of the largest companies to have a federal charter in addition to a state charter. The Nader proposal, coming during a period of continuing disclosure of wrongdoing by some corporations, sparked a significant public policy debate. Federal charter requirements recommended by

Nader included both standards of internal corporate governance and regulations for controlling external conduct, a role traditionally provided by specific regulatory laws. Among the principal requirements were these:

1. Shareholders would nominate and elect a full-time, wholly outside board of directors with a full-time staff available to monitor management performance.
2. Boards would be composed of "constituency directors," each representing a particular interest (e.g., labor, minorities, women, environmentalists, and consumers) in addition to bearing overall responsibility.
3. Boards would establish corporate procedures and could approve or veto management decisions.
4. Shareholder approval of "fundamental" corporate decisions would be required.
5. Corporate disclosure of detailed performance and financial information would be required on such matters as pollution violations, detectable toxic substances in each workplace, minority-hiring practices, lobbying activities, joint-venture investments, annual tax returns, federal sales contracts, and the 100 largest security holders for each class of voting stock.
6. Employee citizenship rights, such as freedom of speech and personal privacy, would be mandated.
7. Presumption of monopoly power would be based on an arbitrary share of market, and mergers in concentrated industries would be prohibited.

Stimulated by growing public concern over examples of corporate misconduct and the Nader proposal, the Senate Committee on Commerce, Science, and Transportation held hearings in 1976 on the conduct and control of large corporations. The hearings had the effect of setting aside federal chartering but provided testimony by corporate leaders as well as corporate critics that further improvements in corporate governance were needed, particularly as to more effective performance by boards of directors.

The 1977 hearings of the Subcommittee on Citizens' and Shareholders' Rights and Remedies of the Senate Judiciary Committee included an examination of federal incorporation. However, Sen. Howard M. Metzenbaum (Democrat, Ohio), chairman of the subcommittee, did not include federal chartering in the protection of shareholders' rights bill which he introduced in April 1980.

In 1980 Rep. Benjamin S. Rosenthal (Democrat, New York) introduced the Corporate Democracy Act of 1980 in the House. The bill
would not have established formal federal chartering either, but it
would have imposed on large companies federal requirements concerning the structure of the board of directors and directors' duties,
shareholder rights to nominate directors and review certain corporate
transactions, disclosure of socially significant information, company
obligations in connection with plant closings, and novel criminal
liabilities and sanctions. No hearings were held on the bill.

Corporate leaders, many attorneys, and professors of law and business have strongly opposed federal chartering and federal legislation
under any other name that affects the internal structure of the corporation. Their principal reasons are these:

1. There has been no failure of state laws. Those laws provide the basis
   of the existence of a corporation and establish standards for its
   internal management.

2. Recent corporate, Securities and Exchange Commission, New York
   Stock Exchange, and American Bar Association initiatives to a great
   extent have obviated the need for any form of federal chartering or
   governance legislation.

3. The stock market, undergirded by the federal securities laws,
   provides adequate means for shareholders to register approval or
   disapproval of management conduct. Together, state law and federal
   securities laws provide necessary protection of shareholder rights.

4. Advocates of federal chartering have used the issue of chartering as a
   means to promote their own social and economic causes, which, by
   and large, they have not been able to sell in the public policy
   process.

5. A single set of standards prescribed for a large number of corporations proposes a simplistic answer to a situation that involves a wide
   variety of circumstances and calls for a flexible response. Disclosure
   is particularly well suited to that purpose.

6. Federal chartering or another version of federal regulation of the
   internal governance of the corporation is an inappropriate way to
   curb errant corporate conduct. Specific legislation for identified
   problems is preferable to a single omnibus bill that would regulate
   governance and such problems as antitrust, pollution, equal opportunity, and occupational health.

In the last several sessions of Congress, various federal chartering
proposals have been introduced. While it appears unlikely that federal

chartering will be adopted in the foreseeable future, there have regularly been introduced at congressional hearings proposals for a federal corporate minimum standards act which, depending upon one's point of view, would establish a moderate form of federal chartering or be a big step toward an extreme form. Consequently, the possibility of some type of federal chartering remains a threat in being as a potentially draconian means of controlling governance and attempting to control the conduct of large corporations.

# CHAPTER 16

# Shareholder Rights

In addition to provisions of state corporation laws that protect the rights of shareholders, various federal securities laws of 1933, 1934, 1939, and 1940 were designed to protect shareholders and other security holders. The federal securities laws were designed generally (1) to assure complete and accurate disclosure by a company pertaining to its securities being sold in the marketplace; (2) to prevent and afford remedies for fraudulent practices in connection with such disclosure and in trading in and manipulation of the securities markets; (3) to provide, in the case of debt offerings, that a corporate trustee meet certain standards of independence; and (4) to regulate investment companies. The Securities and Exchange Commission (SEC) is the regulatory agency responsible for administration of the federal securities laws. The failure of a company subject to the laws to comply with the disclosure requirements of federal securities laws may trigger civil action by investors, administrative proceedings or injunctive actions by the SEC, or criminal actions by the Department of Justice against the company, its officers, or its staff.

The legal model of the corporation conforms to the small, closely held corporation of 80 to 100 years ago. The typical corporation at the turn of the century had relatively few shareholders. Those few elected the members of the board, and significant shareholders also were directors. The board elected the chief executive and other officers, and in many cases those positions were also held by shareholders who were board members. Today, the line of legal authority still runs from the state to shareholders to directors to officers. However, as corporations became national and international in scope and the numbers of shareholders vastly increased and became widely dispersed, owners yielded their right to active participation in management. Early in the twentieth century the authority of shareholders began to shift, and eventually the line of practical authority became the reverse of the legal line. The result is that for decades the managements of most large companies (in some cases, the chief executive officers) have had de facto control over company policies and actions. Yet, few shareholders object in the absence of outright illegal or other reprehensible conduct adversely affecting shareholder interests. The vast majority of share-holders understand that boards and managments cannot account to them individually. In fact, they expect their investment to include competent management without their being obligated to participate in management decisions.

In this modern context, when shareholders are dissatisfied with their corporation's economic performance or prospects, they usually follow the "Wall Street rule": they sell their shares. Nonetheless, critics who are dissatisfied with corporate voluntary action or government regula-tion as means of assuring publicly acceptable corporate performance point to the aforementioned reversal of authority in corporate gover-nance and call for a return to what they characterize as "shareholder democracy." Though often confused with the process of disclosure, shareholder democracy has as its principal objective a more active role for shareholders in major company decisions. While most proponents of shareholder rights have recognized limitations to shareholder partic-ipation in management decision making, they have proposed a variety of ways for shareholders to influence the decision making of boards and managements.

Several proposals concerning shareholder rights were included in Sen. Howard M. Metzenbaum's proposed Protection of Shareholders' Rights Act. One concerned the right of shareholders to nominate candidates for the board; another, the right of cumulative voting to elect directors. Cumulative voting, a shareholders' right in twenty-one states, allows each shareholder to cast for a single candidate a number of votes equal to the number of his or her shares multiplied by the number of directors to be elected or to distribute the total among several candi-dates. Shareholders have shown little interest in nominating board candidates or in cumulative voting. Many observers believe that cumulative voting would foster the election of directors who would represent particular interest groups. Also, over time, cumulative voting could facilitate the takeover of a company by minority financial interests. The Metzenbaum bill also had a provision for shareholders to maintain a civil action in a federal court to enforce any provision of the act. This, of course, would further crowd the dockets of the federal courts and would create confusing and conflicting bodies of state and federal law governing corporations.

In late 1980, the SEC published a comprehensive *Staff Report on Corporate Accountability* based on a 3-year study of its rules regarding corporate governance. The report did not recommend any legislation; it did, however, propose some minor amendments to existing rules and suggested several actions that corporate managements might take to preclude legislation in the future.

An important recommendation of the staff was that the SEC consider requiring corporations to disclose information about their political activities. The report based this recommendation on the 1978 *Bank of Boston v. Bellotti* case, in which the U.S. Supreme Court upheld the bank's right to express its position in a state referendum but suggested that shareholders have a say on the matter.[1] As discussed in Chapter 12, "Political Participation," critics who would like to limit corporate political activity have proposed that the SEC require company disclosure or shareholder approval of company political action committees and company expenditures to support them, as well as shareholder approval prior to the advocating of positions on significant public policy issues.

The SEC staff report stated that an additional requirement for company disclosure of socially significant information is not presently needed but that board public policy committees and voluntary disclosure in annual reports could be regarded as positive corporate initiatives.

Another subject of the staff report involved corporate accountability and the beneficial owners of street-name stock. The staff recommended the development of means to identify the beneficial owners of stock held in a street or other name in order to provide for distribution of proxy material and other company information to all such shareholders. The staff also suggested that in the future the SEC consider means of prohibiting broker-dealers from voting proxies unless they had been instructed by beneficial owners. In April 1981, the SEC established an advisory committee on shareholder communications to develop a uniform system for distributing proxy material and other corporate communications to all shareholders in order to eliminate the voting of proxies by broker-dealers.

About 35 percent of all outstanding corporate shares are owned by institutional investors, such as pension and savings plans and investment funds of labor unions, companies, churches, and universities, as

---

[1]*Bank of Boston v. Bellotti*, 435 U.S. 765 (1978).

well as mutual funds. The SEC staff has taken increasing interest in the voting practices of such institutions. While recognizing that some institutional investors have been developing objective voting procedures, the staff report recommended that the SEC strongly encourage all of them to establish formal procedures to process proxy statements and reach voting decisions, to formulate criteria by which to decide how to vote, and to disclose their voting procedures and criteria. Because of the potential effect of institutional investors on corporate election results, the SEC has promised to monitor this area of concern. As discussed in Chapter 21 in the section "Labor Unions," general interest in that aspect of corporate governance has been spurred by the fact that labor unions are beginning to use their pension fund stockholdings as an organizing and bargaining weapon. In addition to labor unions, church-related organizations, cities, universities, and minority groups have the potential "pension fund power" to affect the policies, decisions, and conceivably, through coalitions, even the control of companies in which they hold substantial shares. Thus, if institutional investors exercise the voting rights of shares held by them, interesting problems will be posed, such as how the ownership interests of labor unions, church associations, and other large institutional investors would be brought into the corporate governance process.

The SEC requires a corporate management to advise shareholders of the nomination and electoral process of its company and to disclose in the proxy statement the fact that any director nominee serves another company that has a significant business relationship with the issues. The staff report, however, concluded that it is not practical for shareholders to nominate directors via access to the proxy statement. Nonetheless, in order to determine whether some form of rule would be necessary, the SEC staff stated that it would be monitoring corporate practices to determine the extent to which companies have nominating committees and are receptive to candidates whom shareholders recommend.

Apart from the SEC staff report, another idea of critics is for the SEC to broaden its definition of acceptable shareholder proposals. This proposal is intended to provide challenges to management on a wider range of questions and afford shareholders more numerous opportunities to express their influence by means of the corporate electoral process. A related proposal has been to reduce the minimum percentage of affirmative votes required for a rejected shareholder proposal to be reintroduced the following year. Other ideas involve facilitating shareholders' lawsuits, providing access to company-held shareholder lists, disclosing a variety of types of company information, and prohibiting what Nader has dubbed "crosstown hypocrisy." The last-named idea would require strict consistency between the statements that corporations make in public disclosures to the SEC and statements on the same subject for lobbying, litigation, or other purposes.

Most advocates of greater shareholder participation wish to change some aspect of corporate noneconomic performance. In fact, most shareholder proposals submitted to large companies in recent years have been made by leaders of public-interest or church-affiliated groups on social and political issues. While such shareholder resolutions have not caused much significant change in company policies and actions, they have attracted the attention of top managements, the media, and some institutional investors.

Reconciling the nineteenth-century concept of shareholder democracy in which some shareholders actively participated in management decisions and the reality of governing today's large corporations has proved to be an intractable problem. Participation by hundreds of thousands of geographically dispersed shareholders, thousands of pension and institutional investment funds, and countless unidentified individuals for whom shares are held beneficially would create problems that defy practical solution. Annual voting on what most shareholders regard as relatively straightforward matters stirs little interest among the vast majority of shareholders. There is little or no reason to believe that shareholders would not be equally or more apathetic if asked to vote on a series of complex management decisions. All but a tiny number of shareholders consider themselves principally as investors who do not have the time, background, or data necessary to be accountable for critical decisions involving difficult business problems. For these reasons, the focus for change in corporate governance has largely been on proposals to improve the performance of boards of directors.

# CHAPTER 17

# Boards of Directors

The extent to which chief executives and their corporate officers have exercised de facto control of large corporations was a key factor in the emergence of the third category of governance issues. While state incorporation laws typically require a company to be managed under the direction of a board of directors, there is considerable evidence that some large corporations have been managed by a chief executive and other top officers without sufficient accountability to or monitoring by their boards of directors. After revelations that some outside directors were poorly informed about conditions leading to the collapse of a number of companies, most notably the Penn Central Transportation Company, the corporate community was forcefully reminded that effective performance of corporate boards is an indispensable factor in the governance process. Subsequently, examples of questionable and illegal payments focused public attention on boards of directors and their accountability not only for legal and ethical behavior by management but for the types of corporate performance discussed in previous chapters.

The questionable and illegal payments that occurred in the 1970s became known through the disclosure process administered by the Securities and Exchange Commission (SEC) under the federal securities laws. The SEC and the Department of Justice subsequently brought civil and criminal suits against several companies and obtained consent decrees that required boards of directors to establish governance procedures to prevent future questionable and illegal acts.

The principal government response to the questionable corporate practices was that the SEC shaped and, in 1977, the Congress passed the Foreign Corrupt Practices Act (FCPA), which requires United States corporations, at home and abroad, to

- Keep financial records which, in "reasonable" detail, accurately and fairly reflect transactions and asset dispositions
- Maintain a system of internal accounting control sufficient to provide reasonable assurance that certain stated objectives are met

As discussed in Chapter 5, "Financial Reporting and Control," the FCPA's provision for accounting controls opened a new area for regulatory effort by the SEC. Authorities have thus described the FCPA as the most significant application of federal law to internal corporate affairs since the Securities Acts of 1933 and 1934, a statement that could be modified by proposed revisions to the act.

As chairman of the SEC during the Carter administration, Harold M. Williams was a leading advocate of improved performance by corporate boards of directors. He believed that voluntary corporate initiatives are by far preferable to further government regulation. The basis of his proposals was that boards of directors should be truly independent of management. He stated that management quite naturally is interested in a compatible and comfortable board membership, whereas large corporations, to assure the public that they are capable of self-discipline, need to create a countervailing force that works against the tendency to comfort.

To achieve a board environment of tension without antagonism, Chairman Williams advocated that the ideal board be constructed as follows: a company's legal counsel, bankers, and other suppliers should be excluded from its board, the only management member on its board should be the chief executive, and the chief executive should not serve as chairman. In a series of speeches during his tenure, he stated that these proposals were a call for voluntary change in order to preclude government action which public pressures would likely generate.[1]

Senator Howard M. Metzenbaum's proposed Protection of Shareholders' Rights Act included three requirements that would have affected corporate boards: (1) the majority of corporate board members would be independent (a requirement defined to exclude relatives, officers, legal counsel, bankers, and suppliers of a company); (2) there would be audit and nominating committees composed solely of independent directors with duties prescribed; and (3) directors would be

[1]Harold M. Williams, "Corporate Accountability—One Year Later," address to the Sixth Annual Securities Regulation Institute, San Diego, Calif., Jan. 8, 1979.

subject to duties of "loyalty" and "care" modeled after the American Bar Association's (ABA's) *Corporate Director's Guidebook* and its Model Business Corporation Act.

The public policy debate about the performance of corporate boards of directors includes the functions, composition, and operation of the corporate board.

## FUNCTIONS OF THE BOARD

The state corporation statutes' provision that corporate affairs be "managed by" or be "managed under the direction of" the board of directors has generally been construed to mean that the board of directors has ultimate company authority aside from matters requiring shareholder approval, such as prior review of mergers and election of directors. The quoted language, although commonly understood as not requiring full-time management duty, is vague enough to have stimulated the interest of members of the legal, business, and academic communities in defining the corporate board's proper functions. Their efforts have largely been concerned with the functions that independent directors can realistically perform in the interest of strengthening corporate accountability.

While expressed in different ways, the generally accepted functions of the corporate board are these: (1) approval or disapproval of proposed major strategic business decisions, (2) election and removal of the chief executive officer and other senior executives and recommendation of candidates for the board of directors, (3) review of financial results and prospects, (4) monitoring of the company's social and political impacts, and (5) establishment of performance standards against which to evaluate both company performance and the performance and compensation of its top executives.

Criticism that the boards of many large companies have not performed some or all of these functions or have not performed them adequately has led to proposals for changes in the boards' composition and operation to help assure the independence of corporate boards.

## COMPOSITION OF THE BOARD

A basic criticism has been that boards of large companies have been predominantly composed of top executives of other corporations, lawyers, bankers, and suppliers affiliated with the companies, and company officers who report to the chief executives. These relationships have created the objection that such board members cannot in practice be sufficiently independent to require the chief executive to be accountable to the board. As Victor M. Earle III, general counsel of the public accounting firm of Peat, Marwick, Mitchell & Co., has put it, "The result of all this was that the managers of the business, the supposed servants of the shareholders, effectively became their own supervisors and the control ostensibly exercised by the board of directors became wholly formal."[2]

This basic criticism has raised a variety of proposals by Chairman Williams, Senator Metzenbaum, various legal scholars, and corporate critics. The principal proposals concerning charges in the composition of corporate boards are these:

### Independent Directors

Critics have alleged that unless at least a majority of the directors on a board are truly independent, the board must be presumed to be subservient to the chief executive. At one time, nonmanagement, or outside, directors were generally considered independent. Today, a more common definition of an independent director is one who is not a member or former member of management or an outside legal counsel, banker, or any other supplier of services to a company. A stricter definition also excludes anyone who has a significant family or economic relationship with the chief executive or another key officer.

In recent years, there has been a trend toward boards of large companies with a majority of independent directors. The executive search firm of Heidrick & Struggles found in its 1980 study on corporate boards of directors that independent directors, without ties as suppliers or family members, constituted a majority of the typical board of large corporations. They also learned that 45 percent of the companies planned to have a greater percentage of independent directors in the future.[3]

The shift to boards with predominantly independent directors has not satisfied those who advocate that all board members except the chief executive officer be independent directors. Nonetheless, that proposal has met with skepticism by corporate leaders who are overwhelmingly convinced that the specific company knowledge of officers cannot be replaced by whatever general qualifications outside directors might have. On the other hand, critics have acknowledged the importance of having company officers attend board meetings and

[2]Victor M. Earle III, "Corporate Governance and the Outside Director—A Modest Proposal," *Washington and Lee Law Review*, summer, 1979, pp. 787–788.
[3]Heidrick & Struggles, Inc., *The Changing Board*, 1980 update.

make presentations but point out that these acts do not require these officers to be members who participate in board decisions. Corporate leaders disagree and stress the importance of having several top officers participate as board members in decisions as well as in sharing the accountability and liability for them. They also stress that top officers should not be supplicants but should serve as full members and acquire board experience as potential candidates for promotion to the office of chief executive.

The importance of having a core of management directors on a corporate board has been emphasized by corporate leaders who have experience as both chief executives and outside directors. Du Pont's Irving Shapiro has affirmed that the objective of an independent board is unassailable but opines that boards without people who understand the complexities of business today would result in incompetent leadership. Shapiro also has noted that there is already a shortage of qualified board candidates and that if some company officers are not included the shortage will be aggravated. Another factor is that the need to avoid potential conflicts of interest precludes selection of many people who know enough about an industry to replace company officers. The net result, Shapiro has pointed out, would be that corporate boards would be composed of members who were less competent than those at present. He also has stated that a board of outsiders could be easily manipulated by a skillful chief executive officer, who would be the board's only member with a close personal knowledge of the business.[4]

The increasing legal liability of directors has become a factor that has contributed to the greater difficulty in finding independent directors, whether qualified by business, public service, academic, or scientific experience. Dean Courtney Brown described this limitation:

> In recent years, a number of judicial decisions have enlarged the requirement of prudence in a director. Federal courts have held that board members must now be fully informed, ultra-careful regarding possible conflicts of interest, and scrupulous not to use inside information for personal benefit. They must develop more than a cursory knowledge of the company and the field or fields in which it operates. They must confirm the accuracy of important reporting documents such as registration statements and proxy material. Self-dealing, inside trading, and conflicts of interest are subject to heavy penalty. Any one or several of these requirements, if violated, can be accompanied by large liability.[5]

[4]Irving S. Shapiro, "Corporate Governance," Fairless Lecture Series, Carnegie-Mellon University, Pittsburgh, Pa., Oct. 24, 1979.

[5]Courtney Brown, *Putting the Corporate Board to Work*, Macmillan Publishing Co., Inc., New York, 1976, p. 107. Copyright © 1976, The Trustees of Columbia University in the City of New York. Reprinted by permission of The Free Press.

As large corporations have become more heavily involved in social and political problems, many of them have searched for talented people to broaden the perspective and improve the effectiveness of their boards. Many large companies have to a greater extent used the long-standing practice of selecting directors with substantial public service and academic or scientific experience who can bring important perspectives to their boards. Corporations have increasingly looked for and selected women and members of minority groups with these backgrounds. These sources, as in recruitment of employees at all levels, were largely untapped in the past. According to Heidrick & Struggles, the proportion of companies with at least one woman director increased from 21 percent in 1976 to 40 percent in 1980; the proportion of those with at least one ethnic-minority member increased from 15 percent in 1976 to 19 percent in 1980. Heidrick & Struggles nevertheless found that 98.28 percent of the members of the total boards in their 1980 study were white males.[6] Many women and minority-group members who obviously meet the traditional qualifications for board membership have already been elected directors of large companies. Some observers believe that, for the numbers of women and minority directors to increase significantly, companies will have to select able people with likely potential rather than hold out for those with fully established credentials.

## The Board Chairman as an Independent Director

This proposal is intended to help make corporate boards truly independent by avoiding any suggestion of conflict of interest, in fact or appearance, between management (if the chief executive were chairman) and the interests of the shareholders and other constituents. Specific examples discussed variously in this book that can be causes of conflict of interest are the pressures on and motivations of management that tend to favor short-term results while the interests of the company and its shareholders tend to be longer-term. Another reason for this proposal is that setting the board's agenda can, in itself, have a powerful effect on the independence and the effectiveness of the board, and thus some authorities believe that it should not be controlled by the chief executive. A third reason is a desire to separate the policy function of the board from the executive and operating functions of management.

The corporate community has strongly opposed the separation of the two positions and has backed up its objection with its practice.

[6]Heidrick & Struggles, op. cit.

Heidrick & Struggles reported that in 75 percent of the companies responding to its 1980 survey the chairman and the chief executive were the same person and that the incidence of this combination increased with company size.[7] According to most authorities, the principal reasons that most companies do not separate those positions are examples of friction that have developed between the incumbents to the detriment of the effective performance of their boards and companies, as well as the anomaly of a chairman who lacks the detailed operational knowledge that his board expects and that comes naturally to the chief executive officer.

A 1978 statement of the Business Roundtable cited the need for strong, independent directors and commented on the separation of the board chairman and the chief executive officer:

> We note first that some companies have at particular times separated the role of CEO and the board chairman and that this has worked well on those occasions where the two individuals involved were compatible and where there was a clear delineation of the two roles. In other cases, however, the separation seems not to have worked well and to have been abandoned.
>
> The general experience of the Roundtable members has been that the board functions well where the CEO also serves as chairman and where there is no sharp organizational line drawn between the board and operating management. It would be a mistake to suppose that the board can perform its mission apart from the chief executive officer or in an adversary relationship with him.[8]

### Constituency Directors

Another idea that has been proposed as a means to help make corporate boards more broadly accountable is the selection of so-called constituency directors to represent respectively consumer, environmental, labor union, racial, and other interests. The idea of constituency directors has been supported primarily by leaders of public-interest groups. Also, except for the special situation involving government, management, and union efforts to save the Chrysler Corporation from bankruptcy, the European practice of codetermination, in which labor union representatives are members of corporate boards, has not appeared in the United States.

Most authorities on corporate governance believe that such single-

[7]Ibid.
[8]*The Role and Composition of the Board of Directors of the Large Publicly Owned Corporation*, Business Roundtable, New York, January 1978, p. 15.

interest directors would create a divisive and antagonistic atmosphere. John K. Tabor, a partner of the Washington law firm of Reavis & McGrath, has criticized constituency directorships in these words:

> Constituency directors by definition would bring to their task a conflict of interest. They would also lack knowledge of how to run a large business enterprise successfully. Their assured political debate would destroy the decisiveness, innovativeness, and risktaking which are the source of the U.S. corporation's success.[9]

## OPERATION OF THE BOARD

Better definition of board functions and changes in the composition of directors have improved the performance of the boards of most large companies. Other factors that are critical to the effective operation of corporate boards are committees, internal company controls, flow of information to the board, orientation and education of board members, and use of public disclosure.

### Board Committees

There has been a trend toward the bolstering of existing board committees and the creation of additional ones. That trend and the movement toward an independent board have propelled independent directors into the chair of or membership on board committees.

For the purpose of corporate accountability, the key board committees are audit, nominating, and compensation. The SEC requires disclosure concerning the existence, membership, and activities of these committees, and the New York Stock Exchange since 1977 has required its listed companies to have an audit committee composed solely of outside directors, as defined by its rules. It is interesting to note that 3 years earlier 80 percent of the exchange's listed companies had audit committees and that, of those, 84 percent were composed of outside or nonmanagement directors. In effect, the exchange's rule largely confirmed a practice that was already commonplace in the corporate world. As working oversight groups, audit committees can convey within the company and to the outside world that corporate performance is seriously monitored.

Audit committees have a wide range of duties, but an agreed key

[9]John K. Tabor, "Federal Chartering and Corporate Governance," address to the Public Affairs Council, Washington, Jan. 27, 1977.

purpose is to monitor the integrity of the corporation's financial information used in decision making and financial reporting. According to Victor Earle, "The audit committee performs this function by reviewing significant financial information, inquiring into the corporation's internal control and accounting practices, consulting with the inside and outside directors, and reviewing changes in accounting principles." [10]

The purposes of the nominating committee are, in the long and short terms, to search for and recommend candidates for the board for election by the shareholders and to select chief executives and other company officers for election by the board. A board with a nominating committee composed solely or largely of independent directors is not as yet common. However, in their 1980 study Heidrick & Struggles reported on a trend toward greater influence by nominating committees in this way:

> In 1976, the chief executive officer was most frequently the initial decision-maker in approving board prospects. At that time, the entire board acting as a group ranked a distant second, followed by the executive committee. The nominating committee served as initial decision-maker in only 8.2 percent of the companies. In 1980 the nominating committee leads the chief executive officer acting alone, and all other alternative decision-makers, in 45.5 percent of the organizations. This committee holds sway in 69.2 percent of the premier-size companies. [11]

A compensation committee of outside directors, particularly one that obtains advice on executive compensation and perquisites from an outside consultant, can help to avoid allegations that the chief executive and other officers are instrumental in setting their own compensation and perquisites.

On the basis of the successful use of these committees, many large corporations have established others such as conflict of interest, finance, and one variously called corporate responsibility, social responsibility, public issues, or, most frequently, public policy. The Conference Board has reported that since the General Motors Board of Directors established its public policy committee in 1970 almost 100 major companies have set up such committees to give board-level attention to matters of special public concern such as corporate performance issues. [12] Most such committees include outside directors who have public policy experience. Examples of such people cited by

[10]Earle, op. cit., p. 802.
[11]Heidrick & Struggles, op. cit.
[12]*Corporate Directorship Practices: The Public Policy Committee*, Conference Board, Inc., New York, 1980.

*Dun's Review* are Anne Armstrong, former ambassador to Great Britain (General Motors); Jerome Weisner, former MIT president (Celanese Corp.); Barbara Jordan, former member of Congress (Mead Corp.); and Paul McCracken, former chairman of the President's Council of Economic Advisers (Dow Chemical Company).[13]

Public policy committees are intended to serve a dual role: they look externally to see how public issues, social trends, and interest groups may impact their company; and they monitor company performance in order to consider appropriate policies and programs to deal with the external environment.

## Internal Company Controls

As discussed in Chapter 5, "Financial Reporting and Control," the SEC, Congress, and corporate executives have directed attention to corporate internal accounting and other control systems. Management attention was spurred by both the New York Stock Exchange requirement for a board audit committee of outside directors and the provision of the FCPA that requires an adequate system of internal accounting controls.

In addition to accounting control systems, other management controls have been adopted or strengthened. As discussed in Chapter 7, "Legal and Ethical Behavior," many companies have systems to monitor such critical matters of their performance as adherence to antitrust and other basic laws, as well as specific areas of public concern such as consumer and environmental protection and equal opportunity. There also has been widespread interest in adopting, updating, or reintroducing company codes of business conduct.

Internal control systems have proved to be most effective when the board and management establish both general standards of business conduct and specific performance objectives that incorporate relevant social and political factors and short- and longer-term profit goals. Such standards and objectives can provide a basis for the board to evaluate company performance and that of responsible key executives in terms of the present and ongoing interests of the company and its shareholders. Company control and evaluation systems help to place the board in the flow of critical information, which itself is an important aspect of board operation and performance.

## Flow of Information to the Board

As the Business Roundtable has pointed out, some corporate failures have been traceable in large measure to the fact that directors were

[13]"A Useful New Tool for Company Boards," *Dun's Review*, October 1980, p. 101.

inadequately informed. The Roundtable has emphasized that cutting across all the board functions is "the board's responsibility to establish in conjunction with the chief executive officer, systems and procedures to assure that there is a flow of information to the board sufficient to permit the effective discharge of its obligations."[14]

There is general agreement that a necessary flow of information should include regular reports by operating management of a company's important businesses and by corporate staff functions such as financial, legal, employee relations, and public affairs. There is also agreement that communication between outside auditors and the board's audit committee should be emphasized, and many companies have adopted a similar type of communication between the board's audit committee and the internal auditing staff.

Some outside directors have stated that they require the assistance of a staff that is independent of management. Their reason is either that they have not been able to get needed information or, as Arthur Goldberg, the former U.S. Supreme Court justice, announced when he resigned from the board of Trans World Airlines in 1972, that directors should avoid being dependent for information on the management they are supposed to monitor. While there is general recognition that outside directors may need outside legal, accounting, or other expert counsel in special circumstances, the idea of a regular staff has been strongly opposed as being divisive and factionalizing. On the other hand, a reference point within management for directors seeking information is a widespread and sound practice.

### Orientation and Education of Board Members

Various authorities have suggested that, in lieu of adopting a potentially divisive and costly separate staff, boards and their managements should provide comprehensive orientation for new directors. One prescription for new directors' orientation has been made by Victor Earle:

> A new director would, for example, review the financial statements, meet with corporate officers, attend some meetings of committees on which he does not serve, meet with the outside auditors and regular corporate counsel, and assure himself that board meetings will be held regularly. A new director should also satisfy himself that an agenda will be circulated in advance, that dissent is acceptable, and that minutes of meetings are kept and circulated.[15]

[14]*The Role and Composition of the Board of Directors of the Large Publicly Owned Corporation*, op. cit., pp. 4–5.
[15]Earle, op. cit., p. 802.

The orientation of new directors whose background is substantial public service, academic, or scientific experience should logically emphasize company and industry fundamentals. Equally important is provision to all new directors of knowledge of the aspects of the external environment and the public policy issues of special concern to the company whose board they are joining. Many company boards provide the ABA's *Corporate Director's Guidebook* as a feature of the orientation of new members.

Another response to the need for more effective boards of directors has been a variety of educational programs for both new and experienced directors. Some are professional meetings conducted by the ABA and the American Society of Corporate Secretaries and by the Financial Executives Institute. Others are intensive programs conducted by universities such as New York University and the University of Michigan. A comprehensive educational program is carried out by the National Association of Corporate Directors (NACD), one of the American Management Associations. The NACD's purpose is to keep its members informed on relevant boardroom issues by publication, briefings, and conferences.

Victor Earle foresees the need for professional schools for new and experienced directors. His proposal is for "institutes of corporate governance" as adjuncts to several university business and law schools. He has likened these institutes to the schools for trial judges and state governors. With a faculty drawn from the sponsoring schools and authorities from corporations and government, Earle visualizes that the institutes would provide directors with these benefits:

> First, they will acquire the vocational skills that they need to do their job. Second, they will contribute to the incremental development, in a scholarly atmosphere, of a body of jurisprudence on corporate governance.[16]

## The Board's Use of Public Disclosure

Not only are internal controls and a flow of information necessary for effective board performance, but they place the board in a position to use the process of public disclosure as a means of building shareholder and public confidence. Irving Shapiro has commented that corporate boards are the first place to look for policies that can help restore trust and respect. He has explained that people are not interested in disclosure of commercial secrets and, in fact, that directors and

[16]Victor M. Earle III, "A Stop at School on the Way to the Boardroom," *Fortune*, July 2, 1979.

managers would be delinquent if they failed to protect proprietary knowledge. Shapiro's point is:

> What people want to know is not what the company is doing commercially, but simply what kind of people are running the show. In effect they are asking "Who are you and what do you believe in?" Neither question is hard to answer and, in view of the leverage that large corporations have on people's lives today, it is difficult to see why anyone in a position of corporate governance would decline to answer.

In endorsing the idea of the establishment by corporate boards of more open policies of public disclosure, Shapiro concludes with this statement:

> The large corporation has long since earned its mark as an effective instrument for production and distribution. The task now is not to bring drastic change to the corporate interior, turning business units into instruments of the national government, but to make those shifts that will best demonstrate that the large corporation is in the hands of people who are not only competent but also cognizant of the world around them, and properly accountable.[17]

In addition to advocating voluntary disclosure, Shapiro and John D. deButts, former chairman of AT&T, as members of Senator Metzenbaum's Advisory Committee on Corporate Governance, stated that the public-disclosure provisions of the securities laws are effective and proper and should not be replaced with prescriptive legislation on matters of corporate governance.[18]

---

[17]Shapiro, op. cit., pp. 14–15.

[18]Irving S. Shapiro and John D. deButts, "Memorandum on Federal Corporate Governance Legislation," written as members of Sen. Howard M. Metzenbaum's Advisory Committee on Corporate Governance, Apr. 27, 1979, pp. 1–2.

# CHAPTER 18

# The Corporate Governance
# Issues in Context

As noted throughout this book, the underlying reason for public concern about the large corporation is the power of corporate executives by their decision-making authority to affect people, other institutions, and the physical and social environments. Acceptable, even exemplary, performance is taken for granted. Corporate performance that adversely affects people or their interests is usually regarded as abuse of management power, and it prompts demands for more effective corporate accountability. The broad public dissatisfaction with many aspects of corporate performance, highlighted by the glaring examples of illegal corporate behavior in the mid-1970s, focused attention on the corporate governance issues as a means of controlling the large corporation at the top.

## RELATIONSHIP OF THE CORPORATE
## PERFORMANCE AND GOVERNANCE ISSUES

The corporate governance and performance issues are clearly interrelated. In the keynote address at the Rice University Conference on Corporate Governance in the 1980s, Robert S. Hatfield, when chairman of the board of the Continental Group, Inc., confirmed this relationship:

> Make no mistake: corporate governance is an important issue but let's recognize it for what it really is. The debate over corporate governance is

a surrogate for the debate over the crucial substantive corporate performance issues.[1]

The causal relationship between corporate performance and corporate governance holds an opportunity for corporate managements. Just
as publicly unacceptable corporate performance was instrumental in
generating (or regenerating from previous eras) the governance issues,
the achievement of publicly acceptable corporate performance over
time will relieve public and political pressures for both specific
regulations regarding performance and the overall regulation of governance. In fact, there is evidence that this is happening. The attention that
the managements of most large corporations have given to assure legal
behavior by their executives and employees since the mid-1970s has
moderated this issue and, in turn, must be credited with lessening the
prospects of many of the governance reform proposals.

There are other reasons that commend corporate managements to
concentrate on effective corporate performance as the basis of resolving
both the performance and the governance issues:

- The corporate performance issues, while often complex, are suscepti-
  ble to action by management. In contrast, except for the types of
  changes involving boards of directors that have already been made or
  are being made, the governance issues are much less tractable.

- The corporate performance issues are well known, remain highly
  visible, and are important to large segments of the American people.
  In contrast, corporate governance is an arcane subject, normally of
  small interest except to certain specialists in business, the law, and
  the behavioral sciences. Existing contemporary public and government interest has been stimulated by fear of the abuse of corporate
  power, illustrated by recurring examples of corporate wrongdoing.

- The proliferation of government intervention to control corporate
  performance is cumbersome to management and costly to consumers
  and shareholders and ultimately can only be threatening to private
  enterprise. Governmental control of governance, however, is an even
- greater threat. Harold Williams, as chairman of the Securities and
  Exchange Commission (SEC), made this point in a speech in which he
  urged voluntary steps to improve board performance and accountability:

> The eventual painful lesson may be that it is one thing for the federal
> government to legislate on discrete social impacting issues, such as safety

[1]Robert S. Hatfield, "The Changing Corporate Environment: Problems and Opportunities," address to the Rice University Conference on Corporate Governance in the 1980s,
Houston, Aug. 8, 1980.

standards; it is another for it to begin to deal directly with the process by which private economic activity is directed and controlled.[2]

## CORPORATE INITIATIVES AND ACTIONS

There is a good deal of evidence that corporate leaders, assisted by others in the private sector and prodded by the SEC and Congress, have made substantial progress in recent years in improving the governance process in most large corporations. As early as 1978, former SEC Chairman Roderick M. Hills, in addressing the American Assembly, characterized that progress as "awesome."[3] Later that year, in a nationwide study, shareholders in publicly held United States corporations expressed basic satisfaction with the composition of boards of directors as structured and elected.[4] Corporate initiatives have mostly been concerned with improving the performance and accountability of the boards of directors. That emphasis has been logical, since the board is the aspect of corporate governance for which corporate leaders have direct responsibility and the most practical opportunity to effect change.

The principal results of initiatives and actions taken by most major companies to improve the quality of performance and accountability of boards of directors are these:

1. Definition of board functions and operating procedures to guide board members and management in their respective and joint roles
2. Independent directors as a majority of the typical board of large companies
3. Increased numbers of directors with public service, academic, and scientific experience, including women and members of minority groups
4. Near-unanimous use of auditing committees composed of independent directors and with access to both outside and inside auditors
5. In many companies, nominating committees with a majority of independent directors that encourage shareholders' recommendations, nominate board candidates for election by shareholders, and

[2]Harold M. Williams, "Corporate Accountability: The Board of Directors," address delivered at the Securities Regulation Institute, San Diego, Calif. Jan. 18, 1978.
[3]Roderick M. Hills, "After Awesome Gains, Caution in Corporate Governance," *Financier,* June 1978, p. 15.
[4]Opinion Research Corporation, quoted in *Roundtable Report,* no. 78-9, December 1978.

nominate the chief executive and other officers for election by the board

6. In many companies, compensation committees composed largely or entirely of outside directors that evaluate top executives' performance and determine the terms and conditions of their employment

7. In about 100 major companies, public policy committees that give board-level attention to company policies and performance on subjects of special public concern

8. Internal management and accounting control systems

9. Codes of business conduct, including standards of executive behavior with their effectiveness monitored and audited by company management and board committees

10. An improved flow of information to board members necessary for them to perform effectively

11. A substantial increase in the voluntary disclosure of company information about policies, activities, plans, and performance as a form of accountability to constituent interests

The Business Roundtable in 1980 referred to these initiatives as a dramatic and continuing evolution in corporate governance mechanisms in a statement prepared under the direction of the Roundtable's Corporate Responsibility Task Force, headed by BankAmerica's chief executive officer, A. W. Clausen, before he became president of the World Bank. In addition to crediting increased reliance on nonmanagement directors and corporate codes of conduct for strengthened corporate accountability, the statement singled out pervasive corporate disclosure as perhaps the most important factor of all.[5]

## OTHER PRIVATE-SECTOR INITIATIVES AND ACTIONS

Beyond the eleven substantive corporate initiatives and actions, other private-sector steps have been taken to help improve the corporate governance process. A section of the American Bar Association (ABA) has written and updated the Model Business Corporation Act. That act, which has been adopted in more than twenty-five states and major portions of it in other states, defines among other things responsibilities

[5]"Dramatic Advances in Corporate Governance Preclude Need for New Legislation," *Roundtable Report,* Business Roundtable, November 1980, pp. 3–4.

of boards of directors and the directors' duty of loyalty and duty of care. The same ABA section has published the *Corporate Director's Guidebook*, which provides orderly advice and reference material for corporate directors on the proper performance of their role. The American Society of Corporate Secretaries has recommended the *Guidebook* to its more than 1700 member companies, and it is in wide use today. W. M. Batten, chairman of the New York Stock Exchange, has testified that these private initiatives have had a desirable influence in deepening the perception of directors of business corporations as to their responsibilities.[6]

A seminal private initiative was the joint business-academic study at the Harvard Graduate School of Business Administration in May 1977, which in turn led to a 1978 statement of the Business Roundtable, *The Role and Composition of the Board of Directors of the Large Publicly Owned Corporation.*[7] The statement recommended:

*Concerning the role of directors,* that directors, prepared by an effective information system, should participate in free and open discussion of corporate policies and actions at board meetings, should cope with key aspects of governance through audit, compensation, and nominating committee work and, as members of the full board, have specific and vital corporate functions to perform.

*Concerning the selection of directors,* that board succession and chief executive officer succession be the responsibility of the board; that a nominating committee composed of a majority of outside directors recommend to the board the choice of candidates for directors and top management; that directors possess "independence, an inquiring mind, . . . and broad experience." The statement endorsed the tendency of United States corporations to move to a board structure based on a majority of outside directors. It concluded that it is difficult to see a board so selected and populated as "submissive."

*Concerning the shareholder role in director selection,* that the SEC revise Rule 14a-8, if necessary, to permit shareowners to propose amendments of corporate bylaws which would provide nomination by shareowners of candidates for election to the board.

*Concerning the knowledge of directors,* that the board in conjunction with the chief executive officer establish systems and procedures to

[6]William M. Batten, "Letter to Senator Howard M. Metzenbaum," written as a member of Senator Metzenbaum's Advisory Committee on Corporate Governance, Apr. 24, 1979, pp. 2–3.

[7]*The Role and Composition of the Board of Directors of the Large Publicly Owned Corporation,* Business Roundtable, New York, January 1978, pp. 4–5.

assure a flow of information to the board sufficient to permit the effective discharge of its obligations and such additional information as any member deems necessary.

*Concerning board homogeneity,* that directors reflect "a variety of experience and background" and be selected from managers, people experienced in public life, academics, scientists, members of minority groups, and women.

*Concerning time,* that time spent on a task is not the sole criterion of effectiveness. A well-designed information system and effective committee work can enable intelligent directors to accomplish the scheduled periodic review of management performance and other important matters responsibly in a limited period.

These corporate initiatives and actions, centering on strengthening board performance and accountability, also protect shareholder rights and respond to some proposals of those who espouse federal governance legislation.

The American Law Institute's project on corporate governance is an additional private initiative. Its principal purpose is to analyze the large amount of existing law affecting directors and "controlling persons" and to make recommendations pertaining to the legal duties incident to corporate management and control.

## THE OUTLOOK

While it is recognized that further changes in corporate governance will emerge, there appear to be only cosmetic or impractical ways that corporate managements could initiate an increase in shareholder participation in corporate decisions. Corporate executives have pointed out that most such "shareholder democracy" proposals range from the unrealistic to the impossible. They reason that to manage a large corporation by the political processes of initiative and referendum would weaken management decision making and enervate the competitiveness of United States business enterprise. Moreover, to encourage the belief that shareholder democracy which would provide for direct shareholder participation in corporate decisions is needed and possible would be a delusion, and to initiate cosmetic forms of participation would be disingenuous.

Corporate leaders find even less reason to support the concept of federal chartering or a federal law of corporate governance. Contemporary corporate developments are providing a continuing strengthening of corporate accountability through increased reliance upon independent directors, effective board committees, independent audit, nominating, public policy, and compensation committees, practical recognition of the right of shareholders to participate in the corporate electoral process, corporate codes of conduct, emphasis upon corporate legal and ethical compliance mechanisms, and, perhaps most important of all, pervasive corporate disclosure.

In addition, there exist effective legislative and regulatory restraints upon corporate conduct by means of state incorporation codes, government regulation of corporate performance when required, and SEC regulation and oversight featuring disclosure directed toward improving aspects of corporate governance.

Finally, federal laws governing the internal structure of corporations and the rights and duties of shareholders, directors, and officers would create a further concentration of federal power. In contrast, chartering the corporation under state law has helped to avoid the conjunction in the federal government of political and economic power and preserves two important aspects of the separation of powers that has served our country well for two centuries.

Harold Williams, when chairman of the SEC, expressed the heart of the matter:

> While some apparently believe that legislation is the key to reform, I am concerned that federal encroachment into the board room would likely cripple rather than strengthen its functioning.
>
> It would be unfortunate if legislation introduced in the name of improving corporate accountability had the effect of stopping private sector initiative in its tracks. Our goal is to change behavior, not the law.[8]

Effective boards of directors and company managements that meet reasonable public expectations of corporate performance are not likely to be faced with the arcane and esoteric issues of corporate governance and corporate legitimacy. Few shareholders other than some avowed social activists want their companies to be governed as a shareholder democracy under a federal charter. The vast majority of shareholders will continue to opt for a well-qualified board of directors and a professional management that is accountable to them, to state and federal laws, and to the discipline of the competitive market system, is sensitive to the constraints of public and peer pressures, and, in addition, conveys a sense of voluntary accountability to the larger

---

[8]Harold M. Williams, statement before the Subcommittee on Securities of the Senate Banking Committee in connection with hearings on the proposed Protection of Shareholders' Rights Act of 1980, Nov. 19, 1980.

society.

William M. Batten, chairman of the New York Stock Exchange, has advised corporate leaders that the arrival of a so-called probusiness administration in Washington did not signal the end to the corporate governance crusade for laws and regulations that would curb managements' freedom to manage.[9] Notwithstanding the corporate and private-sector initiatives and actions taken in recent years, the governance issues remain a threat in being to the corporate community. As in the case of the issue of legal and ethical behavior, whenever significant malpractices in corporate performance occur, the governance issues come to the fore. This consequence, of course, is an important reason for directing management attention to publicly acceptable company performance as a basis for resolving both the performance and the governance issues. To do this clearly challenges the corporate board of directors to provide a system of governance and to insist on types of performance that engender public trust in their shareholders' company and help assure its success and continuity.

[9]William M. Batten, "Why I Do Not Want to Talk about Corporate Governance," Bracebridge H. Young Memorial Address at the National Conference of the American Society of Corporate Secretaries, Inc., June 25, 1981.

# PART FOUR

# The Corporate Executive and the Public Policy Environment

T he corporate performance issues are essentially a product of interaction among the large corporation and its executives, the external environment, and the other participants in the public policy process. The issues are rooted in the many elements of corporate performance and executive conduct, and their development is influenced by the external environment: the social, economic, political and technological factors that cause changes in the larger society. The direction, intensity, and resolution of the corporate issues are, of course, greatly affected by the major participants in the public policy process: government, the media, public-interest groups, the small-business community, labor unions, and the intellectual community.

Chapter 19 deals with examples of executive conduct that have adversely affected public perceptions of the large corporation and its leadership. Chapter 20 briefly describes the social, economic, political, and technological context of the corporate issues. Chapter 21 discusses the status of the other major participants in the public policy process.

While it is not possible or necessary for purposes of this book to predict specific outcomes, it is clear that external forces, both existing and presently unforeseeable, will affect and, in many instances, be affected by the large corporation well into the future. This dynamic alone ensures that the corporate performance issues are not passing phenomena but will continue to challenge management's persistence, courage, and imagination in seeking constructive solutions.

# CHAPTER 19

# Executive Conduct and Public Perception

Among the most subtle but critical influences on the performance of the large corporation, and to an even greater degree on the public's perception of that performance, are the personal behavior and attitudes of senior executives. The conduct of top executives can be a force for good or for bad. The good characterizes most executive conduct. Behavior that meets society's generally accepted standards of integrity, decency, and civility is expected and taken for granted. Behavior that does not is inimical to the executives themselves, their companies, and public perceptions of corporations in general. This adverse behavior is the subject of this chapter.

Inappropriate or insensitive conduct by executives is not an issue comparable to the corporate performance or governance issues. Indeed, such conduct is often welcomed by critics and is cited as evidence of the personal characteristics and motivations of top executives that make them insensitive to the interests of others and impair their ability or willingness to deal with the issues and their causes. In keeping with the objective of understanding better the ways in which large corporations and their executives can regain public trust and confidence, this chapter is intended for self-assessment rather than commendation. It is aimed at helping to understand this nagging question: Why is there so little public confidence and trust in corporate leaders?

It can be argued that the personal behavior and attitudes of executives are not relevant to their business activities and that they certainly should not affect public attitudes about their companies' performance. It can also be unfair to an individual to generalize about executives' diverse styles, behavior, and attitudes. There are, apart from those established in law, few objective standards.

Nevertheless, there is convincing evidence that some types of behavior by executives generate a dangerously negative public reaction toward the large corporation itself. In the public mind executives personify their companies, and public anger or revulsion at the behavior of some executives is readily translated into dissatisfaction with the performance of the corporation. A similar translation occurs in politics, in which, for example, public anger at the personal conduct of Richard Nixon in the White House helped to fuel broader dissatisfaction with his administration.

In reaching such judgments about corporate executives, people make significant distinctions between entrepreneurs and professional managers. Opinion research has consistently shown that the public respects entrepreneurs, especially the founders of successful companies. However, professional managers, even the top executives of the largest corporations, are seen quite differently by the public. In their analysis of opinion surveys, Lipset and Schneider concluded that the public sees most corporate executives as motivated basically by self-interest and that it resents executive conduct which is seen as the use of power for that purpose.[1]

Occasional examples of a flamboyant "executive lifestyle" thus are a reason for concern about the extent and uses of executives' power. They also act to confirm public suspicions that executives are insulated from many inconveniences and adversities and, as a result, are insensitive to the day-to-day concerns of the citizenry, including the adverse impacts of corporate performance on people. Behavior that fosters the twin beliefs that executives misuse corporate power to advance their own self-interest and that they don't care about what concerns the public holds explosive consequences for the large corporation.

While it is difficult to define precisely the conduct that is inimical to public perceptions of executives and corporations (indeed, specific standards change over time), certain broad behavioral patterns can be identified, and some discussion of them may be helpful to executives who want to see executive behavior as others do. This chapter identifies behavior and attitudes that are counterproductive; it consists largely of comments by executives themselves, not by critics of the corporation.

[1]Seymour Martin Lipset and William Schneider, *The Confidence Gap: How Americans View Their Institutions*, Macmillan Publishing Co., Inc., New York, 1981. Copyright © 1981, The Trustees of Columbia University in the City of New York. Reprinted by permission of The Free Press.

## UNDESIRABLE BEHAVIOR

Sometimes the *way* in which executives conduct their business activities creates an adverse impression even though the activities themselves may be desirable and necessary. This section offers some examples.

Executive behavior that generates adverse public attitudes supports the common belief that executives are motivated by self-interest. It leads to a public conclusion that corporate executives *as a group* are greedy and selfish, willing to use their power as company executives for their own advantage. In speaking of the poor track record of business-endorsed economic education programs, Daniel J. Krumm, president of the Maytag Co., was quoted by *The Wall Street Journal* as saying that "like it or not, people simply do not equate businessmen with the free enterprise system. Rather, they see business people as self-serving individuals, trying hard to fortify their own position."[2] How well executives exercise discipline in their use of perquisites such as limousines, aircraft, and clubs strongly influences this perception.

Executive self-discipline is especially important because the combined burden of great responsibility and the prerogatives of high office can breed arrogance or the impression of arrogance. Arrogance can cause officials of any institution to reject criticism out of hand, particularly on such matters as their performance or behavior. With respect to corporate executives, Sister Jane Scully, president of Carlow College and a corporate director, has perceived occasional examples of behavior which suggest that "management knows best for the corporation or the nation, or they know better than you." Executives exhibiting such certainty (or arrogance), she says, sometimes fail to "see the validity of complaints from the outside."[3]

Closely linked to arrogance is infallibility. It is rare for executives to acknowledge that they or their companies might have made a mistake or might be at fault. The common response to corporate error is to use legally correct, often self-damaging statements. A typical example of corporate statements that follow a *nolo contendere* settlement for alleged damage is worded in this way: "Company officials denied any wrongdoing or any liability and stressed that the settlement should not be construed as an admission of liability." Such statements, made to avoid further litigation, simply are not credible to much of the public; they also further erode public trust and weaken the credibility even of

[2]Daniel J. Krumm, in "Notable and Quotable," *The Wall Street Journal*, Nov. 2, 1977, p. 22.

[3]"Sister Jane of Gulf Oil," *The New York Times*, Mar. 7, 1976, sec. III, p. 7. © 1976 by The New York Times Company. Reprinted by permission.

corporate good news. They also are used as evidence of corporate hypocrisy.

Inconsistency or even hypocrisy sometimes is an element in executive speeches and more frequently in advertising and corporate statements, and it vividly contrasts "what we say with what we do." Acclaiming free enterprise while simultaneously subverting it by seeking advantageous governmental favors is an example. Robert Mayo, when president of the Federal Reserve Bank of Chicago, noted several variations of this type of undesirable behavior: "What I see behind much of the talk [about deregulation] amounts to saying 'Let's get rid of the regulation on that industry because I will benefit, but don't deregulate my industry; we're too fragile'; 'Deregulate natural gas prices, but don't let the prices go up'; 'We're for free trade generally, but our industry needs import quotas.' "[4]

The characteristics of arrogance and hypocrisy can sometimes lead to deceptive or even dishonest behavior. As the public has demanded higher corporate standards, continuing examples of illegal and unethical behavior have caused large segments of the public to generalize that dishonesty and deception are characteristic of executive behavior and the profit motive. In accord with the human tendency to accentuate the positive and deemphasize the negative, corporate executives sometimes are unintentionally deceptive. An impression of deception can also be created when companies decide not to announce developments that might be regarded as unfavorable.

The desire to avoid publicity can have adverse consequences. Many of the damaging examples of personal and corporate behavior occur because numerous executives see themselves as private individuals who occupy essentially private positions and are entitled to the personal freedom that privacy and anonymity afford. Even at a time when most corporations are disclosing much more about their governance, policies, and operations, some executives still believe theirs is a private and anonymous role.

Irving Shapiro has argued that "executives are realizing that the day is gone when the spot at the top of an organization chart permitted a private life style. A generation or two in the past, you could get by in business by following four rules: stick to business, stay out of trouble, join the right clubs, and don't talk to reporters."[5]

Irving Kristol, in his *Wall Street Journal* commentary, has noted perhaps the most important effect of executive anonymity:

[4]Robert Mayo, quoted in Gurney Breckenfeld, "Government's Hammerlock on Business," *Saturday Review*, July 10, 1976, p. 24.

[5]Irving Shapiro, "Business and the Public Policy Process," address to the Harvard University Symposium on Business and Government, May 9, 1979.

The power of the large corporation appears "irresponsible" precisely because of the anonymity which cloaks it: one doesn't know who is making all those decisions that affect our lives, or why, and in such a case the nastiest interpretation seems as plausible as any other. And when these decisions become dramatically costly to the average citizen, it is the nastiest interpretation that will come most naturally to mind.[6]

Adverse impressions can also be fostered by injudicious use of corporate facilities or resources. In managing the activities and resources of large corporations, top executives personify the corporation's power. To enable them to perform their duties optimally, the top executives of most large corporations have staffs at their disposal to handle business details and often some personal affairs, such as tax, investment, and legal matters. They also make use of limousines, hotel suites, private clubs, exercise facilities, and corporate aircraft. All these services and facilities project power and wealth, particularly if they are used ostentatiously or for personal purposes. While individually they may be reasonable and useful, in the aggregate they serve to set executives and corporations apart from and above the general society. Photographs of corporate jets parked at the Super Bowl, the Kentucky Derby, or the Masters golf tournament send a powerful and ultimately damaging message to employees and the public alike.

In fact, the personal behavior and attitudes of top executives form a model for their organizations. If the top executives are secretive, or arrogant, or hypocritical, the management team will tend to behave that way, and that behavior will soon become apparent to employees, customers, and critics.

## COUNTERPRODUCTIVE ATTITUDES

Equally damaging can be personal attitudes or opinions that denigrate or criticize other institutions and their leaders. These attitudes frequently serve to generate reciprocal responses, to the detriment of both corporations and executives. Some examples of deleterious attitudes toward other institutions are described in this section.

### Government

A long-standing and pervasive phenomenon is the antagonism and sometimes open hostility between many corporate leaders and govern-

[6]Irving Kristol, "The Credibility of Corporations," *The Wall Street Journal*, Jan. 17, 1974, p. 16.

ment officials. On one hand, this hostility reaches a crescendo in the case of electoral candidates who are running against "big business" and "corporate profiteers"; on the other, in the case of executives who vent their feelings by deprecating "bureaucrats and politicians who have never met a payroll." While executives may not express their attitudes as frequently or as openly as their behavior would indicate, as a group they make enough adverse statements to sustain the feeling of government officials that corporate executives tend to distrust and look down on them. While there may be goodwill and effective collaboration between corporate and government officials in a particular situation, government representatives are sometimes left with the lingering feeling that this occurs only when an executive is seeking a particular favor or result.

John D. deButts, former chairman of AT&T, has said, "Businessmen reserve their loudest applause for the orator who mounts the most muscular attack on government."[7] Irving Shapiro has emphasized the need to modify that mind-set: "Businessmen gain nothing in government by making 'enemies' lists, or by talking only to Congressmen of comfortable ideology." Shapiro pointed out: "We can go a long way toward improving the climate between business and government and ending the ancient, mutually destructive, and unproductive anomosity that has too long discolored the American political and economic environment."[8]

Tension between corporate and government officials is inevitable and, to a significant degree, is both beneficial to and characteristic of the American system of political democracy and capitalist economy. Yet, many observers believe that the threshold of mutual trust is unnecessarily low. As Courtney Brown has commented, "A full rapprochement to achieve candid and sympathetic relations between corporate executives and government officers may be too much to expect. The gap is now so wide, however, that there is much room for improvement."[9]

This is not to say that corporate managements should not be resolute in dealing with government officials. But that can be done far more effectively by eschewing inflammatory rhetoric and investing instead in learning how to participate in the public policy process and to deal with government officials on a basis of mutual respect. Thomas Murphy of General Motors has expressed his conviction that business's relations with government "are better today than they were in the past,"

[7]John D. deButts, quoted in Louis M. Kohlmeier, "A Call for Regulation," National Journal, July 17, 1976, p. 1011.
[8]Shapiro, op. cit.
[9]Courtney Brown, unpublished background paper prepared for the Resource and Review Committee.

and he cited the concerted effort by the business community to "break down the adversary relationship that has been causing so much friction between our public and private sectors." Every company, he declared, should become involved in that effort.[10]

President Reagan, as noted in Chapter 1, has acknowledged the adversary relationship of government and business and has called for leaders of both institutions to lay aside old hostilities.

## The Media

The general corporate executive attitude toward the media has been characterized by James L. Ferguson, chairman of General Foods, in this statement: "At almost any meeting of businessmen, when the topic turns to the press, what comes out is not simply expressions of resentment or anger, but of deep cynicism and bitterness. Those are dangerous emotions. They should not be left unattended."[11] Louis Banks, a former *Fortune* editor and a business professor at the MIT Sloan School of Management, has confirmed that hostility with his comment that "even the best-connected business journalists do not know the depth of emotion about the media's coverage of business harbored in the breasts of most corporate executives."[12]

Disagreements between media representatives and executives are inherent in the different roles and objectives of their respective institutions. Yet, because the large corporation has more to lose than the media from chronic hostility, some corporate leaders are changing their attitudes and adopting different methods of dealing with the media. For example, James Ferguson has recounted: "At General Foods, we have been angry at the press, or outraged or shocked or disappointed or perplexed a considerable number of times in the past few years." However, in considering both sides of the media-corporate relationship, Ferguson concluded: "To the journalist, freedom of the press is a sacred thing. To the businessman, freedom of enterprise and commerce are no less sacred, as are the trust and public confidence on which they rest. But the central question here is not who is right and who is wrong, but whether we can permit an adversary relationship to lead to confrontations."[13] General Foods still has complaints, but Ferguson has credited the news media with an increasing level of competence and

[10]Thomas A. Murphy, quoted in *Roundtable Report*, no. 80-2, March 1980, p. 3.

[11]James L. Ferguson, "Business and the News Media," *Editor & Publisher*, Oct. 23, 1976, p. 28.

[12]Louis Banks, "Taking on the Hostile Media," *Harvard Business Review*, March–April 1978, p. 124. Copyright © 1978 by the President and Fellows of Harvard College; all rights reserved. Reprinted by permission of the Harvard Business Review.

[13]James L. Ferguson, "Truth in Business News," *The New York Times*, Dec. 10, 1976, sec. I, p. 27. © 1976 by The New York Times Company. Reprinted by permission.

sophistication in reporting business news, and a lessened hostility toward business.

The prospect of reconciliation was also recognized by Louis Banks, whose view is: "Once executives work off their emotional hates and fears of the media, . . . they can come to see a broad area of neutral ground where they and the media may even have common cause."[14] From the corporate viewpoint, Donald MacNaughton, when chairman of Prudential Insurance Company of America, recommended:

> We businessmen should understand that adversary relationships with the press will often be normal—a series of contests, if you will. . . . [B]usiness must . . . become more open about its affairs—more free with information, more candid about its plans and problems, much readier than it has ever been to respond to questions and criticisms.[15]

## The Academic Community

With some exceptions, corporate executives have tended to caricature the college professor as a theorist and an adversary of private enterprise. Professors often have reciprocated by caricaturing the corporate executive as a single-minded profit seeker and an opponent of academic freedom.

Robert S. Hatfield, when chairman of the Continental Group, Inc., acknowledged: "Many of us in the past have labeled most academicians as somewhat impractical visionaries, opposed to private enterprise and looking to the public sector first to find the solution to the nation's problems."[16] W. Allen Wallis, chancellor of the University of Rochester and a corporate director, has cited this example of distrust by a corporate executive:

> I am reminded of an incident when one of the country's great corporations was ready, after extensive staff work, to support a university research project. All that remained was the approval of an executive vice-president. He killed the project, after nearly two minutes of thoughtful consideration, saying that with a group of academic men working on the subject, sooner or later one of them would publish a finding the company did not like.[17]

[14]Banks, op. cit., p. 130.

[15]Donald MacNaughton, "The Businessman versus the Journalist," *The New York Times*, Mar. 7, 1976, sec. III, p. 14. © 1976 by The New York Times Company. Reprinted by permission.

[16]Robert S. Hatfield, "Concerned Corporate Citizen," address to the American Assembly of Collegiate Schools of Business, St. Louis, Apr. 19, 1978.

[17]W. Allen Wallis, in "Notable and Quotable," *The Wall Street Journal*, Mar. 31, 1978, p. 14.

There are increasing opportunities for corporate executives and professors to close the gap of distrust: the common problems of government regulations, the need for joint action to improve American technological innovation, and the indivisibility of academic and economic freedom are but three examples. The time is right, Robert Hatfield pointed out in quoting this conclusion made by Lipset and Prof. Everett Ladd of the University of Connecticut from their studies of the attitudes of United States professors: "Eighty-one percent of the faculty members support the private business system. Most importantly, however, over two-thirds of the professors surveyed approved the view that the growth of government in the United States now poses a threat to the freedom and opportunity for individual initiative of the citizenry."[18]

## Labor Unions and Public-Interest Groups

Antagonism by some corporate executives toward labor and public-interest groups has been widely noted. Executives usually display their attitudes toward these groups by frequent opposition to their ideas and proposals while leaving direct attacks on unions to others.

Some corporate managements and public-interest groups are entering into new types of relationships. On several important public policy issues they have identified their areas of agreement and have decided how to resolve disagreement. Successful examples, such as the Food Safety Council and the National Coal Policy Project, have shown that this type of coalition has the promise of avoiding some unnecessary delays in the public policy or judicial processes, adverse criticism for recalcitrance, and legal and opportunity costs.

Some corporate executives and union leaders rarely align themselves in the common interest of their respective organizations. The oil industry has been an example of this, while steel executives and labor leaders, by contrast, have a record of arm's-length collective bargaining and joint political action on important public policy questions.

## The General Public

Despite the fact that the continued existence of the large corporation depends upon the trust and confidence of the American people, some corporate executives convey the impression of lack of trust and confidence in the public. Preston R. Tisch, president of Loews Corporation, has said: "Leaders in almost every field—including business—

---

[18]Everett Carl Ladd and Seymour Martin Lipset, "Professors Found to Be Liberal But Not Radical," *Chronicle of Higher Education*, vol. 15, Jan. 16, 1978, p. 9.

have fallen into a habit of thinking of public opinion as something to be molded and manipulated for their own purposes." He added: "The premise that the public cannot be trusted to make sensible judgments on complex issues is at best unproven. Moreover, the side effects of excluding the public from vital decision-making can be disastrous."[19]

Executives' attitudes often suggest that they believe that the public needs to be guided in economic and political decisions because most people are unqualified to make these decisions. John C. Sawhill, speaking as president of New York University, stated: "Traditional free-enterprise rhetoric lionizes the consumer and the ultimate wisdom of consumer choice. But business is reluctant to trust people in roles other than as consumers. Businesses survive only if they have a keen understanding of people as consumers or potential consumers of their goods and services. Yet business is out of touch with the perceptions and social attitudes of its critics."[20]

This absence of trust in people is a long-standing attitude that is reciprocated. "If trust and respect [in corporations and executives] are lacking," Irving Shapiro noted in 1976,

> it is not just because of recent, well-publicized misbehavior by some companies; it is also because for years we in business have not taken the public enough into our confidence. We have not let people see enough of what we do and what we stand for. All too often the corporate chief executive officer has been a cardboard figure and the company's policies as they relate to the public interest have been unknown, or so wrapped in 'PR' as to lack credibility."[21]

## The Private Enterprise System

Perhaps the most harmful form of executive behavior is ambivalent, inconsistent, or hypocritical attitudes toward the United States private enterprise system. William Simon, former secretary of the treasury, has expressed this point in vivid terms: "They [corporate executives] *say* they believe in competition, but when government offers a subsidy, their competitive standards go out the window. They *say* they believe in free enterprise, but what they want most in the world is a secure, guaranteed future."[22] Thus, corporate executives sometimes give the

[19]Preston R. Tisch, "A Way to Rebuild Public Confidence in Business," *Nation's Business,* April 1976, pp. 22–23.

[20]John C. Sawhill, "The Future Role of Business in Society," remarks before the Conference Board, Sept. 16, 1976.

[21]Irving Shapiro, "Corporate Reform: What's the Real Issue?" address to the Commercial Club of Boston, Apr. 20, 1976.

[22]William Simon, "Education and Ethics Are Greatest Business Challenges," *Treasury Papers,* November 1976, p. 7.

impression that they judge competition and private enterprise for their positive or negative effects on the bottom line rather than for their essential role in the United States system of a capitalist economy and a political democracy.

## CONSEQUENCES OF INAPPROPRIATE CONDUCT

Just as the overwhelmingly beneficial performance of large corporations is taken for granted, so are all the praiseworthy aspects of executive behavior. While it is satisfying and reassuring to review the very great deal that is favorable, some aspects of executive conduct clearly can be detrimental to the corporate community and its leaders.

Beyond the corporate performance that has generated the twelve public issues described in Part Two, executive conduct itself is an important reason why public confidence and trust in corporate leaders are lacking. Furthermore, sometimes perfectly reasonable and sound behavior by a single executive or corporation appears excessive when it is multiplied by many.

Most important, executives who convey such attitudes as hostility, denigration, and distrust engender adverse attitudes by others who are judging the large corporation and will ultimately decide its future. Observers regard the phenomenon of executives' distrust of others as self-defeating. Leonard Silk, a member of the editorial board of *The New York Times*, reporting on his and David Vogel's study for the Conference Board on corporate executive attitudes, pointed out: "Business cannot . . . achieve its own objectives unless it accords to other groups the same respect business seeks for itself."[23]

Personal characteristics that contribute to or mirror deficiencies of corporate performance are an important reason why corporate executives and their companies lack public trust and confidence. Experience has shown that executive privacy and anonymity can personify corporate secrecy and impersonality; individual deceit or dishonesty may portray a variety of corporate malpractices, from deceptive sales methods to illegal political contributions; and the authority of top executives and corporate power are often seen as indistinguishable.

Examples of hostile and deprecating attitudes and negative personal characteristics such as those described in this chapter generate antipathies toward the large corporation and its leaders and help to give

[23]Leonard Silk, address to Conference Board meeting, "The Future Role of Business in Society," New York, Sept. 16, 1976.

credibility to charges of corporate and executive misconduct. At a minimum, unacceptable executive conduct creates a public state of mind in which many close decisions are made *against* the large corporation. At the other extreme, some forms of executive conduct cause unsatisfactory corporate performance. Adverse attitudes toward others are part of the reason why, in many cases, corporate managements do not recognize the need for changes that they could make but that instead are eventually imposed by government.

To respond to the nagging question posed at the outset of this chapter, in addition to corporate leaders being held primarily responsible for unsatisfactory corporate performance, an important reason why they as a group have so little public confidence and trust is that their personal conduct as executives is regarded as unacceptable. In effect, these adverse public perceptions of senior executives and corporate performance are so closely intertwined that the combined impression, when negative, can be devastating.

# CHAPTER 20

# The External Environment

In the past 10 to 15 years, the large corporation and other United States institutions have been particularly affected by social, economic, political, and technological changes. Although these four factors are presented separately in the discussion that follows, they and their elements interact in innumerable ways to make up the kaleidoscopic external environment.

## SOCIAL FACTORS

Extensive criticism of corporate performance exists despite the fact that the quality of corporate performance is better than in previous decades. This anomaly has been caused, in part, by demographic and cultural trends that have influenced public expectations and events and have contributed to these changes:

### Distrust of Large Institutions and Their Leaders

Every measure of public attitudes has confirmed widespread disappointment in the performance of big government, large corporations, and other major institutions. Public disapproval has not centered on the institutions themselves but on their leaders. While a variety of reasons are cited, the principal one given is that the leaders act for their own advantage rather than for the public interest. Corporate profit seeking is frequently cited as an obvious and egregious example.

Accompanying this erosion of confidence in institutional leaders has been a pervasive sense of public doubt, punctuated by bursts of frustration and anger. Whether or not there is a crisis of confidence in American institutions and leaders, as some public leaders have suggested, there are apparent and deep-seated signs of public distrust. One result is that the public looks with favor on the countervailing power that big government, labor, and corporations exert on each other.

## Populism

Contributing to the public distrust of institutions and leaders is a view of society in which the vast majority of people are decent, ordinary citizens who are manipulated by a tiny group of powerful individuals who control corporations, government, labor unions, foundations, and special-interest groups and use them for personal advantage. Populism has, of course, emerged before as a powerful force in American history. In this generation it is essentially a reaction of many individuals who perceive themselves to be powerless in relation to the massive institutions of a highly technological society. The populist image has been conveyed by public figures as diverse as George Wallace, Edward M. Kennedy, and Ralph Nader.

During the past 15 years, campus riots, farmers' tractor marches on Washington, demonstrations for the equal rights amendment, mass protests against the siting of nuclear power plants, and demonstrations against Reagan economic policies have provided some dramatic examples of the depth and breadth of populist sentiment. An antibusiness expression of populism occurred in 1980, when Ralph Nader promised to form a coalition of unions, consumer and other advocacy groups, and intellectuals to curb the power of large corporations.

## Rights and Entitlements

Accompanying populist beliefs have been continuing public demands for improvements in the quality of life in general and in the status of disadvantaged groups in particular. Those demands generally affect all employers. However, when a new right has been recognized in law applicable to business, the large corporation has been the first to be singled out by government enforcement officials. In numerous instances large corporations have been publicly admonished as examples for both smaller corporations and small employers.

The concept of equality of treatment for all persons was a driving force behind what became the "rights explosion" of the 1960s and 1970s. That general concept of egalitarianism, coupled with the political activism of the period, produced equal voting rights in government elections and equal opportunity in education, employment, credit, and housing. As discussed in Chapter 9, the issue of employee citizenship rights is a current manifestation of the pressures on corporations by the rights movement.

Along with, and sometimes preceding, the demand for a right is the concept of entitlement: the claim that status as a citizen, employee, or resident qualifies a person for a particular benefit or privilege. Current pressures for entitlements include such ideas as guaranteed access to health care and other social services, protection against health and safety hazards, and a guaranteed minimum income whether or not an individual earns it. While there is often a greater factor of "more" than there is of egalitarianism in the pressure for entitlements, once an entitlement has been established, a round of pressures follows to make it a right. A recent example was that while some employees were entitled to avoid compulsory retirement before age 70, Congress made this a right for most employees.

Some observers believe the rights and entitlements movement is being shaped by the ultimate egalitarian concept: that a just society requires not only that individuals have equal rights but that they be made equal in all respects, for example, in income, influence, and the quality of life. While the concept of equal results is presently in the realm of social philosophy, to the extent that proponents of rights and entitlements could make it operational, government, corporations, and other institutions would be confronted with another social pressure.

## Social Attitudes

As distrust of institutions, populism, and demands for new rights and entitlements emerged from the events of the 1960s and 1970s, new and different public attitudes were formed. Some attitudes about corporations have resulted in public expectations that executives should manage corporations in ways that:

- Assure quality products at reasonable prices—manufactured, distributed, and disposed of under publicly acceptable conditions
- Help to provide a cleaner environment and lessen risks to human health and safety
- Improve the quality of working life by employee participation in

workplace decisions, job satisfaction, and advances in on-the-job rights and entitlements
• Are open and ethical and provide greater public accountability for corporate performance, including aspects that heretofore were of little public interest

These public attitudes and expectations are regarded as particularly characteristic of the generation of Americans born in the decade after World War II, a group that is of special significance to corporations as employees and consumers.

Another large and growing cohort consists of Americans over age 65. By the mid-1980s, the older population will constitute one in every eight Americans. These people are already a powerful group whose special interests affect corporations beyond the marketplace. Their demands, for example, include extended working life, special employment conditions such as part-time work or phased retirement, indexed pensions, and improved benefit plans that provide health services and long-term nonambulatory care for pensioners.

Substantial changes in the composition of the United States population are another social factor affecting the external environment. The rapid influx of Hispanic people into many urban areas of the United States has created serious problems in employment, housing, education, and provision of social services. As the fastest-growing minority in the country, the Hispanic group has an emerging leadership and is affecting the balance of political power in many areas.

Many of the social factors shaping the external environment are influencing the development and resolution of the corporate performance issues. Some of them also conflict with traditional corporate economic and political concerns. As a result, many of the public issues confronting the nation and corporations will focus on trade-off decisions such as deciding between growth and environmental protection, between inflation and unemployment, and between the costs and the benefits of social programs and government budget constraints.


## ECONOMIC FACTORS

As society's most visible economic institution, the large corporation is held at least partially responsible for national and international economic problems, just as it accepts partial credit for the benefits of prosperity and growth. Corporations, for example, are inevitably saddled with a good deal of the blame for rising prices because their products and services are the interface between inflation and the consumer.

Among the economic problems laid in part on the corporate doorstep are inflation, the energy dilemma, unemployment, low productivity, slow economic growth, environmental degradation, scarce resources, and unfavorable trade balances. As Lipset and Schneider have observed, when things go badly, people look for scapegoats and find them more often than not in the federal government and the large corporation. When serious economic problems exist, public criticism extends to all dimensions of corporate performance. For example, when the nation was confronted with short supplies and rising gasoline prices, the public's attitude toward large oil companies became negative in every respect, even on matters unrelated to gasoline availability and price.

Instead of sharing with government the role of scapegoat, many corporate managements hope that with the Reagan administration they are entering an era of economic achievement. The editor of *Financier*, however, spelled out an important admonition:

> There is a state of near-euphoria in the private sector at the prospect of supply-side tax breaks and relief from burdensome regulation, which is perfectly understandable. These are seen as welcome restorations of competitive capability.
>
> But understood also is a promise upon which the private sector must deliver, and it is here that the leaders stand most accountable. These restorations are almost in the Biblical sense talents; they must be multiplied and not squandered. The political system which, like an ultimate Board of Directors, has approved these general propositions, will expect results, or like a Board, it will adopt other plans.
>
> As Reginald Jones of General Electric points out [in *Financier*], for many of the problems they face today, businessmen have only themselves to blame. And if that has been the case while they have been dealing with a Government they regarded as uncooperative, they must beware of the potential penalties for self-inflicted damage under a Government that is trying to help as much as possible.
>
> So too the leaders of the private sector, as responsible executors of policy in their own realm, must hold the new Administration to account on its main proposals, above all on the need to impose discipline on Federal spending as a necessity in the fight against inflation. Its absence could signal lack of will or competence in the inflation fight.[1]

[1]Editorial, *Financier*, January 1981, pp. 3–4.

## POLITICAL FACTORS

Important consequences of public distrust in institutions and their leaders have been the growth of the populist concept of participatory democracy, the development of single-interest politics, a decrease in public participation in party politics, and the emergence of media politics.

### Participatory Democracy

During the past 10 to 15 years, there has been a substantial growth in participatory democracy. This development was triggered by the emergence of a wide variety of advocacy groups, variously referred to as single-, special-, or public-interest groups, whose status is discussed in Chapter 21. In addition to influencing legislation and the election of candidates, interest groups have rejuvenated the initiative and referendum in the last decade. Although many political scientists believe that these direct-election procedures for enacting or rejecting state and local legislation substitute media politics for the legislative process, the initiative and referendum have been used with frequency and effect. Initiative proposals involving corporate interests have drawn corporate managements into the competition for voter support. As a result, corporate managements now support propositions as well as oppose some propositions launched by others.

Many commentators have concluded that the proliferation of interest groups has contributed to the seeming absence of purpose and priority in federal lawmaking. Other observers disagree and advocate unlimited participation in public policy formulation as a requirement for assuring sound governmental decisions. L. William Seidman, vice chairman of the Phelps Dodge Corporation and former assistant to President Ford for economic affairs, believes that a great many national decisions are made better by the messy process of participatory democracy than by any other method yet devised. Seidman has observed:

> Anyone with a cause can come to Washington and expound it, march for it, sing for it, and pray for it. Our citizens can participate, they can get the attention of their elected representatives, and they do. A not unimportant benefit of such special interest political contests is that the loser knows he's had "his day in court," his chance in combat. Thus, he is more likely to accept adverse decisions because he has been part of the process.
>
> Special interest battles are part of the process of reconciling the diverse views of our citizens. Different interests must be reconciled in some way by any government—better to fight it out in public, and let off

steam in the process, than to use more orderly, more elitist, and more authoritarian decision-making processes.

In the words of Will Rogers—Democracy is just stumbling along to the right decision instead of going straight forward to the wrong one.[2]

## Single-Issue Politics

A number of influential interest groups, such as some concerned with gun control, nuclear energy, or abortion, support or oppose a candidate solely on the basis of his or her position on the group's single issue, regardless of how much they may agree on other matters. Some experts have argued that broad public-interest objectives have suffered when patently qualified candidates have been defeated by less qualified ones who have taken positions that agree with those of powerful single-issue groups. Fletcher L. Byrom, chairman of Koppers Company, Inc., has concluded that to vote for a political candidate on the basis of a single, isolated issue is "a distortion of the democratic process."[3]

## Party Politics

As some forms of participatory democracy have burgeoned, the strength of the political parties has declined. The number of persons claiming to be members of the two major parties has decreased in recent years, while there has been a substantial increase in the number of independents. Participation in political party activities also has decreased, with the result that candidates now create their own campaign organizations instead of relying primarily upon the parties. Another factor is that traditional forms of electoral politics have waned. Registration and voter turnout declined in federal, state, and local elections throughout the 1970s and in the 1980₃ elections. The decline in citizen interest occurred at about the same time that corporate managements began to encourage their managers and employees to become involved in electoral politics.

## Media Politics

The growth of participatory democracy and single-interest politics and the decline of traditional party politics were facilitated by the emer-

---

[2]L. William Seidman, "Lobbyists Democratize Policymaking," *The News World*, Sept. 5, 1980.

[3]Fletcher L. Byrom, "Uncritical Lovers . . . Unloving Critics," address delivered at the Health and Welfare Planning Association's annual meeting of the Citizens Assembly, Pittsburgh, Pa., 1980; reprinted in *Vital Speeches of the Day*, Aug. 1, 1980.

gence of media politics, particularly the use of the visual effects of television. With nearly three-quarters of the population using television as their principal source of news, many politicians and interest-group leaders have learned to arrange carefully orchestrated media events to promote their interests.

## TECHNOLOGICAL FACTORS

Because of their extensive involvement in the development and application of technology, large corporations are both praised and criticized for the effects of technology on society. The principal technological factors in the external environment, as discussed more fully in Chapter 10, "Health, Safety, and the Environment," and Chapter 11, "Technological Innovation," are these:

### Public Attitudes toward Science and Technology

The American people are ambivalent about the role of science and technology. Most Americans point with pride and satisfaction to the achievements and benefits associated with technology. A significant number, however, fear the present and potentially adverse future consequences of technology, particularly those arising from industrial activity. Public responses to that fear have been to demand that corporations anticipate and avoid the negative effects of their technology and to use science and technology to solve countless social and economic problems as well as those arising from technology itself.

### Rate and Nature of Technological Innovation

Public expectations of improved quality of life, including technological solutions to problems, depend upon the rate and quality of United States innovation and its commercial application. Public and corporate leaders agree that a decline in innovation will adversely affect these expectations. Despite the assertion that technological innovation is inhibited by government policies, many critics believe that the burden for reversing the trend and the blame for failing to do so rest squarely with the large corporation.

### Alternative Technologies

Large corporations are closely identified with "hard," or "massive-scale," technology projects, in contrast to the "soft," or "appropriate-scale," technology projects advocated by writers Amory Lovins, the late E. F. Schumacher, and others. A principal benefit of the soft-technology approach, its supporters contend, is that technological resources and their application would not be closely controlled by a relatively few large corporations. Another benefit claimed is that there would be less adverse impact on the environment. Also, in the case of some soft alternatives such as solar energy, resources would be constantly renewable and could be controlled by the users.

When corporate executives point out technological and other short-comings of the concepts of soft, or appropriate-scale, technologies, they are often accused of favoring their corporate interests at the expense of the public interest.

# CHAPTER 21

# The Other Major Public Policy Participants

Corporate performance in the complex and rapidly changing external environment has been the subject of intensive debate by the participants in the public policy process. The other major participants—government, the media, public-interest groups, small business, labor unions, and the intellectual community—have been influenced by the same environmental factors as large corporations. All of them, for instance, have been affected by the erosion of public confidence and inflation and by the changing age mix and social values. Each has power and influence in the formation of public attitudes and, in the end, in the formulation and monitoring of laws and regulations. Because of the important interrelationships between those institutions and large corporations, this chapter describes the other major participants and their respective status in the early 1980s.

## GOVERNMENT

The status of government and the political factors in the external environment together have created a more diffuse governmental and political system. Corporate executives and other private-sector participants in the public policy and electoral processes are contending with greater complexity and uncertainty. As a result, the political and social awareness of corporate executives and the managerial skills required in the public policy environment have become much more important than in the past.

Concurrent with the huge growth of government has been a rising distrust of that enlarged government. This reaction was a major factor in the election of President Carter in 1976, and, ironically, the trend accelerated during his term and contributed to his defeat in 1980. In those consecutive presidential elections, the electorate supported an outsider over the Washington "establishment." Equally important factors in President Carter's defeat were inability to manage the nation's persistent economic problems and a decline in United States prestige internationally.

Despite public dissatisfaction with the performance of government and many of its officials, there is overwhelming support for the United States democratic system. The public's ambivalence toward its government is often registered by demands for less government and lower taxes at the same time that it is requesting more government services that require higher public expenditures.

The following discussion concerns several major developments in government in recent years and their effect on the status of government as the key participant in the public policy process.

### The Presidency and the Power to Govern

Events of the last two decades have adversely affected the power of the presidency. Between 1960 and 1980 there were five presidents, and none served two full terms. As H. Monroe Browne, president of the Institute for Contemporary Studies, has noted:

> The "imperial presidency" has come and gone, leaving President Reagan an inheritance of inflated expectations and widespread public disillusionment.
>
> In light of recent experience, some commentators have argued that a president can no longer govern. They cite variously the huge complexity of the decisions a president faces, the decline of party support, the fragmentation of Congress, the hostility of the media, the intransigence of the federal bureaucracy, or the willfullness of foreign governments.[1]

As chief of state, head of his political party, and widely regarded as leader of the free world, the President of the United States is expected to deal effectively with a myriad of intractable problems compounded by unpredictable events at home and abroad. As President Reagan faces these challenges, much depends upon his ability to formulate and

---

[1]H. Monroe Browne, preface to Arnold J. Meltsner (ed.), *Politics and the Oval Office,* Institute for Contemporary Studies, San Francisco, 1981, p. ix.

administer policies in the external environment described in the previous chapter and to muster support or overcome opposition of the public policy participants described in this chapter.

With respect to the business community, President Reagan has called upon corporate leaders to help achieve what he has characterized as the major goals of this decade: the control of inflation, the reestablishment of United States competitiveness, and the achievement of near independence in energy supplies. "To reach these goals," the President has advised, "both business and government will have to learn to lay aside old hostilities and assume a new spirit of cooperation and shared responsibility."[2]

Industry associations and corporate leaders have responded by urging support of the President's program. They have recognized that there have been and will be disagreements within the business community concerning the program's provisions, but they have called for subordination of individual interests and continuing support of the program as a whole. In this context, John W. Hanley, chairman and chief executive officer of Monsanto Company, commented:

> A failure on our part likely will see a prompt return to overdependence on the government sector and continued low regard for the initiative of business leadership.
>
> Many of us in business have been arguing for years that we could help this economy produce more effectively if Washington would just get off our backs. Now, they've called our bluff. So we've got to deliver in terms of both our economic performance and our social responsibilities.
>
> To do so, we'll have to rediscover some old-fashioned virtues—self-restraint, self-denial and, above all, self-reliance.[3]

Company managements are thus faced with a highly visible and extended test of their willingness to support the President's program even if their interests are adversely affected in the short run.

## Congress and Its Reforms

During the late 1960s and early 1970s, many members of Congress became convinced that the power of Congress had eroded in relation to that of the President. The newer members of the House of Representa-

---

[2]Ronald Reagan, "Government and Business in the '80s," *The Wall Street Journal*, Jan. 9, 1981, p. 18.

[3]John W. Hanley, "Business Gets a Second Chance," *Washington Report*, Chamber of Commerce of the United States, May 11, 1981, p. 14.

tives were particularly frustrated by traditional congressional organization and procedures. Those two phenomena led to a series of reforms, primarily in the House, that have had important effects on the legislative process and on corporations and the other participants in the public policy process.

One reform transferred substantial power and authority from House committees to subcommittees. Another gave greater power to the Speaker, the majority leader, and the Democratic Caucus, largely at the expense of committee heads. The power of committee heads was further reduced when the Democratic Caucus assigned authority for nominating them to its Steering and Policy Committee. This had the effect of eliminating succession by strict seniority and of increasing the relative influence of younger members. Together, these reforms have meant that legislative proposals often come within the jurisdiction of many more committees and subcommittees than previously and that committee heads have less control over committee members. Another factor in the slowing of the legislative process is the plethora of complex and divisive issues that has been the basis for a large growth of congressional staffs. An important side effect in the opinion of many Congress watchers is that numerous senators and members of the House place undue reliance on their staff members for decisions on important issues.

The larger numbers of both committee and subcommittee chairpersons and members of their staffs have, in turn, increased the number of lobbyists and thus added to the difficulty of the lobbying process.

### The Judiciary and Policymaking

As a result of the large amount of social and economic legislation of the last two decades, the judiciary has been faced with many questions concerning the constitutionality of laws and their application. Judges have imposed their decisions on elected officials on complex matters of social policy, such as the details of racial desegregation in schools and the technical requirements of environmental protection. Many important decisions are misunderstood or are unpopular with large numbers of people. Also, the fact that judges reach their decisions in private has added to the criticism that the judiciary has intruded too far into the formulation of public policy.

The litigiousness of recent years has placed an overload of cases on the judiciary that is detracting from its performance. The increasing number of scientific and technological disputes that arise in corporate regulatory and judicial proceedings has added to the judiciary's problems and has generated proposals for "science courts" to help resolve conflicting technical testimony.

## The Agencies and Regulatory Reform

With the unprecedented growth of regulation in the 1970s, the regulatory agencies became such a significant factor in the formulation and administration of public policy that they are commonly referred to as the "fourth branch" of government. The power of regulatory officials, the vast amount of regulations they have produced, and the questionable or deleterious effects of many regulations have led to the regulatory reform movement.

Although disparate groups agree on the need for regulatory reform, the changes they seek and the means to achieve them have caused substantial disagreement. One result has been that progress toward regulatory reform has been uneven. Some structural and procedural reforms, such as inflation-impact and cost-benefit analyses that are required for new federal regulations, have been instituted. President Carter established the U.S. Regulatory Council, composed of chairpersons from principal regulatory agencies and departments, and charged it with improving the regulatory process. In addition, the Ninety-sixth Congress placed limitations on the powers of the Federal Trade Commission.

In the category of economic regulation, the Ninety-sixth Congress, with an impetus beginning in the Nixon and Ford eras, effected substantial deregulation of airlines, trucking, and railroads and laid some groundwork for reduced regulation of the communications industry. With respect to social regulation, initial efforts were made to substitute market-type incentives for some command-and-control regulations applicable to environmental protection.

The Reagan administration is closely examining the whole regulatory structure and is committed to roll back unnecessary and nonproductive regulations. A Presidential Task Force on Regulatory Relief, headed by Vice President Bush, has provided a means of coordinating the review and revision of existing and proposed regulations. A 60-day regulatory freeze gave administration officials and regulators a period in which to identify regulations that most needed review, and a new executive order is intended to require more rigorous cost-benefit analyses of proposed regulations.

The administration's commitment to regulatory reform was emphasized by the President's appointment of Murray L. Weidenbaum, a leading advocate of deregulation, as chairman of the Council of

Economic Advisers. Weidenbaum has expressed the administration's pleasant surprise that the regulatory agencies are responding positively by easing or eliminating counterproductive rules and excessive procedures. He has, however, cautioned that the administration will not discard regulation which is needed to reach laudable goals, such as clean air, but will endeavor to improve regulation which thoughtfully serves the public interest.

### The Larger Role of State and Local Governments

In recent years, there has also been a growth in the size and power of state and local governments, accompanied in most cases by growing public dissatisfaction with their performance. With the federal government unable to solve important problems, many people have looked closer to home for help. Legislation introduced in one state often spreads quickly to other states, reflecting the fact that state legislatures are acting more and more like Congress with full-time staffs and a network for communication with each other. Similarly, state attorneys general are organized and act in concert in suits against large companies.

In several key states, people have registered their disapproval of the costs of state and local government. California's Proposition 13 was the bellwether example of the taxpayers' revolt and served as a warning for federal officials as well as for officials in state and local governments.

Overall, corporate relations with state and local governments have been growing. The importance of these relationships is accelerating as the Reagan administration emphasizes the basic role of state and local governments and as many public-interest groups have decided to conduct more of their activities in the state and local arenas. Participation in the public policy processes of the many state and local governments has long presented some problems as difficult and perplexing as corporate involvement in the federal domain, and they are certain to be compounded.

### Openness in Government

While the United States has one of the most open governmental systems in the world, political abuse of power led to new government ethics laws and to demands for openness in government paralleling those for corporate public disclosure that arose during the same period. The pressures for a more open government created the question of how much secrecy, confidentiality, or openness is needed in the public policy and electoral processes, at what stage, and for how long. During the 1970s, a variety of "sunshine" reforms, such as the Freedom of Information Act, were enacted with the objective of making government decision making and the political processes more visible, public participation in government more accessible, and government corruption less liable.

The need to curb corporate influence on government was cited by consumer, environmental, and other interest groups as a reason for greater openness. They argued that the public policy process was not sufficiently responsive to their views and believed that if government deliberations were conducted openly, public opinion would preclude outcomes which unduly favor corporate interests.

The most noticeable effect of greater openness has been further redistribution of influence in the public policy process from well-established interests such as business, agriculture, and professional associations to environmental, consumer, and other public-interest groups. There is, however, evidence that too much openness has hindered frankness and efficiency, and, as a result, the pendulum swing toward openness has slowed. For example, President Carter found that campaign rhetoric on open government and the reality of governing in the open are not the same.[4]

### International Agencies

United States multinational companies are confronted abroad with increasing governmental and political complexities. In addition to host governments, governmental organizations such as the European Economic Community and the Organization of American States are regulating or are concerned with many aspects of corporate performance. Also, the United Nations and the Organization for Economic Cooperation and Development are endeavoring to influence corporate conduct by establishing codes and standards concerning such issues as corporate legal and ethical behavior, public disclosure, accounting standards, financial reporting, and health, safety, and environmental protection.

## THE MEDIA

Television, radio, newspapers, and magazines are part of the network of pressures on corporations and the other public policy participants,

[4]Charles S. Bullock and Francis W. Steckmest, "Openness in Government: Sunshine or Sunburn?" *Nation's Business*, November 1978, p. 97.

particularly by their selection and coverage of issues and events. While many executives believe that the effect of the media is to place the business community at a disadvantage, government officials and public-interest advocates also complain that the media do not fully and objectively report their activities and positions. Yet, government officials often have better leverage in gaining access to the media, and the immediate publicity that the media often accord public-interest groups is a key reason for their growth in numbers and influence.

Among the media, none has greater impact on the course of public issues than television. Not only does the public obtain most of its information from television, but the impact of what people see and hear on television far outweighs the effect of radio or the print media. The television news format places a premium on spectacular or dramatic events. "The result," says Lipset, "is a steady dose of bad news that portrays the country and all of its institutions as not working well."[5]

With increased coverage of news, television news programming has faced some difficult constraints. Some years ago Walter Cronkite pointed out some of television's problems in covering complex news issues adequately by stating:

> In the compression process forced upon us by the severe limitations of time, the job is incredibly, almost impossibly, difficult. I am afraid that we compress so well as to almost defy the viewer and listener to understand what we say. And when that becomes the fact, we cease to be communicators.[6]

The importance and power of the media, particularly television, is nowhere more apparent than in the attention given to the managed news event. Public figures have tailored appearances, arranged schedules, and adopted programs and positions with an eye to how they will appear on television and with an appreciation of timing needed to coincide with the networks' programming. Business finds itself virtually, if not completely, locked out. Corporations are prohibited from buying time on television to present their positions and find it difficult to attract TV coverage for anything other than "bad news." An exception is the occasional appearance by a corporate chief executive officer on programs like *Face the Nation*.

[5]Seymour Martin Lipset and William Schneider, *The Confidence Gap: How Americans View Their Institutions,* Macmillan Publishing Co., Inc., New York, 1981. Copyright © 1981, The Trustees of Columbia University in the City of New York. Reprinted by permission of The Free Press.

[6]Walter Cronkite, address to the Radio-Television News Directors Association Conference, Miami Beach, Fla., Dec. 13, 1976.

Some years ago, a prominent newscaster reportedly said, "News is what I say it is." Though the remark was likely offered in jest, today many people believe, and some have reason to fear, that news is indeed what television journalists say it is. A misstatement on television news often creates irreparable damage and can rarely if ever be properly corrected in the mind of the audience.

Media representatives on both the management and the editorial sides of their enterprises are conscious of what has been a growing criticism of their news coverage by the other public policy participants as well as by the public at large. They cite the constraints on selection and coverage of news and the impossibility of pleasing the many diverse interests despite their efforts to do so. They also remind their critics of the constitutional protection of freedom of the press with about the same regularity that academics refer to academic freedom and corporate executives refer to economic freedom.

One of the clearest messages on television—on newscasts and in plays, situation comedies, and serials—is that business executives are bad and that big-business executives are the most sinister of all. This picture appears to be shared by a distinct majority of all writers and producers on current TV shows. In TV plays, executives are portrayed in several different roles, all highly unflattering: they are either pompous fools, charlatans, or lawbreakers. Most communications experts believe that against this backdrop of malevolence, the viewing public, either consciously or subconsciously, is bound to be conditioned to believe the worst about corporations and their executives.

In addition to fictional portrayal, America's large corporations and how they perform have become big news. Each of the corporate performance and governance issues has been the subject of news reporting, editorials, and feature magazine articles on many occasions. In recognition of the important relationship between the media and corporations, the 1980 Business Roundtable *Report on Corporate Constituencies* recommended that the business community "openly probe the rationale behind certain news practices and policies that inhibit or distort the flow of information. The publicized attempts of Mobil Corporation and Kaiser Aluminum and Chemical Corporation are examples of this new activism among corporations."[7]

Many corporations have improved their ability to interact with the media, particularly the print media. And journalists in general have an improved understanding of business affairs. The public interest is served by encouraging both forms of improvement.

[7]*A Report on Corporate Constituencies*, Business Roundtable, New York, March 1980, pp. 16–17.

## PUBLIC-INTEREST GROUPS

Citizen advocacy organizations are an old vehicle of political action and social reform. Since the mid-1960s, a modern version has achieved unprecedented effectiveness as aggressive, vocal public pressure groups. With the attention of the media and politicians, the self-styled public-interest groups have frequently been able to focus national attention on public issues and exercise substantial influence in the public policy process.

The concept of an interest group representing the interests of the public has been discounted as presumptuous and incorrect. Yet, because some groups generally act as proponents of unrepresented noncommercial interests and as adversaries of government and the corporate world, they see themselves and are commonly known by that name. In practice, the public-interest group is a special-interest group, just like countless other groups that represent interests ranging from the professions to state and local governments, to universities, and to the many segments of the business community.

The reasons for the rapid growth of contemporary public-interest groups are numerous. A foremost reason was the model of the civil rights and antiwar groups of the 1960s. In the view of many people, the political parties did not serve to promote their specific interests, and thus they turned to single-interest groups. Also, changes in primary election laws and particularly Democratic party rules that stressed equality of representation strengthened the development of single-interest groups to the detriment of the political party system. The media and some politicians found a common interest in the investigative and publicity-generating functions of public-interest groups and provided them with exposure to national audiences. Some intellectuals began to give their support when they discovered that they were influential in the education of some prospective activists and that public-interest groups could promote their ideas for societal change more effectively than they themselves could. Another factor was financial support by private foundations. Also, beginning in the mid-1970s the federal government provided limited funds for direct support of public-interest groups to testify at congressional hearings and before regulatory agencies. While such intervenor funding established a precedent for limited public financing of the activities of public-interest groups, late in 1980 the Ninety-sixth Congress balked at continuing such support.

Members of public-interest groups are largely drawn from the upper-middle-income sector. In structure most groups are oligarchic. Policy is determined by staff officers in most of them, by directors in a few, but rarely by members. The leaders and members of activist groups are not necessarily advocates of more government intervention in the economy. John L. Holcomb, when research director of the Foundation for Public Affairs, found: "The ideology and opinion of many public interest group leaders were anti-statist and even libertarian in outlook and they were far more interested in having citizens, rather than bureaucrats, exercise political power."[8] It is with such leaders that corporate executives who recognize the legitimacy of public-interest groups have an opportunity to engage in dialogue and to mediate differences and develop coalitions on matters involving government intervention. In some cases, however, cooperation is hampered because, as Lipset has pointed out, "Some public interest group leaders who are anti-statist also are anti-materialist, and disdain the corporate pursuit of profits and the labor union drive for higher wages and benefits."[9]

Public-interest groups of particular relevance to corporate managements are those that deal with the environment, energy, health and safety, equal opportunity, consumerism, economic structure, and tax policy, multinational corporations, and corporate accountability. The political strategies used by such groups vary with their character and mission. National organizations with a goal of influencing government policy rely on the traditional political strategies of lobbying, legislative testimony, litigation, policy research, coalition building, and support for elected officials. Lobbying has increased while litigation, with some notable exceptions, has decreased, in part because private lawyers are litigating environmental, consumer, and equal-opportunity cases. Grass-roots organizations more frequently resort to boycotts and demonstrations, while church bodies and some universities, in their roles as investors, support shareholder resolutions to change management policies on socially oriented issues. Increasingly, public-interest groups also have launched initiative and referendum campaigns that challenge corporate interests and have become more deeply involved in recruitment of candidates for public office and in campaign activities.

A range of political strategies on the various corporate issues is evolving. For instance, Ralph Nader lobbies at the national level on corporate issues, while in California, Tom Hayden, chairman of Campaign for Economic Democracy, uses grass-roots strategies to promote the concept of local control of corporate decisions. Research and action on corporate issues are pursued by a growing number of organizations.

---

[8]John L. Holcomb, unpublished background paper for the Resource and Review Committee.

[9]Lipset and Schneider, op. cit.

The Center for Law in the Public Interest sued several companies guilty of illegal payments, with the result that outside directors were imposed on their boards of directors by the courts. The Institute for Public Representation has promoted the principle that corporate legal counsel should disclose evidence of client misbehavior. The Interfaith Center on Corporate Responsibility has proposed shareholder resolutions calling for disclosure of corporate social impacts as well as on questionable corporate behavior and executive compensation. Moreover, a coalition involving Nader, labor unions, and other groups drafted the proposed Corporate Democracy Act of 1980. Another group, composed of unions, public-interest groups, the Democratic Study Group, and the Congressional Black Caucus, has expressed interest in corporate governance, corporate public disclosure, limitations on mergers, class-action suits, plant closings, and an employee bill of rights.

The impact of public-interest groups has been felt directly by both government and business. John Gardner, founder of Common Cause, has expressed concern about a special-interest state that tends to create paralysis in government decision making. Moreover, some members of Congress have complained about the adverse impact of single-issue groups on their daily functions and in their reelection campaigns. Of course, the challenges of public-interest groups have not been uniformly successful. They have, however, stimulated the corporate community to improve existing business associations and form new ones that are emulating many of the political strategies used against them. The traditional business interest groups, such as the Chamber of Commerce of the United States and the National Association of Manufacturers (NAM), have substantially increased their public policy analysis, lobbying, and communication staff support on public issues. The business community has also formed new organizations, such as the Business Roundtable and the American Business Council. Another new type comprises legal foundations that represent corporate views of the public interest.

The importance with which some corporation managements view some of their public-interest adversaries is exemplified by their efforts to coalesce with them on issues they hold in common. For example, the U.S. Chamber of Commerce joined with Nader's Congress Watch and the Sierra Club against proposed disclosure requirements of grass-roots lobbying activities. Allstate Insurance Company cooperated with Nader in the campaign to require automobile air bags although they still opposed each other on no-fault insurance.

Dialogue meetings to explore areas of agreement and mediation efforts to reconcile differences between industry and some of its critics are also occurring. A leading example is the National Coal Policy

Project, through which industry representatives and environmentalists were able to reach agreement on about 200 specific measures to encourage energy development.

What is becoming clear to some leaders of public-interest groups, government officials, and corporate executives is that regulatory and judicial determinations are no longer the only or necessarily the most desirable ways to resolve some public policy issues. Decisions reached by those means usually divide the parties into "winners" and "losers," and the losers often lack commitment to the decision and may act to obstruct or delay its implementation.

Some observers of the contemporary public policy process believe that opportunity exists for corporate executives to encourage dialogue and consultation with diverse interests and that such initiatives can lead to creative resolutions and even coalition of interests. They point out that since many major policy decisions facing society must be made with "uncertainty," the interests of all parties may best be served through dialogue and consultation. They aver that the major problems facing the nation will not go away with a change in administration and, therefore, that new initiatives are needed not only to resolve issues but to rebuild public confidence in the leaders of all institutions, who, of course, are the participants in the public policy process.

Observers of the interest-group movement believe that membership and foundation funding of liberal national public-interest groups peaked in the mid-1970s, although most local groups have continued their growth. Also, public-interest groups are confronted with personnel problems. In addition to the legal skills used in lobbying for the social legislation established in the 1970s, public-interest groups now need various technical skills to participate in the process of formulating standards and regulations that implement those laws. Today, with the government's emphasis on reviewing the technical requirements and feasibility of regulations, key roles are played by a variety of professional specialists such as biologists, epidemiologists, economists, toxicologists, and engineers. Qualified people in these specialties are in great demand, and public-interest groups have not been able to attract them as easily as the relatively abundant pro bono lawyers.

Another personnel problem may be leadership. Many of the leaders of public-interest groups who joined the Carter administration have not returned to the public-interest-group movement. Observers point to that loss as a cause of a dearth of well-known, charismatic leaders. Yet, others see a change in leadership style rather than in leadership effectiveness. They point to a number of leaders who are quietly influencing public policy formulation by interacting with government, business, and other interests and eschewing flamboyant tactics.

While some people expected that the advent of the Reagan administration would discourage public-interest groups, the opposite effect has occurred. Many groups have had a resurgence in membership and money, particularly those concerned with the environment. National public-interest groups are forming alliances to pool ideas and resources to help maintain their influence. At the state and local levels, they are also joining in support of each other. Most group leaders are convinced that there is strong public support underlying their particular interests and that many activists who were reasonably well satisfied with the Carter administration's stance on their issues are being stimulated to action by the Reagan White House. Some groups are developing new issues such as state and local taxation of oil company profits. Others are using the administration's policies to promote their ends; for example, by endorsing free market principles, some environmentalists have encouraged Congress to refuse or limit appropriations for the U.S. Synthetic Fuels Corporation. Some groups seek support of industries or companies whose economic interests coincide with theirs; for example, they hope to coalesce with companies whose energy costs are so intensive that they favor various forms of energy regulation.

## THE SMALL-BUSINESS COMMUNITY

One of the relatively recent phenomena of government-business relations has been the organization of the nation's small-business interests as a major public policy participant. While the small-business community and large corporations traditionally have held the same general positions on most public policy issues, the potential for opposition exists.

Two major national groups have become the primary representatives of small business: the National Federation of Independent Business (NFIB) and the National Small Business Association (NSB). The NFIB has grown from fewer than 300 member companies in 1971 to some 600,000 in 1980. With a substantial lobbying organization in Washington, the NFIB plans to expand its state lobbying operations from twenty-four to all fifty states. The NSB has a membership of about 50,000 small-business executives. Its major lobbying efforts are exerted in conjunction with the Small Business Legislative Council (SBLC). The SBLC is made up of more than seventy-five national trade associations and several state trade associations, representing 4 million small businesses.

Perhaps the foremost reason for the rising political influence of small business is that the roughly 14 million operators of small enterprises are everywhere and that such operators are constituents of every officeholder. As Lipset and Schneider have pointed out, the public has a much more favorable opinion of small businesses than of large corporations. Thus, legislators' support of small business is less likely to be publicly objectionable than alignment with major corporate interests, particularly on business-versus-consumer issues. A less obvious factor is that many members of Congress have owned or managed small businesses themselves. Government officials recognize the importance of small business and its collective strength. For example, President Carter received the report of the White House Commission on Small Business in 1980, and members of Congress and state legislators are paying more attention to small-business executives and their association representatives.

The intense efforts of recent years by small-business executives to make their voices prominent in Washington are primarily concerned with their opposition to government regulation. Small-business operators contend that Congress and federal regulators frequently have failed to consider the impact of their actions on small businesses.

While a coincidence of interest between small business and the large corporation still exists, small business has already staked out its special interest in less government control and more economic advantages for itself than for large corporations. The agenda of small business for the early 1980s includes such issues as these:

- *Regulatory flexibility.* Less restrictive regulatory compliance standards for smaller businesses than for larger ones.
- *Technological innovation.* Increased federal research funds for small business, programs to promote small-business innovation, and increased control of innovations made by small businesses as a result of federally funded R&D.
- *Taxes.* Special tax advantages such as a more graduated corporate income tax, accelerated depreciation, credit for investment in new stock issues of small companies, and reserves for future research.
- *Special compensation for court action.* Provision for small businesses to recover attorneys' fees and other expenses in suits in which "unreasonable" government action is proved.

Among the responses of the Ninety-sixth Congress to this agenda was the Regulatory Flexibility Act. In addition to other provisions, the act requires federal agencies to consider the ability of small companies to comply with regulations and required paperwork.

In addition to the small-business associations, the U.S. Chamber of Commerce in 1976 established a staff unit and an advisory group to focus exclusively on the concerns of small business. While the NAM has not assigned staff to deal specifically with issues of concern to small business, its representatives are routinely expected to consider small-business views.

Behind the growing success of Washington's small-business lobby, some observers believe that there is an increasing opposition to big business. Former Colorado Congressman James D. McKevitt, chief lobbyist for the NFIB, has characterized that organization in this way: "We're populists. That's what gives us credibility."[10] Some observers believe that the new populism of small business and the growth of its lobby may prove increasingly troubling rather than helpful for large corporations.

As public policy differences occur between large and small companies, umbrella associations like the U.S. Chamber of Commerce and the NAM may find it more difficult to develop consensus positions. The Business Roundtable, with its membership of large corporations, has already faced questions about the effects of its positions on the interests of smaller business. Although these organizations have worked closely with the NFIB and other small-business interests, divergent positions have been taken. On the issue of regulatory flexibility for small business, the Roundtable favored a more comprehensive approach to regulatory reform, while the NFIB supported Senator Kennedy's proposal to curb corporate mergers. While unanimity among all business groups cannot be expected on certain narrow issues, business leaders of large and small companies alike have emphasized the importance of remaining together on fundamental issues.

Another component of the business community is the middle-sized corporation. Arthur Levitt, Jr., chairman of the American Stock Exchange, Inc., has formed the American Business Council, a lobbying group similar to the Business Roundtable but composed of middle-sized growth companies. Levitt, who served as chairman of the White House Commission on Small Business, has maintained that the interests of medium-sized companies are not sufficiently served by either the Business Roundtable or the various small-business organizations.

Whether the full power of small business is realized may depend on how far small business is willing to delve into electoral politics. The NFIB has established a political action committee (PAC) to make contributions to congressional candidates whom it rates highly for their support of small business. The NSB, in contrast, has rejected the idea of

---

[10]James D. McKevitt, quoted in Kevin Phillips, "Big Business Hasn't Built a Political Constituency," *Business and Public Affairs Fortnightly,* Sept. 1, 1979, p. 2.

a PAC; however, numerous small-business PACs have been organized by trade associations.

## LABOR UNIONS

The American labor movement is at a crucial turning point. Lane Kirkland, as a younger, less conservative president of the AFL-CIO than his predecessor, George Meany, is representative of leaders who are in line to replace older heads of member unions. Power within the labor movement is shifting from the private-sector unions, whose rate of growth is declining, to public-sector unions, which have been growing more rapidly. An attitude of confrontation has been engendered among many labor union leaders as a result of difficult economic and demographic conditions, combined with the defeat of legislative proposals backed by unions, such as those for labor reform, a consumer protection agency, and common-situs picketing.

Corporate personnel programs that many employees perceive as constructive alternatives to unionization have contributed to a decline in the union "win rate" in representation elections and to an increase in decertification elections. The union movement placed great emphasis on its sponsorship of the 1979 labor law reform bill, which was buried by a filibuster in the Senate. The provisions of that bill, which would have strengthened the organizing abilities of unions, are still a union objective. Unions also support in both Congress and state legislatures proposed plant-closing legislation that would require corporations to give advance notice and financial assistance to workers and communities when plants are to be closed.

Unions have begun to use direct and secondary applications of their financial power, both as a weapon in their organizing activities and in an effort to change corporate performance and governance. As discussed in Chapter 16, "Shareholder Rights," unions are using their pension fund stockholdings to influence companies whose practices are antithetical to union goals by means of shareholder resolutions, threats to sell their shareholdings, and voting their shares rather than leaving them to be exercised by trustees who in the past have generally voted with management. In the aggregate, union-controlled pension funds have significant stockholdings in many large corporations, and various union leaders have stated that union pension power will become an important organizing and bargaining weapon.

While recognizing labor's attitude of confrontation, there is evidence that important labor leaders are concerned about adverse public attitudes toward the labor movement. "Public opinion toward labor unions," Lipset has observed, "is less favorable than toward business. The predominant opinion is that unions are 'selfish, inefficient and corrupt.' Nonetheless, a majority of the public believes that unions are needed to protect employees."[11]

With union membership declining, there is a resurgence of argument that the cause, rather than the ineffectiveness of the unions themselves, is increasing management hostility. With labor increasingly frustrated in its strategy of pursuing ad hoc legislative objectives, calls by labor leaders for different political tactics have increased. As the public unions have become more prominent, and with the government as the "employer" of the people in these unions, there has been some acceptance of the view that nationalization of some industries would be an acceptable solution for economic ills. The militancy of public-sector unions in Great Britain, France, and Japan provides an instructive parallel for assessing the probable direction of the American labor movement. The new breed of labor leader could well endorse a more expansive role for government in the economy. In August 1979, for example, the AFL-CIO endorsed some form of nationalization of the oil industry.

The increasingly protectionist mood of United States labor in the last decade is another factor that will tend to draw the labor movement into the public policy process as a competitor of the corporation. Organized labor some years ago showed its opposition to some aspects of the multinational company by support of the Burke-Hartke bill, which would have imposed stringent limitations on American-based multinational companies, and through the formation of international trade union structures and bargaining arrangements. The internationalization of the American economy and of the market for labor has further provoked changes in the AFL-CIO's attitudes toward foreign trade. Historically, organized labor has generally supported expanded trade. That position has reflected the consumer interests of the AFL-CIO and the fact that only small, selective segments of the labor force were directly affected. However, with the deep penetration of imports in markets in which trade unions have a substantial membership, the AFL-CIO has been shifting toward a position of outright resistance to expanded international trade.

The labor response to the surge of illegal immigration has also been to favor increased restrictions. The AFL-CIO has supported legislation that aims at diminishing and/or controlling the movement of immigrants to the United States. In particular, the federation has thrown its weight behind a provision that would impose penalties on employers who hire illegal immigrants.

[11]Lipset and Schneider, op. cit.

While corporate executives have long had their share of differences with union leaders, the American trade union movement is one of the most conservative in the Western industrialized world. The labor movement generally has accepted democratic capitalism. Union political action has been concentrated largely on economic gains via collective bargaining, and broad social changes have been a secondary objective. This commitment to capitalism and a modified market system has come under considerable stress in recent years. While some labor leaders may try to turn their unions toward new ideological directions in response to the conservative policies of the Reagan administration, the American labor movement as a whole is unlikely to change its ideology.

According to Arnold Weber, professor of economics and president of the University of Colorado, the Reagan election effectively dashed the union movement's hope for legislation to bolster its organizing efforts and for such social goals as national health insurance. Weber believes that the impact of the changed environment on labor-management relations will have these paradoxical effects:

> On the one hand, there will be extended efforts to establish coalitions of convenience between organized labor and management in distressed industries in order to lobby for government relief. This pattern has emerged in the auto, steel, and electrical equipment industries. Unions will be congenial to this approach because an alliance with business can lever their influence in a Republican Administration.
>
> On the other hand, unions will press aggressively at the bargaining table for gains that were formerly pursued through legislative channels in a more favorable political environment. This displacement to the bargaining table will focus on issues such as health and safety, the protection of pension funds, affirmative action, advance notice of plant shutdowns and income security during layoffs.[12]

## THE INTELLECTUAL COMMUNITY

The term "community" exaggerates the cohesiveness of this large and varied group composed of professors, writers, editors, artists, and think-tank scholars. Nonetheless, most observers agree that many of its most influential members do share a common culture of beliefs and attitudes, particularly with respect to the economic and corporate world.

Some intellectual critics of business are powerful individuals,

[12]Arnold Weber, "The Outlook for Organized Labor under the Reagan Administration," *Dun's Review*, January 1981, p. 13.

ranging from philosophers to scientists, whose ideas interact with those of other intellectuals and reach many public leaders and millions of students. While those critics usually do not form or lead pressure groups, they are often participants in them. Their greatest influence results from their books, articles, speeches, and classroom teaching. For example, Harvard Professor John Kenneth Galbraith's books such as *The New Industrial State* have proclaimed the large corporation as an anticompetitive institution and a detrimental influence on society. Similar pressures on business are applied by scientists. Rachel Carson's book *Silent Spring* was instrumental in focusing public attention on the need for environmental protection. More recently, Amory Lovins's writings that have posed the questions of soft and appropriate-scale solutions versus hard and massive-scale solutions to energy problems are being used by proponents of restrictions on corporate size and economic growth.

Many of the challenges to the large corporation are based on complex and rapidly changing knowledge. Whether an issue concerns the health effects of an industrial activity or the extension of employee citizenship rights to the workplace, the role of the expert is an increasingly critical factor in shaping the very terms of the public policy debate on the performance issues. The experts are often members of the intellectual community, and they frequently share many, if not most, of the concerns of their colleagues about the large corporation. However, experts who are employed by or are in some way affiliated with the business community often find that their expertise is denigrated and their motives questioned.

For reasons such as these, corporate executives traditionally have been suspicious of (in some cases, hostile toward) some intellectuals. During the 1970s, for example, many executives felt that many university professors lent their prestige to proposals for greater government control over corporations. In that period, however, an important countervailing force developed. A number of influential intellectuals such as Irving Kristol, Norman Podhoretz, and Daniel Bell, who had been allied with leftist or socialist ideologies earlier in their careers, came to recognize that intellectual freedom is dependent on economic freedom as well as on the other freedoms. That recognition developed in the context of their anxiety about the expansion of communism. While still critical of various aspects of corporate performance, intellectuals such as Kristol have become staunch advocates of the United States private enterprise system. They, in fact, level their criticism at corporate executives who do not support and defend that system by personal advocacy that is backed up and illustrated by the performance of their companies.

The intellectual advocates of capitalism have been attracting other intellectuals to their general point of view by their writing and speaking, by association in editing scholarly journals such as *The Public Interest*, and as scholars in think tanks such as the American Enterprise Institute for Public Policy Research, the Heritage Foundation, the Brookings Institution, the Hoover Institution, and the Institute for Contemporary Studies.

There are other factors that have been creating a closer relationship between corporations and higher education, the principal institution of the intellectual community. Higher education is faced with a financial squeeze because of decreasing enrollments, reduced government support, and higher costs associated with inflation. There are also fewer academic positions for many of its own doctoral graduates. As a result, colleges and universities have been turning increasingly to corporations for financial support, placement of graduates who were trained to be professors, and, more often than in the past, for grants to do research on national problems of importance to business such as productivity, technological innovation, and various aspects of the environmental and energy dilemmas.

In the last 10 years, higher education has been beset for the first time with the adverse effects of extensive federal government regulation. Recognition of the commonality of this problem with business is resulting in greater understanding and cooperation by the higher education community, many of whose members had long espoused the regulation of business. A signal example of the opportunity for cooperation between academia and the corporation is the Business–Higher Education Forum, an organization of corporate chief executives and university presidents founded by the American Council on Education. One purpose of the forum is to address problems shared in common and to engage in coordinated activity in the public policy process. Another is to facilitate understanding of corporate enterprise on the campuses of the nation's colleges and universities.

Notwithstanding some encouraging examples of joint interest and cooperation, the intellectual community by its nature will continue to produce some powerful critics of the large corporation. As the 1980 Business Roundtable *Report on Corporate Constituencies* advised, "Many of the trends in public opinion originate on campus, and the business sector could ignore this fact only at its peril. There are, moreover, increasing opportunities for constructive relations between the corporate and the intellectual communities that are being nurtured by thoughtful people in both groups."[13]

---

[13]*A Report on Corporate Constituencies*, op. cit., p. 1.

# PART FIVE

# Findings and Conclusions

Т he rapidly changing business environment of the last 10 years has been highlighted by criticism of aspects of corporate performance that previously had not been serious matters of public concern. Many of the public policy issues that have resulted have important societal implications and political consequences.

Chapter 22 reviews how the corporate public policy agenda and managements' response have broadened the economic role of the large corporation. The dilemmas that company managements face in accepting the reality of a corporate social and political role are discussed, and examples of changes in corporate organization and function are cited. The concept of "voluntary corporate accountability" is introduced as an alternative to government-imposed accountability, and this emerging process is described, and examples of management actions to implement it are given. The chapter closes with a brief analysis of the need for the development of corporate executives who are as effective in dealing with the public policy dimension of their business as they must be in managing its other functions.

In Chapter 23, the many pressing public policy issues described in this book are brought together in terms of their significance to the future of the large corporation and the private enterprise system. These findings and conclusions are set forth as a challenge to corporate managements to operate their companies successfully and to help assure the survival of large corporations and the private enterprise system.

# CHAPTER 22

# The Evolving Role of
# The Large Corporation

The basic economic role of the large corporation has not changed. It remains that of providing goods and services with profit the end or the means, depending upon one's point of view. What is different about the economic role is the greater complexity of performing it well. Corporate economic performance has been hampered by unprecedented government regulation, high inflation, inadequate productivity, the energy dilemma, severe foreign competition, and insufficient technological innovation. These and other economic factors have created a condition of uncertainty in which corporate managements face unusual risks in planning expenditures and anticipating revenues. In effect, the traditional corporate economic role has become fraught with major problems of the national and international economies.

In addition to the severe economic problems, managements are challenged by the social and political implications of these problems and by the emergence of specific social and political issues involving their businesses. As a result, the traditional role of the large corporation has come to include social and political components that are inextricable from the economic role and that vastly complicate it.

## THE EVOLVING SOCIAL ROLE

An important factor in the business environment is the evolution of public attitudes from the principle that the large corporation is basically private and accountable to its stockholders and the marketplace to the concept that the large corporation is "quasi-public." In addition to their basic obligations to shareholders, corporate boards of directors and managements have become more and more accountable to innumerable laws that are intended to protect and promote the interests of consumers, employees, and other groups.

An important aspect of the business environment has been the continuing public interest in the social impact of corporate performance. An important reason for this interest is that corporate social performance has been joined with the issue of corporate governance. For example, in a study of corporate governance, the Business Roundtable stated:

> Another major board responsibility is the consideration of significant social impacts of corporate activities and relatedly the consideration of views of substantial groups (other than shareholders) affected by such activity.[1]

Also, studies and proposals by the Securities and Exchange Commission, the Federal Trade Commission, the Department of Commerce, and Congress have been directed at assuring management accountability for its company's social impact as well as for the economic interests of its shareholders.

Corporate executives who have been career-conditioned in an environment of profit maximizing usually find it difficult to accept the idea that the corporation has a real social role. Courtney Brown commented on this point:

> The disciplined and aggressive executive committed to continuous improvement in efficiency and growth is a social resource of real value. He or she is, however, unlikely to fit comfortably with the specifications of the socially aware. In fact, just the reverse is more likely. Compassion may and does play a part in one's personal life, but in business affairs it enters for the most part only when mutual benefits result. The effort to minimize costs and maximize returns is continuous and unrelenting. That is the source of the corporation's strength; of its ability to achieve the tasks to which it is committed.

In that context, Brown concluded:

> The transition of the corporation from a purely business organization to an activity that accepts enlarged social purposes is proving to be difficult. But there seems to be no real alternative. As it has grown in size, even its business decisions have a larger component of social signifi-

[1]*The Role and Composition of the Board of Directors of the Large Publicly Owned Corporation*, Business Roundtable, New York, 1978, pp. 11–13.

cance. In fact, in the large modern corporation there is no longer the possibility of it being purely business, whether the issue is siting a new plant or dismantling an old one, producing new products or refining old ones, hiring older people or training new ones.[2]

As discussed in Chapter 13, "Social Performance," a new definition of and consensus on the proper corporate social role is still evolving, and its limits are not yet clear. When chairman of the General Electric Company, Reginald H. Jones spoke of the future of the corporate social role in these terms:

> Economic performance is no longer enough. Business is properly expected to act in the public interest, as well as the share owners' interest, and serve the larger aspirations of society. Some of today's managers seem to be uncomfortable with their new social responsibilities, but it's like fish swimming in new waters—either we'll adapt or we won't survive. The successful managers of tomorrow will be those that swim as comfortably in the societal waters as their predecessors swam in the waters of technology and finance.[3]

John H. Filer, Chairman of Aetna Life & Casualty, believes that a social role for business should not be considered as a separate, peripheral function unrelated to the mainstream of the business. Addressing the Conference Board in 1981, Filer proposed a concept of "corporate public involvement" rather than that of a "corporate social role." In explaining his broader concept, he said:

> We are talking about the impact, for good or bad, of all facets of corporate activity—voluntary and involuntary, intended and unintended —on the public or society at large.

Filer stressed that if these impacts are regarded as a concept divorced from the primary economic roles of production, pricing, and sales, "we will be frustrated in achievement and create counterproductive tensions with seemingly inconsistent demands upon our own managers."[4]

Whatever terminology one chooses, the many impacts of corporate performance on people have created public issues whose resolution continues to affect the traditional role of the large corporation. This phenomenon, in turn, has drawn company managements more actively

[2]Courtney Brown, unpublished background paper for the Resource and Review Committee.

[3]Reginald H. Jones, "The Manager of the Future," remarks on acceptance of the Joseph P. Wharton Award at the Wharton Graduate School of Business Club, Mar. 23, 1976.

[4]John H. Filer, "Corporate Public Involvement Enlarging under Challenge," *Financier*, May 1981, p. 33.

into the public policy and electoral processes and has accelerated the evolution of the corporate political role.

## THE EVOLVING POLITICAL ROLE

As discussed in Chapter 12, "Political Participation," there has been a resurgence of corporate interest in both the public policy and the electoral processes, which, in turn, has raised the question of the appropriate corporate political role. Chairman James L. Ferguson of General Foods Corporation believes:

> The chief executive has a fundamental responsibility to look realistically at the way the world works today, to acknowledge what business can and cannot do—and should and should not do—in meeting the needs of society, and to take the lead where appropriate.
>
> Fortune magazine made a good point some time back. In a discussion of the perennial efforts on the part of businessmen to educate people about the way the American economic system works, it argued that the primary responsibility of the businessman is not to educate others but to educate himself about political, social and economic reality, and to put that knowledge to work through meaningful participation in the political process.[5]

In contrast to the reluctance of some executives to recognize a real corporate social role, the idea of a corporate political role is popular among most executives. In fact, a recurring decision facing corporate managements is to determine the optimal nature and extent of their political activity. In this regard, Du Pont's Irving Shapiro has observed:

> There are some dangers. One is that the public will perceive that businessmen are running around Washington acting like elected officials, trying to take over the running of the country. If business steps over that line, it will be in worse trouble that it has ever known before.[6]

In his valedictory address as chairman of the Business Roundtable in June 1980, Thomas A. Murphy urged corporate leaders to strive for a less adversarial relationship toward those in government: "Wherever, however, and whenever we can do something or say something or print something to restore public confidence in our political system, we must

[5]James L. Ferguson, "The Chief Executive's Responsibility for Corporate Public Service," Sloan Management Review, vol. 20, no. 1, p. 77, by permission of the publisher. Copyright © 1978 by the Sloan Management Review Association. All rights reserved.

[6]Irving Shapiro, remarks to the Media Awards Luncheon, Amos Tuck School of Business Administration, New York, May 23, 1978.

do it—not only as members of this organization, but also as officers of our corporations." By following that course,, Murphy said, the Roundtable would continue to move ever closer to its stated goal: to help build a sound cooperative relationship among the various sectors of American society in which "the national interest takes precedence over all others—over the purely political, over the purely business, over the militant coalition. The underlying conviction at the beginning of the Roundtable was—and remains today—that the furtherance of the national interest will benefit all the others, including our own."[7]

## THE EVOLVING SOCIAL AND POLITICAL ROLE

The social and political aspects of the large corporation have similarities and differences. Two important similarities are that both are causing changes in corporate organization, policies, and performance and are requiring greater public disclosure. Disclosure particularly involves corporate performance, both as to its impact on people and as to its influence on elections and public policy.

The social and political aspects of the large corporation also have two important differences. While many corporate managements find it difficult to accept a real social role, they would like to have a stronger political role. The former is seen as a drag on economic performance; the latter, as a boon to it. The second difference is that the trend of public policy has been to require a larger corporate social role in contrast to public pressures that would limit the corporate political role. In effect, increased corporate participation in social problem solving is generally regarded as beneficial; extensive corporate political influence is seen as threatening.

The evolution of a joint social and political role has been stimulated by the interrelationship of the social and political components of business. The social impacts of corporate performance have caused public issues which have hastened the development of a corporate political role. In turn, in the exercise of a political role, corporate managements have advocated more numerous positions on corporate-related and social issues with the result that they are expected to have a more active social role, e.g., being accountable for publicly acceptable performance under the conditions of less social regulation that they have advocated.

While the large United States corporation has always had some

[7]Thomas A. Murphy, valedictory address as chairman of the Business Roundtable, June 1980.

social and political characteristics, the two roles generally have been managed separately from each other and apart from basic corporate functions. However, the evolution of a joint social and political role has also been accelerated by the public's concern with the broader aspects of corporate performance, the dynamic interaction of the corporation with the social and political environment, and the legislation of recent years and its ongoing implementation. These developments have created a dilemma: Should corporation managements either resist and give lip service to a social and political role for their businesses, or should they accept it as an integral factor in managing the affairs of their companies?

The first horn of the dilemma is hardly attractive. Irving Shapiro, for example, feels: "In view of the decades of opposition by some business representatives to almost every step government decides to take, it ought to be clear that knee-jerk opposition is at best a delaying tactic."[8] That resistance has resulted in a progressive loss of corporate managements' ability to manage: individually they have lost some of their ability to control the destiny of their companies and, as a leadership group, to shape the evolving role of the large corporation. The second horn of the dilemma also has undesirable aspects. Modification of corporate policies, structure, and performance to manage the evolving corporate social and political role has resulted in some loss of economic vitality by diverting executive attention from economic performance.

For all practical purposes, the dilemma has already been resolved for large, highly visible corporations that are regarded as "quasi-public" despite their private ownership status. Their managements' task, perforce, has become that of helping to shape the future of their companies and to preserve private enterprise by effective participation in the public policy process. As a result, many large corporations have adopted new types of staff support to assist their general managements in two ways: in improving the performance of their companies and in participating effectively in the public policy process by which laws and regulations affecting the business community are considered. The following are principal examples of changes in corporate organization and functions that have occurred in recent years and are continuing to occur:

- Equal-opportunity and urban and consumer affairs staffs were established.
- Most large corporations established or greatly bolstered their government relations function.
- The concept of public issue "management" was adopted.

[8]Irving Shapiro, "Business and the Public Policy Process," address to the Harvard University Symposium on Business and Government, Cambridge, Mass., May 9, 1979.

- The traditional public relations function of publicity and media relations has been upgraded and has become more frequently involved with management's communication with the corporation's constituents on public policy issues.

- Corporate community relations and philanthropy are maturing as business functions.

- When the nature of companies so requires, departments have been established to provide corporatewide scientific expertise and policy guidance concerning environmental protection and the prevention of health and safety hazards to employees, customers, and the general public. In some cases, those departments have been combined to form a new corporate function concerned with the integrated problems of health, safety, and the environment.

- Many large companies have combined or provided for the close coordination of the foregoing staff groups into the overall management function of public affairs or corporate affairs. The purpose of that function is to assist the chief executive and senior officers in dealing with the external relations and public policy dimensions of the business.

- Most large companies have established or improved their internal financial, legal, and administrative controls on the sensitive matters of corporate performance, governance, and executive conduct by such means as board committees on public policy, audit, and executive compensation, each predominantly or entirely composed of outside directors.

Those organizational developments confirm that the large corporation has an evolving social and political role. The predominant importance of the corporation's economic role is not questioned. In fact, most business observers would agree that such needs as improved productivity and efficiency make the economic role more challenging than in the past. At the same time, there is growing recognition that the large corporation has a social and political role which is inextricable from its economic role and that together they must be managed successfully for the well-being of society as well as for that of the large corporation.

## THE EVOLVING ROLE AND VOLUNTARY ACCOUNTABILITY

The evolving corporate social and political role, with attendant changes in organization, policies, and performance, has significant implications. One implication is an emerging process that is an alternative to government-imposed accountability. This process, which might be called "voluntary corporate accountability," is based on effective management participation in the public policy process and sensitive interaction with company constituent interests that (1) contribute to management attitudes and performance standards which are in tune with the social, economic, and political environment, (2) foster publicly acceptable company performance, and (3) manifest a sense of voluntary accountability to the broader society.

While standards of performance and internal controls are routinely used for the traditional aspects of corporate performance, such as financial, production, and sales activities, they have not been applied as generally or as successfully to matters of public concern, such as the social and environmental impacts of corporate activity, legal and ethical behavior, and corporate political participation.

An increasing number of corporate managements are finding that by interacting with constituent groups and participating in the public policy process, they are better equipped to set standards and conduct their business affairs in harmony with the external environment. In addition, appropriate interaction with employee and external groups can result in a mode of voluntary corporate accountability; in effect they express a sense of accountability to constituent interests. As chairman of AT&T, John D. deButts presaged this concept when he advised chief executive officers "to demonstrate their accountability not only through right action but by their readiness to respond to every reasonable public inquiry about the policies and practices of their businesses."[9]

The concept of voluntary accountability is taking shape because of corporate management actions such as these:

• Defining the social and political role of their companies and setting policies and procedures for managing that dimension of their business, including legal and ethical behavior, openness and public disclosure, governmental and political relations, and social performance

• Establishing internal financial, legal, and administrative controls and company codes of business conduct to help assure legal and ethical behavior as well as publicly acceptable conduct on other sensitive matters of corporate and executive performance

• Creating more open and candid relations with shareholders, custom-

---

[9]John D. deButts, foreword to Chester Burger, *The Chief Executive: Realities of Corporate Leadership,* CBI Publishing Company, Inc., Boston, 1978, p. x.

ers, the media, government, host communities, employees, and other constituents who make up "their public"

• Dealing with government representatives by or through advocacy based on presentation of factual data, recognition that there is always disagreement on how the public interest may be affected, and appreciation of the dilemmas confronting government decision makers

• Being available to the media by such means as quick response to inquiries, briefings for editorial boards, and appearances on radio and television programs

• Establishing new forms of communication and cooperation with employees, from rank-and-file employee participation in workplace decisions to involvement of managerial employees in government, media, and other constituency relations

• Meeting with representative community or regional groups concerning matters that might be of concern to their interests

• Meeting with consumer, environmental, civil rights, health, and other interest groups and with government officials to learn their concerns firsthand and to explain company plans or actions that they could misunderstand or object to

• Meeting with proponents of adversary shareholder resolutions in an endeavor to resolve differences

• Seeking or joining ad hoc coalitions with labor unions and selected environmental, consumer, or other nonbusiness interest groups to develop areas of agreement on important public policy questions and, in some cases, to coordinate public communication and lobbying

As would be expected, company managements that have reached out to interact with their constituencies have found that some interest groups have "hidden agendas," including radical change in the private enterprise system, and that such groups attempt to advance those purposes by interaction with corporate executives. Also, executives have found that they cannot expect easy agreement by adversary groups on specific issues or changes in their basic positions.

On the positive side, most managements have learned that many media representatives are receptive to interaction, with the result that treatment by the print media, particularly, is generally more accurate than in the past. They have discovered that they and many interest groups are more in agreement on important issues than either expected; they have learned that ad hoc coalitions can achieve results on some specific issues. Further, they have seen that improved understanding and cooperation by legislators and regulators sometimes results.

Reaching out to interact is a tangible and visible expression of voluntary corporate accountability. In addition to facilitating the process of managing the social and political aspects of a company's performance, actions that convey voluntary accountability can help a company management to relieve public pressure for government-imposed accountability. Effective participation in the public policy process, including interaction with constituent groups, fairly and openly and without attempting to dominate other interests, can convey a management's willingness to be accountable to those whose interests are affected by the performance of its company. Innovative application of this concept of voluntary corporate accountability may be corporate management's best means to help assure that in the future the large corporation remains a private enterprise institution.

## EXECUTIVE DEVELOPMENT FOR THE EVOLVING ROLE[10]

Another implication of the evolving social and political role of the large corporation is the need for corporate executives who are as effective in dealing with the public policy dimension of their business as they must be in managing its other functions. As the large corporation has evolved, a broader-gauge executive is needed to deal with the social and political role. Thomas Murphy, when chairman of General Motors Corporation, pointed up the significance of this new role by his comment that "today's chief executive officer . . . must be a public figure."[11] By the term "public figure," Murphy was not referring to public visibility or prominence per se. He was characterizing chief executives who are as skilled in managing the public policy dimension of their businesses as they are in managing their traditional functions.

### The Need for Executives with Public Policy Skills

With notable exceptions, many corporate executives eschew direct business contact with representatives of the media, government, public-interest groups, the intellectual community, and labor leaders. Many corporate executives find that going public on behalf of their companies is not a comfortable experience. Reginald Jones has ac-

[10]For a fuller development of this subject see Francis W. Steckmest, "Career Development for the Public Policy Dimension of Executive Performance," *Public Affairs Review*, 1981.

[11]Thomas A. Murphy, address to the Business Roundtable annual meeting, New York, June 12, 1978.

knowledged that his service as a business activist in the fevered atmosphere of Washington was light-years away from the relatively cool and rational processes of life in General Electric. Nonetheless, large corporations need executives with the knowledge, skills, experience, and attitudes to become effective in the public policy arena. Murphy has asserted that "the day of the cloistered chief executive is past."[12]

Public policy skills are needed not just by chief executives but by both functional and general managers who interact with government, the media, or interest groups. Looking ahead, Shapiro has stated:

> The generation of managers who will direct our evolving private enterprise system will have to be adept in many roles beyond the details of their business operations. We will have to be skilled in dealing with government, with the news media, with investors, with employees and with the general public—and in recognizing that none of them is any sort of enemy.[13]

### Why There Are So Few Executives with Public Policy Skills

People become executives of major corporations by virtue of almost total absorption in traditional business affairs. Little in their education or business experience prepares them for participation in the untidy and often bruising public policy process. Equally important are a variety of corporate practices that, in effect, serve as barriers to the development of the broader-gauge executive that corporations need. The first is that potential public policy skills are not a consequential factor in the corporate recruitment of future executives. The second principal barrier is that, initially and often for years, individuals are judged by performance in the specialty for which they were hired.

Further barriers exist throughout the corporate career span. As people advance in management, their assignments, training, and education emphasize management methods and company knowledge that seldom involve the public policy aspects of corporate performance. Another important obstacle is that managers are seldom rewarded or even commended for the social and political aspects of their work. Similar discouragement occurs when the corporate public policy function is centralized to the extent that management participation is limited to public affairs officers or a few top corporate executives.

[12]Ibid.

[13]Irving Shapiro, "The Future Role of Business in Society," address to the Conference Board, Inc., New York, Sept. 16, 1976, p. 14.

A particularly insidious barrier is erected by some senior executives who themselves ignore the public policy dimensions of the corporation or do not play their role in the public arena. In this regard, Reginald Jones calls for business executives to "study the issues, develop constructive positions, and then speak out in public forums, in Congressional testimony and in personal contacts with our representatives in government."[14]

## The Status of Relevant Executive Development Activities

There is a growing recognition by the managements of some large corporations that steps should be taken to provide for executives who are proficient in the public policy dimension. This need is apparent in the growing number of companies in which formal standards of performance include requirements to participate in public policy matters. The most common developmental activities conducted by corporations are ad hoc government relations assignments, which, however, are generally available only in limited numbers. The most popular activities are university courses in economics and government and training by consultants in radio and television appearances, presenting legislative testimony, and being interviewed by reporters.

An initial step in the development of corporate executives skilled in public policy is their understanding of economics, government, the social and political environment, and the key participants involved in the public policy process. In addition to this initial grounding for the relatively few individuals who may advance to senior executive positions, there are important benefits to company managements in seeing that many middle managers have opportunities to acquire the same basic understanding. The dearth of managers and professional staff with understanding and interest in the public policy issues confronting their company is a basic reason for top management's typical lack of success in garnering employee, even middle-management, support for many of its positions and actions in the public arena. A cadre of managers who are informed about and sensitive to the social, economic, and political aspects of the business can be an effective force in building employee and community understanding and support.

Although there are some proven external educational activities and types of experience, they are presently a small part of a universe of over 10,000 management programs conducted by about 3000 "education suppliers" to United States corporations. Institutions capable of help-

---

[14]Reginald H. Jones, "The Legitimacy of the Business Corporation," address to the Graduate School of Business of Indiana University, Bloomington, Ind., Mar. 31, 1977.

ing develop public policy executives have largely dedicated their resources to their primary purposes: universities concentrate on research, publication, and teaching regular students; public policy institutes hew to their scholarship and publication; and industry associations emphasize lobbying. As a result, there are relatively few external activities available to accommodate the potentially large number of managers.

### The Corporate Stake in Developing Executives
### Skilled in Public Policy

Thomas Murphy, speaking as chairman of the Business Roundtable at the 1979 annual membership meeting, expressed his confidence in the chief executive officers who make up the Roundtable. He praised an increasing number of them for their public activism and spoke of "the need to draw more chief executive officers out into the glaring lights of public debate."[15]

Filling that need ought to be a top priority of American corporate management. Large corporations are highly vulnerable targets for public criticism and government control. Survival in their present form will depend, to a significant degree, upon the efforts of chief executive officers to make certain that their successors and the oncoming generation of executives develop the ability to participate in the public policy process and to manage the evolving role of the large corporation as effectively as executives must manage the other aspects of their work.

[15]Thomas A. Murphy, address as chairman to the annual membership meeting of the Business Roundtable, New York, June 11, 1979.

# CHAPTER 23

# The Challenge to Corporate Managements

This book has described a number of pressing but seemingly unrelated public policy issues arising from the performance of large corporations and their interaction with society and its other institutions. While no one can forecast the future of large corporations, it is clear that the policies pursued by managements in response to the performance issues strongly influence public trust and ultimately the degree to which these leading enterprises remain private in character. What is at stake, then, is not merely corporate reputation but corporate success and even survival of the large corporation as a private institution. If the large corporation is to continue to prosper, the following findings and conclusions are of particular significance to corporate board members and chief executive officers.

*The performance issues demonstrate that corporate performance is a broader concept than economic performance.* Corporate perform-ance is at question for old reasons that have new dimensions. People no longer measure performance solely in terms of the corporation's economic role. People today are concerned with all the ways in which corporate performance affects them and their interests.

No matter how hard corporate managements have been trying to reconcile diverse and conflicting public pressures, no matter how unfair it may seem to executives to be stung by criticism in the very areas where they can point to progress, many people still find a large gap between what they see corporations doing and either what they hear corporate executives claiming or what they think corporations ought to be doing. How well corporations perform in all aspects of their business as manufacturers, marketers, employers, neighbors, and citizens is still the fundamental public concern.

*The performance issues are not passing phenomena.* Many of the issues began emerging with the advent of the large corporation, and for decades they have waxed or waned in relation to public regard for corporate performance and executive conduct. Some have been compounded by recent developments. For instance, the long-standing issues of corporate profit, legal and ethical behavior, political influence, and marketplace performance have been exacerbated by the more recent corporate issues of health, safety, and the environment.

*The performance issues are interrelated.* They cannot be isolated from each other. Each issue increases public concern about others. For example, a product failure or an environmental problem that raises a safety and health issue may also be attributed to lack of ethical standards, social insensitivity, and avoidance of legal requirements as well as to pursuit of profit to the exclusion of other considerations. Each performance issue by itself is troubling enough; together they erode public trust and raise profound challenges to the leaders of large corporations.

*Public concern with corporate power suffuses all the performance issues.* The view of substantially unrestrained corporate power and discretion is among the most important fundamental public concerns about large corporations. From marketplace malpractices to abuse of executive perquisites, the causes of each performance issue are seen to arise from corporate executives' misuse of their authority. Thus, the real or perceived power of corporate executives to affect people's lives adversely, to affect the political process unduly, and to operate for their own self-interest has led inexorably to public support for broader and more pervasive government controls in efforts to assure management accountability.

Public concern with corporate power has increased the degree to which some critics and leaders of public-interest groups expect to have a voice in corporate and government decisions that are intended to assure acceptable corporate performance. This has occurred because public trust in the leaders of large companies has diminished. Many people view corporate executives, as a group, as self-seeking, pursuing profits with little regard for the public interest or for ethical considerations. As a consequence, public pressures have emerged to hold corporate executives individually accountable and, in some cases, criminally liable for corporate misconduct.

*Corporate accountability is the key to the issue of corporate power.* While corporate managements make a host of decisions that affect people and society broadly, their discretion is limited and restrained by federal and state laws and regulations, competitive constraints of the market system, pressures of public-interest groups, the media, and other corporate constituencies, and voluntary corporate accountability.

The popular formula for resolving corporate performance issues has been more government regulation. This often is preceded by appeals from interest groups and corporate constituents for management to take voluntary action. While management clearly cannot and should not accede to every call for change, failure to keep the elements of corporate performance voluntarily in consonance with the external environment has usually led to more and more government regulation.

*The performance issues are affected by environmental factors and the other participants in the public policy process.* The entry of corporate performance issues into the public consciousness in the last decade is significant because actual corporate performance had not markedly changed from the previous decade. What has significantly changed, as a result of the dynamic interplay of the environmental factors and the public policy participants, is the public attitude toward large corporations. The corporate performance issues thus are not just a discrete set of problems. Rather, they are a manifestation of a broader and basic discontinuity between the traditional goals, policies, and performance of large corporations and the goals and expectations of many Americans. This discrepancy is particularly worrisome; given public beliefs about the extent of corporate power, many people think that executives should be held to even higher standards in managing corporations than individuals are in their personal lives.

*The performance issues have led to the even more critical and intractable corporate governance issues.* The corporate performance issues have not yet been resolved to the satisfaction of many people by voluntary management action or conventional government regulation. As a result, some critics have come to believe that corporate executives can only be held accountable for their use of corporate power by such extraordinary measures as federal government control through chartering of large corporations, the establishment of a form of "shareholder democracy" wherein shareholders would participate in important company management decisions, and the restructuring of boards of directors in ways that would replace some company officers and experienced business executives for directors who represent consumer, environmental, labor union, racial, and other interests.

*The performance issues are affecting the role of the large corporation.* The issues have substantially contributed to the broadly held perception that the large corporation has social and political dimensions in addition to its economic role. Among the critical public concerns about the large corporation and its executives, the following are having the most adverse effects:

- *Consumer dissatisfaction.* Failure to meet reasonable consumer expectations is evidence of failure to perform the basic mission of the corporation. Customer dissatisfaction also has adverse effects on the public's view of other aspects of corporate performance and thus contributes disproportionately to erosion of public trust.

- *Overemphasis on profits.* Executive overemphasis on maximizing profits conflicts with the general public's view that the primary corporate purpose is to provide goods and services, with profits the result of doing so successfully. Specifically, the pursuit of short-range profit goals can adversely affect a company and its shareholders' long-range interests. Also, such management strategy is seen as negatively affecting United States technological innovation, productivity, and balance of trade. Of overriding importance is the fact that because corporate misconduct is so often ascribed to a singular dedication to profits, continual emphasis on profits by top corporate executives tends to sustain the popular conclusion that the pursuit of profits leads to illegal and unethical behavior and other corporate misconduct.

- *Illegal and unethical corporate behavior.* Instances of illegal or unethical behavior convey or confirm the impression of uncontrolled corporate power and tend to substantiate claims of other forms of unacceptable performance.

- *Corporate secrecy.* Given public suspicion that corporate secrecy provides a cover for corporate misconduct, it follows that openness and candor in responding to bona fide public inquiry are necessary.

- *Disregard of adverse corporate impacts.* Because of the pervasive impact that large corporations have on people, corporate executives are expected to manage all aspects of their business in a publicly acceptable manner. Adverse corporate impacts on human health and safety and on the environment are among the principal causes of loss of public trust.

- *Excessive corporate political influence.* There is long-standing public concern that corporate money and resources tend unduly to influence and undermine the public policy and electoral processes.

- *Unsatisfactory executive behavior.* The foregoing critical concerns both accentuate and are accentuated by the public perception of corporate executives as a group. When, for example, chief executives in effect establish or appear to establish their own compensation or use perquisites for personal gain, they help to verify charges that corporate misconduct is widespread. To the extent that corporate executives convey adverse attitudes toward members of other institutions, they create reciprocal feelings toward their companies and themselves.

Unlike most questions about corporations, these critical concerns have raised fundamental questions about the role of the large corporation and its executives. They have focused attention on corporate power and the ways in which executives should be held accountable for its use. They are complex and, in most cases, nontraditional in nature and can engender inertia in corporate managements that, like other institutional leaders, already have many more problems than solutions.

If large corporations are to endure, all aspects of their performance must continually merit public trust. Corporate managements must address the performance issues and make progress in dealing with them in their own companies. They will need to instill in the oncoming generation of executives a full recognition that "performance" means more than financial results and that these executives must be capable of dealing with a broad array of public policy issues and their perceived or actual causes. And if corporate executives are to avoid ever more burdensome governmental constraints on their freedom, they will need to innovate and perfect new forms of voluntary accountability to the constituents of their companies while maintaining the large corporation as a private enterprise institution that can continue to generate notable economic, technological, and social achievements.

# Management Assessment of Company Performance in the Public Policy Arena

This book has examined the most critical corporate performance and governance issues and their effects on the evolving role of the large corporation. As explained in the Introduction, the purpose of the study which preceded it was to serve as a basis for chief executive officers to evaluate the broad performance of their respective companies in order to determine what, if any, changes they should make in their companies' policies, strategy and tactics, organization, or performance. Therefore, in addition to the findings and conclusions set forth in Chapters 22 and 23, the Resource and Review Committee formulated the recommendations contained in this section.

With full recognition of the complexities of the issues, the many differences in companies and industries, and the variations in company policies and management viewpoints, the committee made six recommendations. All of them are concerned with the assessment of a company mamagement's ability to deal with the causes of the performance and governance issues and to participate in the public policy arena. Each recommended area of assessment is followed by questions for chief executives to ask in order to stimulate the information and insights necessary to make the particular assessment. Completion of all six is intended to provide a set of assessments that would help chief executive officers reach an overall evaluation of the performance of their respective companies and the ability of their managements to deal with the causes of the issues and to participate in the public policy arena.

Assessment methods will vary, of course, and action that may be taken must be tailored to each company. Nonetheless, the assessments should be done rigorously and not merely be a review of company policy statements. They should consider the extent to which important aspects of company performance vary from company policies to the detriment of the company and members of the general public who are affected, as well as employees, shareholders, and other constituents.

The six recommended areas of assessment and the related questions to stimulate self-examination are these:

**First:** *Assess the relevance of the corporate performance issues to your company's performance.*
- Which aspects of the corporate performance issues or combinations of them are of particular concern to our company and our businesses?
- What changes should we endeavor to make in our corporate performance?
- What changes in our company policies and practices are required?
- What changes are required in the attitudes and behavior of our top-level managers?

**Second:** *Assess the relevance of the corporate governance issues to your company's performance.*
- Which aspects of the corporate governance issues or combinations of them are of particular concern to our company and our businesses?
- What changes should we endeavor to make in our corporate governance?
- What changes in our governance policies and practices are required?
- What changes are required in the attitudes and behavior of our board members and officers?

**Third:** *Assess the role of your company in today's society.*
- What is our economic role?
- What are the social and political implications of our economic role, if any?
- If we have a social and political role, what is it?
- To what extent is our overall corporate role in tune with the most critical contemporary public concerns about the large

corporation? With the social, economic, political, and technological factors that make up the external environment? With
our ability to interact with the other participants in the public
policy process?

- What, if any, changes should we make in our overall corporate
  role?
- What action, if any, should we take to make certain that our
  corporate role is understood by all levels of our management
  and by employees, shareholders, and other constituents who
  are interested in or affected by our company?

**Fourth:** *Assess the ability of your company to manage the functions
that are central to the corporate performance and governance
issues.*

- Are the members of our board of directors and company
  officers sensitive to and well informed about the corporate
  performance and governance issues and their relationship?
- Are our executives whose functions are concerned with the
  corporate performance or governance issues sensitive to and
  well informed about them?
- To what extent are our policies, organization, and staffing
  effective in managing those functions successfully? What
  changes are necessary or desirable?

**Fifth:** *Assess the performance of your company in the general
management function of dealing with the external environment, particularly the public policy process.*

- Are we as a management sufficiently sensitive to and well
  informed about the changing external environment and the
  other public policy participants that can affect our company
  and its interests?
- Do we have an effective process and the necessary competence for:
    *a.* Identifying the relevant public issues, environmental fac-
    tors, and public policy participants concerned with each
    issue?
    *b.* Assessing the status and impact of the issues, factors, and
    participants?
    *c.* Monitoring our performance that is or is likely to be
    affected by each of the issues?
    *d.* Anticipating the need for and formulating company ac-
    tion plans dealing with the issues?

- Are we able to translate public and constituent concerns into consideration of ways to achieve publicly acceptable performance? To communicate effectively about our performance?
- To what extent do we consider the interests of others in arriving at our positions on public issues?
- Are we able to interact effectively in the public policy process with government, business associations, public-interest groups, and the media?
- To what extent has the concept of corporate voluntary accountability or elements of it been used by us? To what extent should we use it?

**Sixth:** *Assess the ability of your company to develop executives who are as adept in dealing with the public policy dimension of the business as they are in managing its traditional functions.*

- To what extent are our top executives effective in dealing with the public policy aspects of our company's business?
- To what extent are our senior functional executives (e.g., those in charge of manufacturing, marketing, and finance) effective in the public policy aspects of their work?
- To what extent are our senior public affairs managers effective?
- To what extent are our candidates for succession to the foregoing three types of executive positions qualified to perform effectively in the public policy aspects of those positions?
- What practices, if any, that serve as barriers to the development of such executives exist in our company? What are we doing or should we be doing about them?
- To what extent do our executive development and succession-planning activities provide experience, education, training, and motivation to help high-potential managers prepare for successful participation in the public policy dimension?
- What, if any, changes or additions should be made in our executive development and succession-planning activities?

# Index